Principles of
Consecration

Principles of Consecration

Charles G. Finney

BETHANY HOUSE PUBLISHERS
MINNEAPOLIS, MINNESOTA 55438

Published by Bethany House Publishers
A Ministry of Bethany Fellowship, Inc.
6820 Auto Club Road, Minneapolis, Minnesota 55438

Printed in the United States of America

Library of Congress Cataloging-in-Publication Data

Finney, Charles Grandison, 1792–1875.
    Principles of consecration / Charles G. Finney ; compiled and edited
by Louis Gifford Parkhurst, Jr.
       p. cm.
    Sermons originally published from 1841–1842 in the Oberlin
Evangelist.

    1. Sermons, American. I. Parkhurst, Louis Gifford, 1946–
II. Title.
BV4253.F435   1990
252'.3—dc20   90–41325
ISBN 1–55661–051–3   CIP

DEDICATION

This book is dedicated to all of the faithful readers and supporters of the Charles G. Finney "Principles Series," both known and unknown to me, over the past eleven years since the series began. This book is also dedicated to those who have yet to discover the riches of God's love, truth and grace that Charles Finney reveals through his works. May all of us rejoice as we think of greeting our Lord and Savior Jesus Christ personally in the future, and as we think of speaking face to face with Mr. Finney, who has so deeply influenced our lives. We are some of his works that will follow him. May our own lives bring a similar blessing to others as we follow him where he followed Christ.

CHARLES G. FINNEY was one of America's foremost evangelists. Over half a million people were converted under his ministry in an age that offered neither amplifiers nor mass communication as tools. Harvard Professor Perry Miller affirmed that "Finney led America out of the eighteenth century." As a theologian, he is best known for his *Revival Lectures* and his *Systematic Theology*.

LOUIS GIFFORD PARKHURST, JR., is pastor of Christ Community Church in Oklahoma City, Oklahoma. He garnered a B.A. and an M.A. from the University of Oklahoma and an M.Div. degree from Princeton Theological Seminary. He is married and the father of two children. This is his fourteenth volume of the works of Charles G. Finney for Bethany House Publishers.

BOOKS IN THIS SERIES

OTHER BOOKS BY FINNEY

CONTENTS

INTRODUCTION

Principles of Consecration probably brings to a close the Charles G. Finney "Principles Series," which I started eleven years ago. When I began to edit *Principles of Prayer* in March of 1979, I had no idea I was beginning a series that would reach fifteen volumes. The Holy Spirit had simply impressed upon my mind that Finney's lectures on prayer from his massive *Lectures on Revival* needed to be published as a devotional book for today's Christian readers. My impression was confirmed when Bethany House Publishers so quickly decided to publish that book.

Over the years, Bethany House Publishers has published over 150 of Finney's complete sermons and lectures in the "Principles Series." In addition, they have printed other sermons as daily devotions in such books as *Principles of Union with Christ* and *The Believer's Secret of Spiritual Power* (with Andrev: Murray). They have also published Finney's complete lectures or sermons in *The Heart of Truth*, *The Promise of the Spirit*, and books edited by others. They have published all of Finney's letters from *The Oberlin Evangelist* in *Reflections on Revival* and *Principles of Discipleship*. You will find a list of the lectures and sermons they have printed, along with the book and page number, in the Appendix of this volume.

At some point, the publishers and the editor had to agree that the series needed to come to an end. There are, perhaps, about 130 or more previously published sermons by Finney that are still out of print. However, other than Finney's sermons on the Beatitudes, and a few other minor topics of interest, the material Bethany House Publishers has made available to the public is so extensive that those who master what is available will be blessed in the endeavor and made more effective Christians. If you have appreciated this series, please write to Gary and Carol Johnson of Bethany House Publishers, 6820 Auto Club Road, Minneapolis, MN 55438, and tell them how much you appreciate their making this series possible. So often, publishers are the unknown servants of God who work in the background and who get little thanks for their efforts to make good Christian books available. Thank you, Gary and Carol!

The sermons in *Principles of Consecration* are from *The Oberlin Evangelist,* from 1841 to 1842. With this book, Bethany House Publishers has printed all of Finney's sermons and lectures from *The Oberlin Evangelist* from 1839 to 1843. Later sermons are scattered throughout the rest of the "Principles Series."*

May God bless you as you study and apply the principles you discover in this book, consecrating your life wholly to the service of God our Father. May your heart be full of love for God as you praise Him for all He has done for you through our Lord and Savior Jesus Christ in the cleansing power of His shed blood and in the Holy Spirit, our Comforter.

With love in the Risen Lamb,
L. G. Parkhurst, Jr.

---

*For tapes on Finney's *Basic Revival Theology* and tapes of Finney's sermons still out of print write: Revival Resources, P.O. Box 571, Edmond, OK 73083–0571. A copy of *Revival Resources Newsletter* will be sent on request.

1

SUBMISSION TO GOD*

"Submit yourselves therefore to God" (James 4:7).

Submission belongs to the will. True submission consists of the will being entirely subdued and under God's control. It is the attitude, the voluntary state, of the will that God requires.

True Submission and God's Providence

True submission includes a joyful acquiescence in or consent to all the providence of God. Perhaps everyone, no matter how wicked (and perhaps even the devil in hell), is pleased with *some* of the providential acts of God. Some of God's actions may secondarily favor people's ambitious and selfish schemes. For example, the murderer who prowls at midnight to plunge a knife deep into his neighbor's heart might be very willing for God's providence to favor him with a dark and stormy night when few would be around to detect his foul deed. The pirate might rejoice in fair winds or in any other providence that might favor his diabolical designs. Satan himself may rejoice at some providential dispensations that might give him the opportunity of extending his rebellious operations against God. Though wicked, a farmer may rejoice in weather that favors his occupation. Thus the worst and best of people may be very pleased with the providence of God as long as it favors their particular designs.

Those whom I have just mentioned have no piety in their submission to God. One element of true submission is a *joyful* yielding to the *whole* providence of God. A truly submissive soul cannot know what an adverse providence is: his will is not independent of God. He wills

---

*The Oberlin Evangelist, lectures 25 and 26 combined (January 6 and 20, 1841).

11

only that the will of God be done. Whatever the weather, whatever the providential occurrences—these events show what, *on the whole,* is the will of God; therefore, the truly submissive person is pleased with them, whatever they may be.

If the providence of God interferes with what the submissive person has intended, he is just as pleased as if the providence had been different. His intention to do a certain thing, to go to a certain place or to attempt anything, is founded upon the supposition that such is the will of God. If the providence of God prohibits his carrying out any such intention, the submissive soul regards that as a revelation from God that the objective was not according to His will. In this case, he is just as well pleased to relinquish his design and pursue any course that at present seems to be according to the will of God. Unable to continue his previous intention, he is just as pleased with his new course, because he has learned that his first plan was adverse to the providence and will of God.

Having no other intention than to do the whole will of God, the truly submissive person is perfectly satisfied with whatever may be the providence of God. He has no self-centered interests to promote. He has no ends of his own to accomplish. He has no ways, schemes or wishes that he believes are not according to the will of God. Therefore, in a state of supreme sweetness and serenity, he waits in an attitude as yielding as air to be led in any direction toward which the will of God is revealed by His providence, by His Spirit, and by His Word.[1] He is equally well pleased to be sick or well, to be rich or poor, to live or die, to enjoy his friends or part with them, to be employed in any way, in any place, at any time, wherever the providence of God shall lead him.

True Submission and God's Will

Another important element of true submission is a wholehearted, joyful, and *practical obedience* to all the known will of God. Perhaps there is no person so wicked that he does not find it in his own self-interest to do many of the things God requires. He does not do these things in obedience to the will of God *as such,* yet he gives himself credit for good behavior. The person is very pleased that God requires some things, because it so happens that the *letter* of these requirements coincides with what he finds to be most agreeable to himself and his own interest under the circumstances in which he is placed. Obviously, in doing these things there is no virtue, since the unbeliever does not

---

[1] See Finney's *Principles of Prayer* for how God leads us by His providence, His Spirit, and His Word.

do them because of God's requirements. He obeys God only because this course of conduct accords with the selfish ends he has in view.

Always remember that true submission consists in a spirit of universal obedience to the whole will of God *because it is His will*. A truly submissive person will regard the will of God on all subjects as the highest good. He has no goal in view other than in everything to be directed by the will of God. For him, nothing is so dear, so desirable, so preferred as to have the whole will of God done on earth as it is in heaven. Consequently, a submissive person does no picking and choosing among the commandments of God, being pleased with some more than others, and preferring obedience to one rather than another. The revealed will of God (however it may be made known, whether by His Word, providence or Spirit) is the principal and universal law to which he yields a universal and joyful obedience.

True submission includes the practical and joyful holding of ourselves and all our possessions and interests at the disposal of the divine will. This attitude is opposite that of a reluctant yielding that complies with the stern demands of conscience without in reality taking any pleasure in giving in. There must be a *practical* yielding of ourselves and our possessions as opposed to a *fancied* willingness in which people often profess to be willing to do anything but in reality do nothing. They profess to hold themselves and all they possess at the disposal of God, but in reality they will never allow Him to dispose of themselves or their possessions until He disposes of them by sending them to hell or of their possessions by putting them into the hands of those who will use them for His glory.

By a *practical* and *joyful* holding of ourselves and our possessions at His disposal, I mean that the whole body, soul, spirit, time, talents, property, and all things over which we have control are yielded up to the advancement of Christ's kingdom in the world. We do not do so grudgingly or by compulsion, but with a ready, willing, and joyful mind. We find our greatest joy in this course. We feel it is true in our own experience that "it is more blessed to give than to receive" (Acts 20:35).

True submission includes an unconditional consent to be used—body and soul, both in time and eternity—for the promotion of the best interests of the universe and the glory of God. Undoubtedly, God wills that every moral being make the most of his influence to promote His glory and the interests of His kingdom. True submission is the intense desire to be used up for God—to be wholly given over to promote the vast interests upon which the heart of God is set.

True Submission and God's Justice

True submission includes a joyful willingness to have justice take its course with us if the interests of God should demand it. Every sinner in the universe deserves to be in hell. Since sin exists, it is indispensable that there be a hell, that the justice of God should be vindicated by sending those who sin to hell. And certainly it is the duty of all who are in hell to be entirely reconciled to their condition.

I do not mean that sinners in hell are compelled to adjust to living in sin. They are able to repent, are obligated to repent, and should love God with all their heart and soul.* But should the interests of the universe demand it, however, it is the duty of God to send them to hell. If sent there, they are ultimately required to rejoice in being there. They are impelled to be willing to obey Him and rejoice in being used in the best possible manner for the promotion of the interests of the kingdom of God. And since, under the circumstances of the case, the best thing that can be done with them is to put them in hell for eternity, they must accept and concede to it.

Just so in the case of every sinner on earth. He deserves to be put in hell. And if, under the circumstances, this is the best that can be made of him for the glory of God and the advancement of His kingdom; if the moral government of God can be better supported by his punishment than by his forgiveness, he is obligated not only to consent to being punished but to be pleased to let justice take its course.

By this I do not mean that the pains of hell should be chosen for their own sake, or that any pain whatever can or ought to be chosen for its own sake. It is contrary to the very nature of moral beings, to the moral constitution of man and to the will of God, that any degree

---

*Finney does not teach here or in the following paragraphs that a person who has been sent to hell can repent *and be saved*. Finney opposed Universalism and universalistic teachings throughout his ministry. The sinner *should* repent in hell and love God with all of his heart, because he is being used to establish God's justice and bring glory to God. However, once the sinner is in hell he will never embrace Jesus Christ as his personal Savior, since he will have no motives for doing so. Once he is in hell, he will have no promise from the Bible that he can be saved from eternal hell, and he will have no influence from the Holy Spirit to persuade him to come to Jesus Christ for salvation. Regardless of what the sinner does or does not do in hell, God will be glorified by the sinner's presence there (see especially *Principles of Christian Obedience*, pages 83–92). Remember, Finney teaches the sinner *can always* repent; the problem is the sinner is so stubborn he *will not* repent apart from the influence of the Holy Spirit. Because he will not repent apart from the work of the Holy Spirit, he is all the more guilty for his sin. Because the Holy Spirit is not in hell, the sinner in hell will never be saved from hell, and will never exercise saving faith in Jesus Christ. The sinner will eternally regret that the possibility of salvation was before him when he lived upon the earth, and now in hell the possiblility of salvation is behind him. With this realization, he should repent of his sins and glorify God for His justice, and be happy that he is bringing honor to God by spending eternity in hell—and that justly. (See also pages 280–282 in this book, *Principles of Consecration* for why hell must be eternal.)

of pain should be chosen for its own sake, either in this or any other world. But while the infliction of pain on the part of God is indispensable to the upholding of His character and authority, whenever the endurance of pain is demanded by the same end whether in this or in any other world, true submission consists of choosing and joyfully submitting to or consenting to the endurance of pain, not for its own sake, but for the sake of the end to be accomplished by it. A person is just as much required to be willing to endure the pains of hell in vindication of the moral government of God, should the interests of the universe demand it, as he is obligated to be willing to endure the pains of bodily disease when physical law has been violated and the vindication of the ways of God demand that he should suffer bodily pain. He is as compelled to be willing to suffer the pains of hell in support of the moral government of God as he is to endure a burn when he recklessly thrusts his hand into the fire in defiance of God's physical government.

Please understand. I am not saying that a person should be willing to remain in eternal rebellion against God. I am not saying that God is as much gratified with the damnation of sinners as with their salvation. I am not saying that God's glory demands, or that it is consistent with the glory of God, that any repentant sinner should be damned. I am not saying that God desires the damnation of any soul for its own sake or that the interests of the universe can be best promoted by the damnation of anyone who can be persuaded to repent and accept salvation. But I am saying that when anyone is so sinful and unrepentant as to render it necessary for God to inflict the pains of eternal hell upon him, he is duty bound to allow it in the end.

Suppose a person has committed the unpardonable sin, or a sin of such a nature that it cannot be forgiven and be consistent with God's character. Can it be right for that sinner to be unwilling to have justice take its course in this case? Can it be right for him to make himself miserable because the supreme good of the universe demands his damnation? Of his own folly he may complain. Of his sin he may and ought to repent and be unutterably ashamed. But with being made use of in this way for the promotion of the highest interests of God's kingdom, he ought to be ultimately pleased. Why, he was made to glorify God! It was always his responsibility to desire above all things that God might be glorified and the universe benefited, and to consecrate his whole being to the promotion of this end. In this he was always bound to find his supreme happiness. And now, if because of his own voluntary wickedness, he has placed himself in such a situation that the glory of God and the best interests of His kingdom demand that he should be put in hell rather than in heaven, then he has no right to disagree with this, to refuse to be used for the glory of God, to refuse to consecrate his whole being to that which will in the highest degree promote this infinitely desirable end. I say again and do insist that in such circumstances he is solemnly obligated to consecrate his whole being to the glory of God and the support of His government in this particular way. He is obligated to willingly lie down upon the bed of eternal death and give up his whole being to suffering the penalty of the law of God.

True Submission and Sin

True submission includes a deep and continual longing for the whole will of God to be done on earth as it is done in heaven. This is the state of mind that God requires and that Christ directed to be exercised and expressed in prayer to God. "Thy will be done on earth, as it is done in heaven" is to be the constant daily language of our soul (Matt. 6:10).

Several things are implied in true submission to God. First, it means the forsaking of all known sin. It is absurd to say that an individual is utterly submitted to God if he still indulges in any known sin. To suppose that true submission is consistent with any degree of known sin is to overlook the very nature of submission. Submission belongs to the will and consists of the total devotion of the heart to the whole known will of God. How unmistakably foolish it is to say that a man can be utterly devoted to the will of God and still knowingly indulge in some things, or even in one thing that is inconsistent with God's will! Whoever lives in the indulgence of any known sin of heart or life has not one particle of true Christianity. This is not a rhetorical flourish. It is not a random, haphazard assertion. It is the unalterable truth of God. *By this I do not mean that if a man is sometimes overcome by temptation and falls into occasional sins that this demonstrates his character as that of an unregenerate sinner.* But I do mean that where any form or degree of sin is catered to, where it is habitual, connived, allowed and practiced by the mind, there is not one vestige of true Christianity.

Second, true submission implies a recognition of the universal providence of God. God is concerned in all events—either actually or in a permissive way—directly or indirectly. Many people hide from themselves their animosity against God by overlooking the fact that God has an active power in the area that irritates them. They ascribe many things to Satan and to wicked men, and seem to feel it is right to be angry and very rebellious in view of many things that occur, because they think God has no agency of any kind in their situation. Now, a submissive spirit views God as so concerned in everything that the person remains calm, undisturbed and joyful amid all those occurrences that keep the ungodly in a state of constant agitation.

Third, true submission implies an honest, earnest and diligent inquiry to know the will of God. A great many profess to hold themselves and all their possessions at the disposal of the will of God. They purport a willingness to do, be, or say anything that God requires of them. *But you will find it impossible to convince them that anything inconsistent with their selfish schemes is the will of God!* They claim to hold all their property at the disposal of God; however, the agents of benevolent institutions may labor with those people for months without being able to convince them that it is the will of God for them to part with some of their possessions to promote good causes. The attitude of their minds is apparently an unwillingness to *know* the will of God in relation to the use of their possessions. They demand a *kind* and *degree* of evidence to satisfy their minds that cannot be had (and ought not to be expected) and would not be demanded by them if they were not totally selfish. Therefore, while they allege to hold themselves and all they possess at God's disposal, they can always manage to quiet their consciences by shutting out the light and refusing to be satisfied with what really is the will of God.

I knew a man who professed to be converted, and who planned to give all of his property to God. At one time he was about to give it to one charitable institution and then at another time to another person or organization. Thus he had excited hopes and expectations—sometimes in one direction and sometimes in another—that he would give at least his surplus of worldly goods to the promotion of great benevolent people and organizations of the day. But alas! He never seemed to find any object to which he believed it the will of God to donate his property. No existing evidence would satisfy him. It seemed that nothing short of a direct revelation from God would convince him. He wanted to hear something like this: "Know you, A.B., it is my will and pleasure that you devote such a portion of your earthly goods to the advancement of the interests of the Redeemer's kingdom, and that you deliver to D.C., the agent of such a society, the specified amount without delay." He wanted an order from God by some direct miracle, or thundered in a voice from heaven, in order to furnish the required evidence.

I know others, who, while they grandly proclaim to hold themselves and all their possessions at the disposal of God, can always find some excuse for doing little or nothing for the promotion of any benevolent enterprise. If a church is to be built, these people can avoid giving anything by imposing some precondition to which the congregation cannot and ought not to consent. If the minister's salary is to be paid, they can always find some excuse for not believing it is the will of God to do anything for the pastor's support. If money is to be given to the cause of foreign missions, these reluctant givers can always find some fault with the proceedings of the board as a reason for not giving. If anything is to be done for the poor, they always have some evasive measure to propose, some other and better way to supply the poor than the one proposed. If anything is to be done for moral reform, they have some objection to the course pursued by its advocates and friends. In short, whenever called to self-denial or to give of their possessions to the promotion of the glory of God, they always have some objection to what is done. They may make some proposal to have something else done, which, if not complied with, constitutes in their mind a sufficient reason for not assisting in any way with that project.

Remember, true submission implies an earnest desire to be convinced of the will of God, to have a diligent, honest inquiry after His will. It is a perfect readiness to decide and act on any reasonable degree of evidence, and to follow the slightest preponderance of evidence, to make whatever self-sacrifice or self-denial it may lead to in the service of God.

True Submission and Punishment

True submission implies a thankful spirit for all the past and present providential dealings of God with us. It especially implies a thankful spirit for those providences that have been and are most deeply afflicting to us. "For he doth not afflict willingly, nor grieve the children of men" (Lam. 3:33). And in all the afflictions of His children, the tender heart of God is afflicted. People are very apt to suppose themselves to be thankful to God for those providential dealings that seem, at the time, matters of great joy to them. Yet, they think themselves excused from being thankful for times of great affliction. Indeed, they suppose themselves to be very virtuous if they fall short of being downright rebellious at such providences.

Do you feel grieved when you are obliged to discipline your children? Do you feel grief when you must resort to using the rod, or to taking some prompt measures to subdue their wayward tempers? Are you not more tried and saddened by it than by all your other pains to do them good? Would you not rather take the blows yourself if it could bring about the same result? Indeed, do you not consider it the very climax of parental kindness, self-denial, and love to inflict punishment when the good of those you love so well requires it at your hand?

Now, what would you say of a child if he, when he had grown to manhood, looked back upon his life and said, "I feel grateful to my mother for watching over my helpless infancy. I thank my father for the trouble and expense of my education, for giving me a farm, and for all the good things of his providence. But, ah! There are many dark spots in the history of my father's dealings with me to which I find it difficult to be reconciled and for which I feel that I am far from having any cause to be thankful. At such and such a time he disciplined me. This I did not like. I remember that he did it with tears; how he trembled when he took the rod. I recall how he lifted up his streaming eyes to heaven. I remember well that when he had repeated the blows he turned away and wept. I saw and knew that it cost him much, that his heart was bleeding at every pore, that much sooner would he have received the blows himself than have inflicted them on me."

Let me ask you, Are children under great obligations of gratitude for needed discipline that so deeply wrings the parent's heart? Will you say, "Of all the trials that I have ever had with my children; of all that I have ever done for them; and of all their obligations to me; I feel that the greatest are those which compel me to deny myself when I must inflict wounds on them"?

Christian, do you think that you do well to barely keep away from downright murmuring and rebellion when you are disciplined by your heavenly Father? Do you remember how much more deeply you have afflicted Him than He has wounded you? Do you remember how much it costs Him to chastise you in this way? Can He, who loved you so much as to give His life for you, rebuke and distress you without affliction? Of all the things that He has ever done for you, you are bound to be the most grateful for His stripes. For when He has been obliged to strike, He has been obliged to touch the apple of His own eye and reach the deep fountains of compassion in His own heart. Oh, how His heart has pitied you when He has lifted up the rod! Oh, how His heart yearned over you when His rod fell upon you; and when you wept, how deeply did He sympathize with your grief! And as soon as you relented, how instantly would He smile and wipe away your tears. How readily He forgave you. And like the prodigal when he returned, He saw you a great way off, and ran, and fell upon your neck, and wept, and kissed you (see Luke 15:20). He took off your rags of shame and guilt. He clothed you in the robes of gladness. With His love He chased away all your grief. Now, can a spirit of true submission imply anything less than deep gratitude to God for all His providential dealings, and the deepest of all, for those in which He so deeply wounded himself in wounding you? Do you need to repent of those idolatries and sins that lay upon Him such a necessity?

True Submission and the Future

True submission to God implies the absence of all worry or perplexing anxiety in regard to His future dealings with us. A person certainly cannot be reconciled to God if he is supposedly willing to let

God deal with him in the future in any way He desires, while at the same time is anxious, worried and fearful in respect to His future dealings. True submission leaves all such questions in the hands of God without distress, distrust, anxiety, or fear.

Furthermore, true submission rejoices in the fact that the wisdom and goodness of God will mete out all His changes for him in a way that best promotes His own glory and the highest good of the universe.

True submission also implies that you have no other will except that "the will of God be done on earth as it is in heaven." "Thy will be done" is the constant language and breathing of a submissive soul. And whenever the will of God is known, the submissive person does not merely consent that it should be so, but rejoices in having it so. He prefers that this take place rather than any other possible course of events, because he regards the will of God as absolutely wise and good.

True submission implies that you are equally well pleased with whatever God does. The submissive soul does not make a virtue of necessity, only consenting or assenting to what God does because resistance would be of no avail. Submission is not simply the absence of murmuring and complaining about the providence of God. Rather, it is the most joyful and hearty acquiescence and delight in what He does; and that too, not merely in those dispensations of providence that are usually accounted merciful and joyous, but also in those that are usually regarded most painful and severe.

True submission implies the subjugation of all our appetites and passions to His will and glory. God requires that whether we eat or drink, or whatever we do, we do all to the glory of God (1 Cor. 10:31). True submission implies that this requirement be completely obeyed.

It implies implicit confidence in God. True submission is impossible when there is not true, real, heartfelt, and practical confidence in God. To submit and rejoice in whatever He does requires perfect confidence that what He does is right and best. Implicit faith is always implied in true submission. And this faith must respect the goodness and power of God, that He is wise, good and powerful enough to do in all respects that which is best.

True Submission and Repentance

True submission implies true repentance for sin. Repentance is that change of mind which takes the part of God against all sin. Repentance condemns all sin in every form and in every degree. It fully and heartily justifies God in all the measures of His government. It is not only an intellectual change of views, but a change of heart, a thorough radical change in the controlling disposition or affection of the soul in regard to sin and the government of God—a thorough reformation of heart and life.

True submission implies a cordial acceptance of the salvation of the Gospel. And here, when I speak of the salvation of the Gospel, I mean far more than the mere acceptance of a pardon because of the atonement of Christ. I mean an acceptance of Christ as a risen, reigning Savior from sin—not merely as an outward, but as an inward Savior, as a glorious deliverer from all iniquity. This is proffered in the Gospel. Nothing is true submission short of a cordial and practical obedience to and acceptance of the Gospel of the blessed God. It implies actual holiness of heart and life.[2]

True submission implies a deep abhorrence of sin and sinners. Said the psalmist, "Do I not hate them, O Lord, that hate thee? Am I not grieved with them that rise up against thee. I hate them with perfect hatred. I count them mine enemies" (Ps. 139:21–22). This hatred is a benevolent hatred. It is a hatred mingled with compassion. Nevertheless, it is a real and deep abhorrence of those who rise up against God.

We need to guard against various delusions practiced by many upon themselves. They confuse desire with will. They suppose themselves to be willing, because they desire to be reconciled to God, to give up their sins, to be pious, and similar such things. They do not consider that willingness and desire are very different. People often desire, and strongly desire, that which *upon the whole* they are very unwilling should occur. For a great many reasons sinners desire to be Christians, but they are unwilling to forsake all and follow Christ. Multitudes are deceiving themselves with regard to the very foundation of their moral character by confusing desire with will. If you ask them if they are deeply engaged in the service of God, they will reply, "I desire to be. I am willing to do anything. But I am a poor creature and cannot do as well as I would." Then fleeing to the seventh chapter of Romans, they believe they are just like Paul in their experience. They interpret that chapter to say that "when I would [am willing to] do good evil is present with me." Whereas in truth it should have been rendered, "When I desire to do good evil is present with me; so that the good which I desire to do I do not, and the evil which I desire to avoid, that I do." The case presented by the apostle in this chapter is one in which the soul is in bondage to sin, and strong desires for deliverance are excited, but the *will* is still under the dominion of sin.[3]

Many deceive themselves by misconstruing emotion with the heart

---

[2]See especially Finney's *Principles of Salvation* for his sermons that make a comprehensive proclamation of the Gospel.

[3]See Finney's *Principles of Victory* and *Principles of Liberty* for his sermons on Romans, especially his expositions on chapter seven.

or will. *Emotions,* or what are commonly called *feelings,* are involuntary states of mind. Emotions are necessarily excited in the senses whenever the thoughts are intensely occupied with those considerations that are calculated in their nature to produce such feelings. Now these feelings or emotions are commonly understood to be identical with the heart. In reality, however, they are no more the heart than the conscience is the heart. And their existence is no more certain evidence of piety than the convictions and remonstrances of conscience are evidences of piety. While the heart is entirely selfish, any kind or degree of emotion may exist in the mind. Submission belongs to the will or heart. When the emotions are confused with the heart, there is a destructive delusion. This accounts for the fact that so many mistake simple excitement for religion. While in all their business transactions these people are supremely selfish, they nevertheless maintain a hope of eternal life because of their religious feelings. Under inspiring preaching, encouraging circumstances, or other measures they find themselves strongly excited and exercised with deep emotion. They call these feelings the feelings of their hearts, and thus take it for granted that their hearts are changed—while their lives demonstrate that their hearts are supremely selfish.

They confuse conviction, remorse and emotions of sorrow for the repentance that forsakes sin. Repentance belongs to the will. Emotions of sorrow for sin should be a consequence of repentance and not that which constitutes it. Indeed, however, emotions of sorrow for sin may and often do exist in a high degree without repentance, or without that change of will that actually rejects or forsakes sin. Always remember that a truly repentant person cannot live in sin. John says, "Whosoever is born of God doth not commit sin; for his seed remaineth in him: and he cannot sin, because he is born of God" (1 John 3:9). Now by this seed is not meant some root or kernel; it represents the voluntary attitude of the will. The will controls the thoughts and the outward actions. Repentance is a fixed choice, preference or intention of the mind, and consequently controls the volitions that direct the thoughts and actions.

Suppose a person chooses or intends to go to Europe. This choice or intention will be the cause of all those volitions that move the muscles, direct the thoughts, and use all the means necessary to accomplish the intended end. Now, if the will or heart is right with God, if a man is in a state of repentance, it is impossible for him to live in sin, for him to act against His will. By this I do not mean that a regenerate soul cannot fall under the power of temptation and not commit a sin. A single choice, or even a series of choices, may under the pressure of temptation be put forth by the mind that are inconsistent with the healthy or ruling decision or preference of the mind. But in all such cases, if the heart is truly regenerate, as soon as the pressure of temptation is removed, as soon as the thoughts cease to be diverted from the great object or end that ultimately engrosses the mind, the whole being will at once come back under the influence of the heart or the supreme choice and intention of the mind. People are often convicted, experience the deep agonies of remorse, deeply regret their having sinned on a great many accounts, and yet, after all, know nothing of that submission to God that puts and keeps the soul strongly on its guard against sin.

Many make the mistake of thinking that conviction and assent are synonymous with faith. Overlooking the fact that faith belongs to the will, they suppose themselves to believe, while, as a matter of fact, they do not *practically confide*. Faith is a practical confidence in God. It is a practical confidence because it is the confidence of the *heart*. To call that faith which does not produce a corresponding practice is absurd. It is no more an act of faith than an act of vision is an act of faith. The mere apprehension of truth by the intellect, the mere conviction of the understanding, is just as distinct from faith as an act of vision is distinct from the effect of an act of vision.[4]

I might see a house on fire; but this is not faith, it is perception. I perceive, know, and am convinced that the house is on fire; but this is not faith. Faith is that act of the mind which is produced by this perception. Faith is an act of will. In perceiving this truth, the mind goes into action. It puts forth choice, volition, and the whole being into motion to extinguish the flames or to rescue the inhabitants of the house.

Just so, when the great truths of Christianity are perceived by the mind, the mind grasps and knows these things to be true. But this is an involuntary state of mind. It is not confidence. It is mere apprehension or knowledge. It may be the *occasion* of confidence or faith, or it may not. Faith is that act of the will, that choice, that confidence and trust, which results from the intellectual apprehension of truth; but faith does not consist in this intellectual apprehension. Now, to confuse "conviction" with that act of the will or heart which constitutes faith is a ruinous mistake. I say again, *faith always consists of a practical confidence, because it is an act of the will that naturally and of necessity produces corresponding practice*.

Many mistake a foolish and wicked antinomian state of mind for true submission. They have such absurd views of the sovereignty and agency of God that they think it unnecessary to make any efforts to accomplish their own salvation or the salvation of others. They suppose

---

[4]See Finney's *Principles of Faith* for his sermons on how to have and maintain Christian faith.

themselves to be truly submissive with respect to the salvation of their own children, while they make no more efforts to bring about their conversion and sanctification than they would to produce a storm of thunder.

Many mistake a legal and outward reformation for Christian faith. Others take it for granted that the standard notions of the Church in respect to what constitutes true Christianity *is* real Christianity. They especially regard the notions of their particular denomination as correct, looking away from the Bible and calling Christianity whatever accords with the views of their church or denomination. And still, more especially, do they think that Christianity is whatever their minister describes as being such.

Now, suppose a minister mistook conviction for conversion, as thousands who claim to be Christians really do, and as, no doubt, many ministers really do. Naturally, in his preaching he would be guided very much by his own experience of what constitutes Christianity. He would describe Christianity as that which he himself had experienced. Whenever anyone in his congregation came into the state of mind in which he himself is in, he would think them converted and encourage their uniting with the church. Both he and they, thinking themselves converted, remain securely entrenched under their delusions. The church formed upon this model has a disastrous notion of what constitutes true Christianity.

Out of this church young men are sent to prepare for the ministry. They also have confused conviction with conversion. They form and gather churches sharing the same notions of what constitutes Christianity. Thus, this delusion extends itself until great multitudes of churches and ministers have radically defective views and consequently a radically defective experience. Naturally, all such ministers, and all such professors of Christianity, would take great offense at anyone intimating that they were not truly converted. That such is the fact, at least in some large branches of the church, cannot be reasonably disputed or doubted. The longer I live the more ripe and painful is my conviction that great numbers of ministers have mistaken conviction and a mere legal religion for conversion and the Christianity of the Gospel.

Many deceive themselves by ascribing to benevolence or true Christianity what is in fact the result of other and radically different principles of action. Some call that which is the result of constitutional temperament true benevolence. Others mistake actions stemming from the influence of public sentiment and a regard to personal reputation for kindness. They do and omit many things because of their reputation, which should have been done or omitted from pure benevolence alone. Without questioning themselves with respect to what the motive is or under whose influence they are acting, they take it for granted that it is real Christianity, because outwardly it is in conformity with the principle of benevolence. Or, they attribute to benevolence and true Christianity in the heart those duties that are performed under the influence of hope and fear, or merely legal considerations. In short, they deceive themselves because they are too careless or too uncandid to thoroughly discriminate between the undoubted and conscious results of benevolence and those things that result from other and opposite principles.

Still others deceive themselves by confounding a boisterous, legal, bitter zeal with true Christianity. They forget that nothing is true Christianity except love and its fruits. They mistake a vociferous and highly excited state of mind for that sweet, composed, heavenly, and yet energetic love that constitutes the true Christianity of the Bible. Such people are very apt to confuse Christian faithfulness with a very harsh and vituperative manner of reproving and rebuking sin. Instead of manifesting a deep desire to instruct and reclaim self-deceivers and backsliders, they seem to think they are doing God a service in using such language as the Bible reserves for addressing those who are the most hardened reprobates and blasphemers.

Many deceive themselves by saying that they are *willing* to do anything, when in fact they really *do* nothing. They say they are willing to give up sin; yet, as a matter of fact, they do not give it up. They are willing to forsake all and follow Christ, and yet really do forsake nothing to follow Him. This is a deep delusion. I have more than once said, so please remember, that as the will is so the conduct is, and that *to will* is the very thing which God requires. It is a principle in the government of God, that "if there be first a willing mind, it is accepted according to that a man hath, and not according to that he hath not" (2 Cor. 8:12). Under the government of God, this is always true. To *will* the rejection of sin is the rejection of it. To *will* obedience to Christ, is obedience to Christ. In other words, to will what Christ requires is to do what He requires; since the will and the action consequent upon the will are connected by a natural necessity. Many are deceiving themselves by saying and thinking that they are willing but unable to obey God, when the fact is that they are able enough but entirely unwilling to do His will.

Others deceive themselves by imagining themselves to be pious, when in fact they do not possess even common honesty. They have been guilty of lying, fraud and a multitude of sins which have injured their neighbors; and yet they refuse to make confession and restitution. Even when they are in what they call their best frame of mind, they are overreaching and selfish in their dealings. Perhaps they will even defraud the post office by sending or receiving double letters while paying single postage, or take any other selfish and unlawful means to promote their own interest when they have the prospect of concealment and impunity.

Without true submission salvation is naturally impossible, because God must and will govern the universe. This He will do whether you consent to it or not. If He governs without your consent and contrary to your will, you are of course miserable because of it; for His government will continually conflict with your own desires and intentions. Since His government will be in direct opposition to your will, it will be a source of continual vexation and annoyance to you.

He will dispose of you for His own glory, whether you consent or not. Now, if this conduct on His part is not consented to by you, if His use of you is not that which you would make of yourself, you are very naturally made miserable by it. You cannot possibly be happy unless your will perfectly coincides with His in relation to the disposal that is to be made of you. Unless it is the supreme choice and delight of your soul to be disposed of for His glory, in whatever world it may fit your destiny and under whatever circumstances your lot may be cast, you are not and cannot be happy under His government. On the contrary, if you have a will of your own and would make a different disposal of yourself, property, time, talents or any thing which you possess, than that which is agreeable to the will of God, you are naturally rendered wretched by having your own feelings crossed by one whom you cannot resist. You see, then, that it is naturally impossible for you to be saved any further than you are truly submissive to God.

Unless your will is completely subdued to the will of God, it is naturally impossible for you to have peace. When you become so dead to your own interests as to have no will of your own, except that the will of God should be done, then, and not till then, can your "peace [be] as a river, and thy righteousness as the waves of the sea" (Isa. 48:18). Peace is opposed to war. War is a state of conflict. Every moral being whose will is not in entire conformity with the will of God is striving with his Maker. It is certainly and naturally impossible for you to have peace while your will is in a state of conflict with the will of God. He cannot yield to you. He ought not to. His will is absolutely good and should not be given up to gratify any being in the universe. Therefore, you must yield. Your will must be entirely submissive. You must come into such a state as to feel utter satisfaction and delight in the will of God, not only in all other things, but also in His will in respect to yourself, or your salvation is forever and naturally impossible. God cannot possibly save you in any other way.

Unless you are in all things submissive to His will, God has no right to save you. I have already said that His will is supremely good. For this very reason He is obligated to insist that every moral being shall be entirely conformed to His will. Therefore, in just so far as you resist His will, He is bound to treat you as an enemy of the universe.

Unless you are entirely conformed to His will, He cannot by any possibility save you. What is salvation? If salvation implies holiness and happiness, then it is self-evident that He is entirely unable to save you in any other way than by your being entirely conformed to His will. Suppose He should change His will, and for the sake of gratifying you and to avoid a conflict between your will and His own, suppose He should submit to you instead of your submitting to Him. This would do you no good; but it would ruin Him and yourself too. The laws of His being would remain forever the same; and He has no power to change them. God cannot by any possibility be happy any further than He conforms to the laws of His own being. Absolute and universal benevolence is in entire conformity with the laws of His being, and therefore naturally and necessarily constitutes His happiness. You are a moral agent. If God should so alter your nature as to destroy your moral agency, He would render it impossible for you to be holy or morally happy. But without a change in your very nature, happiness to you is as naturally impossible, without holiness, as it is to God. The fact is, there is but one possible rule of conduct that can make a moral being happy, and that is the law of perfect and universal benevolence. A moral being can be happy only so far as he is holy. *For holiness is nothing else than exact conformity of heart and life to the nature and relations of moral beings.*[5]

True Submission and Salvation

With true submission, salvation is naturally inevitable, because, let God do what He will with you, if you are submissive, you cannot help but be happy. Remember, submission is not a mere negative state of mind. It is by no means a passive state of the will. *True submission is an active, joyful, supreme acquiescence and delight in the will of God.* If, therefore, you are in a state of true submission to God, you are supremely pleased and delighted with whatever disposition God shall make of you and are therefore naturally happy; whether in heaven or in hell, whether in heathen or in Christian lands, whether poor or rich, whether sick or in health. In whatever circumstances you may be, if you are truly submissive, your "peace is as a river, and your righteousness as the waves of the sea." You are supremely blessed, because you are fully pleased, gratified and delighted with the will and providence of God respecting you. Now what is this but salvation? What other idea

---

[5]In 1843, Finney preached and published in *The Oberlin Evangelist* a series of sermons on holiness. These have been collected and published as *Principles of Holiness*, and follow chronologically the sermons in *Principles of Consecration*.

can you form of salvation than what is implied in this state of mind?

With true submission, salvation is naturally inevitable, because, whatever God does, or may do, would be just as you would have it in all respects. If He saw that His duty was to send you to hell, and certainly He will never send you there unless He sees it to be His obligation to do so, this would be just as you would have it. In view of all the circumstances of the case, if left to your own choice, hell would be the very place which you would select for yourself. If you believed it to be God's duty to send you there, you would feel it to be your duty to consent to go there. If He saw that the interests of the universe demanded and could be better promoted by making you a monument of His justice instead of in any other way, that this would be the most economical disposition that He could make of you, that by sending you to hell He could accomplish a greater good than by making any other disposition of you, this is the very election which you yourself would make, if you were in a state of entire submission to God.

If salvation consists of holiness and happiness, true submission will put you in actual possession of salvation in any world. If you were truly submissive to Him, God himself could not prevent your happiness, even if you were in the depths of hell. For even there you would shout forth His praise, for putting you there, and would be totally delighted that you were in circumstances in which you would be of the greatest possible service to the universe.

Now, if to do good is your delight, if you are truly and perfectly benevolent so that you find it more blessed to give than to receive, if you truly or more than anything desire to do the utmost good in your power, then if you are put in any possible circumstances, in any possible world, with the knowledge that you are now in these circumstances to do the greatest possible good that you can do, then you are supremely blessed, delighted and gratified to be just in those circumstances. Talk then of making you miserable! For while you remain in that state of mind, it is naturally impossible for you to be miserable. Happiness is a state of mind. All happiness and all misery belong to the mind, and are the natural and necessary result of conformity or non-conformity to the laws of our being. When in all things we are submissive to God, the whole machinery of our mind works with a most divine sweetness, like an excellent machine, in which there is no friction, no jarring: Everything is exquisitely balanced, and a divine sweetness is shed over all the soul in its harmonious results. It is like a fine instrument, so exquisitely tuned and touched with such divine skill that it breathes the very harmony of heaven. The mind, in a state of entire submission to God, not only harmonizes in all its own movements, but also entirely harmonizes with the workings of all the machinery in the universe. God's mind, government, plans, and the minds of all holy beings, work together with the most divine and exquisite harmony whenever each mind exactly keeps its place, and the law of order is so fully realized that there is not a point of friction, or a note of discord, among all the holy minds in the universe.

We read of music in heaven. Do you suppose we shall need instruments there to create our music and feast us with their harmonies? Why, the true idea of music is this very harmony of mind with mind of which I am speaking. The mind is so constituted that when all its powers harmonize in action, and when all holy minds act precisely in accordance with their nature, it produces of necessity a universal harmony, a universal sweetness, and a ravishing delight that needs no instruments and audible sounds to enable the mind to realize that which is intended by the music of heaven. Universal submission to God is universal harmony, while, on the other hand, opposition to the will of God is the friction and discord of the soul. There is an infernal grating, mutiny and rebellion of the mind which naturally and necessarily produces misery. And while a holy soul is like an exquisite instrument that breathes forth nothing but the harmonies of heaven, a sinful soul is like a wretched discordant and infernal instrument whose keys are touched with a diabolical agency, groaning forth the very dissonance of hell.

Submission and Chastisement

There is no submission any further than there is true peace and happiness. If this is true, and certainly it is self-evident, how little submission is there in the world! If all the unhappiness, vexation and misery of earth is due to a lack of true submission to God, then there is certainly very little true submission.

A submissive soul can know what it is to agonize in prayer, and can know the pain of struggling with temptation; but these are not at all inconsistent with perfect peace in God, and with that happiness that is the natural result of holiness; because this agony in prayer, and this painful struggle with temptation, are only emotions of the mind and are not at all inconsistent with deep repose of the will in God. On the contrary, they are evidences that the will is in a state of true submission to God. For, if the will were not in a state of submission to God, this earnest resistance would not be made to temptation. Nor would there be an agonizing prayerful struggle in the soul for the salvation of sinners.

No one has salvation who is not really saved; that is, any further than his will is subdued to the will of God. Salvation consists in true submission. It is vain to talk about salvation while that in which it consists is overlooked. Many people entertain the hope of salvation, who self-evidently are not saved, and who, so far as human observation can go, are not likely to be saved. They are continually annoyed by the providences of God, and are never happy any further than the providence of God favors their selfish schemes. Everything else irritates and displeases them. If the weather is not just as they would have it, if their business operations do not go just so as to favor their own interests, if their health and the health of their families are not in accordance with their selfish views and aims, then they are left miserable by what they call adverse providences of God. In short, they have a will of their own. They have interests of their own. They have aims and ends upon which their happiness depends. If God's providence favors them in these respects, they are happy and think they enjoy Christianity. But if otherwise, they are miserable and think themselves to be highly virtuous if they do not go into downright open rebellion against God. They understand submission to mean nothing more than the absence of murmuring, complaining and accusing God of wrong. They do not understand that submission implies a delightful acquiescence, a sweet yielding and a delightful choosing that in all respects the will of God should be done. Obviously such people understand salvation to consist in a change of place, rather than in a change of mind. They think that to be taken to heaven is to be saved, that to be pardoned is to have eternal life. But certainly this is an infinitely dreadful mistake! Heaven is a state of mind that may be enjoyed in any world. Hence the saints or truly submissive souls are represented as already being in the enjoyment of eternal life. Hell can also be a state of mind. Hell does not require a change of place to give the wicked a foretaste of the pains of eternal hell. Why talk of salvation, when you are not saved? Why talk of happiness, while you are not holy? Why hope for heaven, while you have the spirit of hell?

An unsubdued will is conclusive evidence of an unrepentant heart; or, an unsubdued will is nothing else than an unrepentant heart. In a sinner, the lack of true submission and the lack of true repentance are the same thing. There are multitudes who profess to be Christians, who of course profess to be repentant, while at the same time they continually manifest a very unsubdued will. They are not submissive either to God or man. They sometimes have emotions of sorrow. They weep and pray and confess their sins; but to yield up their own will is out of the question. They know not what submission is. They are kept almost in a constant state of fermentation, rasping excitement and distress by the providence of God; yet, they suppose themselves to be repentant. What oceans of delusion exist upon this subject among those who profess to be Christians!

This subject shows the immense importance of teaching children, at a very early period, lessons of true and unconditional submission to parental authority. Parents should remember that they stand to very young children in the place of God. They should lay the hand of parental authority and influence upon the will at a very early period. If their will is not early subdued, it is not likely to be subdued at all. If unconditional and sweet submission to parental authority is not learned early, it will never be learned. If submission to parental influence is not learned, it is almost certain that no true submission to God or man will ever be attained. I have witnessed a great many cases of protracted seriousness and distress of mind on religious subjects, when, after all, there was not, and I fear is never likely to be, anything of the peace and sweetness of unconditional submission to the will of God. Upon inquiry, I believe that I have found it to be universally true that lessons of submission have never been learned by such persons in early childhood.

Do you see from this subject how to account for the dealings of God with many people? They are almost continually in a course of sore discipline. They are smitten, stripe upon stripe. Now in such cases we may rest assured that there is some good reason for this, as God "doth not afflict willingly, nor grieve the children of men" (Lam. 3:33). Under such chastisement, we often hear people saying that they cannot understand why they should be thus dealt with. They seem to think there is something very mysterious in God's dealings with them, and are ready to say, "What have I done, that I should be treated thus?" Now this state of mind at once reveals the reason and shows the necessity of such dealings on the part of God. He sees that the will is not subdued. If you want any other reason for His dealings than that this course of providence is agreeable to His will, an unsubdued will is itself a sufficient reason why He should cross your plans and disappoint you.

It is indispensable to your salvation that you should be supremely pleased with whatever is agreeable to His will. Whatever His providence toward you may be, if you are not completely pleased with it, if you ask for any other reason why He has dealt so with you than that it has seemed good in His sight, this shows that you are not submissive: You do not have entire confidence in His benevolence and wisdom and insist that He give you the reasons of His conduct before you will fully consent to what He does. This demonstrates the necessity for Him to cross and re-cross your path until you will submit. God can never make you understand all the reasons for His conduct. Until you have sufficient confidence in Him and are sufficiently submissive to His will to be happy in what He does, even though you do not know and understand the reasons for His conduct, you need to be and must be disciplined until you unconditionally submit, or else be given up and sent to hell.

From this subject you may see how great a blessing it is to be disciplined by God until we do submit, and that we ought to devoutly beseech God not to spare us until our submission is perfect.

You can see from this subject what to think of sinners and backsliders who live and prosper without providential discipline. "As many as I love, I rebuke and chasten," says Christ (Rev. 3:19). "If ye be without chastisement, whereof all are partakers, then are ye bastards, and not sons" (Heb. 12:8). If then you are without chastisement, especially if you do not live and walk with God, do not infer from your temporal prosperity that God approves of your course of life or that you are the favorite of heaven. On the contrary, you have reason to fear that God has given up on you; that God has abandoned you to your own ways and left you to fill up the measure of your iniquity.

Do you see from this subject the indispensable necessity of thorough discrimination in respect to what does and what does not constitute true Christian submission? Some have seemed to suppose that true Christian submission consists of a kind of dreamy, heartless indifference to what they call the mysterious sovereignty of God. They suppose that submission respects fore-ordination and decrees. They seem to have no idea that true submission consists in voluntary conformity to the revealed will of God. This class of people are never for making any efforts to save and sanctify the souls of others. They think this should be left to the sovereignty of God, and that submission respects the unrevealed rather than the revealed will of God. Now it is impossible for us to submit to the unrevealed will of God, for the obvious reason that we do not know what it is and therefore cannot possibly submit to it. It is, therefore, a delusion for the man who neglects scrupulously to conform himself to all the revealed will of God to suppose himself submissive to the sovereignty of God.

True submission and entire consecration are the same thing. In other words, no one is truly submissive to God any further than he is consecrated to God. And it is very obvious that there can be no *true* submission, unless for the time being there is *universal* submission. A person certainly does not submit to God in one thing, who at the same time refuses submission in something else. It is possible that the same mind may be submissive at one time and not at another. It is certainly impossible that the same mind should both submit to and rebel against God at the same time. Present submission is present consecration; continued submission is continued consecration, and permanent submission is permanent consecration or sanctification to God. Do you know what this is by your own experience?

2

SELF-DENIAL*

"And he said to them all, If any man will come after me, let him deny himself, and take up his cross daily, and follow me" (Luke 9:23).

As we begin to look at the subject of self-denial, we must look first at what self-denial is not. Self-denial is not giving up one form of selfishness for the sake of another form. In other words, self-denial is not the triumph of one form of selfishness over another form of selfishness. Self-denial is not breaking off from any form of sin because you fear the consequences. After all, this is only consulting self-interest. Neither is breaking off from any form of sin for the expectation of reward self-denial, but rather a concern for self-interest.

Forsaking any form of indulgence for prudential reasons, such as a regard to health, wealth or reputation, is not self-denial. This is only a regard to self-interest. It is only one form of selfishness triumphing over another. Self-denial does not consist in either doing or omitting anything whatever from selfish motives. It is impossible to deny self for selfish reasons. It is absurd to talk of denying self to promote self-interest; for this is not self-denial. Self-denial does not consist in denying self in one respect for the sake of gratifying self in another respect. After all, self is still the motivation. Self-interest is the grand reason for every change of this kind.

Self-denial does not consist in abandoning the use of whatever is injurious to us, simply because it is so. Nor does self-denial consist in giving to others that for which we have no use, or the use of which could be of no service to us. There is no denying of self in this. Nor does self-denial consist in giving or doing that which subjects us to no

*The Oberlin Evangelist, lecture 28, March 17, 1841. Lecture 27, "Love Worketh No Ill," can be found in Principles of Liberty, Finney's sermons on Romans, p. 167.

privation, inconvenience or trouble. What self-denial is there in this? If it is for any selfish reason, self-denial does not consist in that which subjects us to any degree of expense, inconvenience, trouble, reproach, or even death itself: This is only consulting self-interest. It is self-indulgence, instead of self-denial.

True Self-denial

Self-denial is the denying of self, not for the sake of a greater good to self, but for the sake of doing good to others. This is really denying self. Self-denial is a real sacrifice of self-interest from disinterested motives; that is, from a singleness of eye to glorify God and do good to others.

True holiness of heart or supreme selfless love for God is implied in self-denial. If God's glory is so preferred to our own happiness or convenience that we deny ourselves for the sake of glorifying Him, it proves that our love for Him is supreme.

Self-denial also implies unselfish love for other people. If we deny ourselves for the sake of promoting their happiness, whenever their happiness is a greater good than our own, it shows that we love them according to the requirement of the law of God.

Self-denial implies giving up that which might be a real good to us. It is no proper denial of self unless we might benefit by the thing which is given up. If the use of it would be an injury to us, and it is abandoned for that reason, this is self-indulgence rather than self-denial.

Self-denial implies the joyful giving up of what we need or what might contribute to our comfort for the purpose of doing a greater good to others. For example, suppose a man has been to the baker's and purchased a loaf of bread for his supper. He has labored hard and really needs food. Yet, in passing an impoverished home, a little, pale, emaciated child stands at the door. Stretching out his little beggar hands, he asks for bread. The man enters this abode of wretchedness, and finds a widowed mother, sick and famished, surrounded by her starving babies. He is hungry himself, but they are starving. He has no more money. If he gives his bread, he must retire without his supper. If he gives all that he has, it will afford but a scanty pittance to this starving family; but he gives it instantly. He gives it joyfully. He retires to bed without his supper with tears of joy and gratitude that by denying himself he has been able to keep a fatherless family from absolute starvation. This is self-denial. Because of self-denial God sent His Son to die for sinners, and Christ practiced self-denial to undertake and accomplish the great work of our salvation.

Remember, if what we possess will be less beneficial to others than to ourselves, or if depriving ourselves of anything will promote the good of others less than it will detract from our own, enlightened benevolence would forbid the sacrifice. For example, it would not be enlightened benevolence for a man to give up his life for a mere animal, because a man's life and happiness are worth more than the life and happiness of a beast. Nor would it be virtuous for a man to starve himself for the sake of feeding his dog.

Every sacrifice of lawful enjoyment, of ease, convenience, health, time, talents, property, reputation or whatever might be lawfully enjoyed, stemming from a desire to promote the glory of God and the greater good of the universe, is self-denial. In short, self-denial implies the death of selfishness. Self-denial and selfishness cannot exist in the mind at the same time. They are exact opposite states of mind.

Taking Up the Cross

Taking up the cross does not consist in performing the social and public duties of religion. It does not consist in refusing the bodily appetites for the good of the soul, or in denying our pride for the good of our soul, or in rejecting any of our inclinations for the same reason. Taking up the cross cannot include doing anything in any degree for any selfish reason whatever. Taking up the cross does not consist in submitting to any kind or degree of evil, persecution or privation for any legal or selfish reason with respect either to our temporal or eternal interests: For all such things are only some modifications of selfishness.

Taking up the cross consists in refusing self from disinterested benevolence. It consists in suffering reproach and persecution meekly and joyfully for the same reason; that is, for true generosity to others and supreme love for God. It consists in denying natural and artificial appetites and inclinations, lest their indulgence should dishonor God and injure the souls of others. We hope that by thus refusing ourselves we may possess the means and opportunities of doing a greater amount of good to others. Thus, bearing the cross is only a modification of self-denial. This is true of all the Christian graces. They are only modifications of one great principle: Benevolence.

Several things are implied in taking up the cross. It implies true holiness of heart or selfless benevolence for God and others (just as self-denial does). It implies deadness to the influence of appetite, to the influence of the world, and to a regard for reputation. A man will never take up the cross in the denial of his appetites to meekly suffer persecution and reproach unless he has become dead to such things.

Cross-bearing implies the death of selfishness in general. It implies true faith or confidence in Christ. Certainly no one will bear the cross of Christ and patiently and joyfully suffer persecution for His sake unless he has great confidence in Him. It implies such an attachment to Christ as to be willing to suffer shame and the total loss of reputation in the world for His sake. It implies doing this with joy and not reluctance. The apostles departed "rejoicing that they were counted worthy to suffer shame for his name," when they were scourged by the Sanhedrin and almost hissed through the streets of Jerusalem (see Acts 5:41).

Taking up the cross implies a state of mind that is ready to forsake all things, and endure all things, for Christ's sake. For example, a loving wife will forsake all things and joyfully go into banishment with her husband and count herself happy in so doing; feeling that if her husband was spared to her it mattered little of what else she was deprived. In short, the true spirit of cross-bearing for the sake of Christ is a state of mind that feels Christ to be such an all-sufficient portion as to perfectly satisfy the soul in the absence of everything else.

Following Christ

Following Christ is not a change of place. When Christ was upon earth, following Him might have implied going after Him from town to town to attend upon His personal instructions. But even then, simply following Him from place to place was not what He intended. The Savior had His eye upon the state of mind. A person might have followed Him from place to place with selfish motives.

Following Christ does not consist in following Him for a reward, as He accused some in His own day. Some followed Him for the loaves and fishes. It does not consist in any service of any kind rendered from any legal or selfish motives. Christ was not selfish. No selfish mind can in any proper sense be said to follow Him, for following Him does not consist in imitating His life from any fear of evil or hope of reward. He was influenced by no such motives.

Following after Christ consists of having the same mind, spirit, motive and purpose that Christ has. It necessarily involves being truly and as disinterestedly devoted to the glory of God and the good of the universe as He is. Following Christ means to possess the zeal and activity of the Son of God in promoting this great end. It inherently requires denying self as Christ did, for the glory of God and the good of men. It lies in using the same means, from the same motives, with the same diligence, and in the same temper of mind, for the promotion of the same end. In short, it consists of imitating His example, respecting His spirit and life, and following His motives for exertion.

Several things are implied in following after Christ. Following Christ not only implies great confidence in Him, but also self-renunciation. You must renounce yourself before you can follow Christ. Christ pleased not himself. He did not seek His own glory, but the glory of the Father who sent Him. Hence, let no one think that he follows Christ until he has renounced himself.

Following Christ includes trusting Him to supply all our needs. It involves giving up our self-interest as the object of pursuit, and devoting ourselves to the glory of God and the good of the universe. We must cheerfully and confidently leave our own good and all our interests to be provided for and disposed of by Him.

Following Christ further implies the death of selfishness. It presupposes not merely and negatively the death of selfishness, but also true holiness of heart and life; or an absolute, disinterested benevolence for God and equal benevolence for others. It entails the final forsaking of all else for His sake, the everlasting renunciation of all ways, ends, employments and things that are inconsistent with the glory of God and the highest good of others from a truly unselfish love for Him and others.

Following Christ daily does not imply a mere experiment for a day or a month. Following Christ is an embarkation for eternity: An eternal commitment of the whole being to the same great end that Christ is pursuing. The text of Luke 9:23 assures you that you must *daily* take up your cross and follow Christ. It is to be a permanent state of mind, a *state* of mind in opposition to a single exercise.

Denying yourself, taking up your cross, and following Jesus Christ are indispensable conditions of salvation because anything short of this virtue only confirms your selfishness. The nature of the case shows that these conditions are naturally indispensable to salvation. The prime idea of salvation is deliverance from sin and a confirmation in a state of holiness. Those states of mind called denying self, bearing the cross, and following Christ are holiness itself; self-evidently, they are naturally indispensable to salvation. The text is an affirmation of this truth: "If any man will come after me, let him deny himself, and take up his cross *daily*, and follow me" (italics added).

Some Mistaken Notions

It is easy to perceive the mistake of those who suppose that self-denial *implies* selfishness. A few years ago I preached in the congregation of a fellow minister on the self-denial of God in the work of Atonement. Some of the members of the church were disturbed with the idea that God could exercise self-denial. They supposed that self-denial implied selfishness, and that no one but a selfish being could deny self. I was told that one of them went to his minister to see whether he accorded with me in my views of self-denial. The minister informed him that he did not agree with me, and that he thought it wrong to affirm that God exercised self-denial since it implied selfishness in God.

It pains me to say this, but it has become more and more evident to my mind from personal observation, reading, reflection and prayer that to an alarming extent the very nature of Christian graces is radically misunderstood by the church and by multitudes of ministers. In innumerable cases simple emotion is mistaken for faith, and to a truly shocking extent selfishness is mistaken for true piety.

Not long ago, the question was proposed by a brother whether a mind in a state of entire sanctification could exercise self-denial at all, and whether anything could be possibly called self-denial in one who is entirely altruistic. Now what an amazing mistake this is. What? Seriously ask whether a benevolent mind can exercise self-denial! Why, it is the most apparent thing in the universe that self-denial *implies* benevolence—it denies self from charitable motives. Therefore, so far from being true that self-denial supposes selfishness, it must be that selfishness is entirely inconsistent with self-denial. They are exactly opposite states of mind and can no more co-exist than light and darkness can co-exist. This mistake is very extensively made in the church. I do not hesitate to say that in just so far as it is made, it is a fundamental error. It is mistaking darkness for light, and sin for holiness. I must confess, it is extremely difficult for me to understand how a mind that has ever truly exercised self-denial could fall into so strange a mistake. How can a person who has ever known what it was to deny himself from unselfish benevolence ever afterwards suppose that self-denial implied denying one form of selfishness for the sake of gratifying another form of selfishness?

True self-denial implies entire consecration or entire sanctification. I do not speak now of continued or permanent sanctification, but of *present* sanctification. To deny self from motives of disinterested benevolence is for the time being to obey God. It is to do your duty. In other words, it is to be in a state of entire conformity to the will of God. Nothing short of this is denying self, taking up the cross, and following Christ.

The fact that so few know what self-denial is by their own experience shows how few there are who exercise self-denial. It would seem as though ministers are the only ones, in the estimation of the church, who are expected to actually exercise any self-denial. They only are expected to labor without wages from motives of selfless generosity. In scarcely any case, the churches do not pretend to give the minister anything like a compensation for his labors. In multitudes of cases they give them nothing at all. They feel as though ministers are to labor for the glory of God and the good of souls and not for "filthy lucre." It seems to be generally understood what self-denial in ministers is: They are to labor from motives of disinterested benevolence. They may visit the sick and spend as much time as the physician (or more than he does) without anyone dreaming that they ought to have any compensation for this expenditure of time and strength. They may travel about the country at the earnest request of churches and spend a Sabbath, a week, or even a number of months laboring almost night and day until they are prostrated and ready to die with fatigue without so much, perhaps, as their traveling expenses being paid. In all this they are expected to labor in selfless charity. They will spend as much time and strength in promoting the good of souls as a lawyer would do in attending to secular affairs where his charge would be at least five hundred or a thousand dollars; and if the minister should ask for a dollar of compensation he would be accused of selfishness and laboring for "filthy lucre," while it would not be so much as expected that a lawyer or a physician would expend so much time and strength without charging enough to buy him a house.

Now the question is, why is there such a public sentiment as this? What would be said of a minister if he made a charge of attending on the sick and officiating at funerals, if he should charge as physicians charge, or as lawyers charge, for services rendered at home or abroad? Even if he did this when he had no salary and no earthly means of support, it would not alter the case in the public estimation. He would be denounced as a mercenary, as a selfish and ungodly minister. Now I ask again, why does such a public sentiment as this exist in the church and in the world? I answer, it is founded in this fundamental mistake that ministers, and ministers alone, are expected to serve God and others from motives of unselfish benevolence. Ministers are bound to do all they can to glorify God and save the souls of others whether they receive any earthly compensation or not.

Churches are as solemnly bound to contribute to the minister's support and give him what is reasonable and just for his services as they are to support their own families, to pay their physician's bill, or to pay the laborer who tills their ground. I am not advocating the principle that ministers should either be allowed or find it necessary to charge for preaching a sermon, or for visiting the sick, or for any such services. But I maintain that for all these services they have the same right to expect a compensation as do lawyers, doctors, merchants and mechanics.

All people are bound to be as self-denying, to perform all their services from disinterested motives, to be willing to spend and be spent and used up in works of benevolence, as ministers are bound to. Anyone and everyone has a right to expect such compensation for his labors as is reasonable and just under the circumstances of the case. But no one has in any instance a right to make his wages the end at which he aims, and that without which he would not perform the service. The minister is to preach and labor for the glory of God and the good of souls, and not for the sake of a salary. The mechanic, the merchant, the lawyer, the physician, are all to do the same. No one has a right to demand or expect any compensation, when, under similar circumstances, a minister might not do the same.

Now, the thing I wish to impress upon your mind is this, the public sentiment of which I am speaking reveals this alarming fact: The church has to a great extent lost sight of that which constitutes true Christianity in everybody else except ministers. They expect and insist upon those things in ministers which really constitute true Christianity; but they expect of themselves and require of others nothing but sheer selfishness. They have set up one standard for ministers and another for lay men and women. Selfishness is the substance and essence of all sin; and disinterested benevolence is the substance of all true Christianity. And in such a world as this, to say the least, there cannot be any true Christianity without true self-denial. And what shall we say when the real spirit of self-denial is so misunderstood that only so far as it is applicable to ministers does it seem to be recognized as even obligatory?

No one can be saved without the true self-denial for the good of others which he feels that a minister ought to exercise. Whatever your calling, unless you pursue it with unselfish motives—as much for the glory of God and the good of men as you feel and know that ministers ought to do—you cannot by any possibility be saved. The same rule is applicable to both. What will ruin a minister's soul will ruin your soul. The requirement with respect to both is, "Whether therefore ye eat, or drink, or whatsoever ye do, do all to the glory of God." (1 Cor. 10:31). And now let me ask you, "In how many instances have you charged and received pay for services, when it would in your own estimation have ruined a minister to have done the same?" Would you not feel an abhorrence of and contempt for a minister, and be one of the first to complain and avow your convictions of his hypocrisy, should he charge for his services as you have charged for yours, and show the same reluctance to laboring without wages as you yourself do?

True Self-denial and Happiness

From this subject it is easy to see that self-denial does not abridge the happiness of those who exercise it. On the contrary, it is the quickest way to promote it. To be sure, our own happiness must not be the object at which we aim; for this would not be self-denial. The Lord Jesus Christ has said, "It is more blessed to give than to receive" (Acts 20:35). It is truly blessed to deny self for the good of others.

Take the case I just mentioned of the man who gave the loaf of bread to the starving family. Tell me, did he not experience a more noble, elevated, and soul-satisfying happiness in saving that famished family from starvation than he would have from eating the bread himself, although hungry and really needing it? Who can doubt that he was really compassionate and unselfish? I do not hesitate to say that he who can doubt it knows not what benevolence and self-denial are. Just so with all acts of *real* self-denial. Such acts always afford the mind more satisfaction than an opposite course would have done; that is, the denying of self for the sake of doing good to others is that course of conduct most ultimately pleasing and gratifying to a benevolent mind. To suppose the contrary is a downright absurdity, a contradiction, and an overlooking of the very nature of self-denial.

True self-denial is wholly indispensable to happiness in this world. Certainly a person cannot be happy, in any proper sense of the word, who is not benevolent. But if he is truly benevolent, in such a world as this, the wants, woes, ignorance and wickedness of those around him would keep him in a state of unspeakable agony unless he were making self-denying efforts to do them good. Can a person act continually against the supreme and the strongest affection of his soul without being made wretched by it? No, he cannot. In other words, a truly religious person, a person who is truly unselfish, cannot be at peace with himself unless he lays himself out for the glory of God and the good of others. I might indeed say this of all people, whether they are benevolent or not. It is an absurd contradiction to say that in a world of woe and want such as this one, a truly unselfish mind can be otherwise than miserable if he does not put forth the most strenuous exertions to relieve the woes, instruct the ignorance, and save the souls of men.

It is impossible for a truly benevolent mind, a truly religious person, to not exercise self-denial in a world like this. Benevolence is good-willing. It is willing or choosing the good of others in proportion to its relative value. The will governs the conduct. If a person, therefore, wills the good of the community in which he lives more than he does his own individual good; if he loves his neighbor as himself, and all his neighbors much more than he loves himself, as their happiness is more valuable than his own, it is impossible for him not to exercise self-denial for their good, just as it is impossible for him to act against his will. This brings out the demonstration that no person is a truly Christian person who does not live a life of self-denial.

From this subject we see why so many seem to suppose that self-denial must necessarily deprive us of our own happiness. It certainly is only because they do not understand what self-denial is. They call giving up one form of selfishness for another self-denial. They call it self-denial when they are whipped out of some form of selfishness, and driven by the terrors of conscience, the thunders of Sinai, or a regard to reputation, to deny themselves some indulgence for the sake of avoiding some great evil or attaining some great good. And being conscious that it is to them a grievous privation and vexation, they of course suppose that self-denial is a great burden.

I have often thought that most of those who profess to be Christians feel secretly as if God's service was a hard service. They feel that Christ's yoke is hard, instead of being easy; and His burden heavy instead of being light—that wisdom's ways are not, in their estimation, "ways of pleasantness, and all her paths . . . peace" (Prov. 3:17). They feel that Christianity is a task, an irksome, difficult, up-hill, laborious business. It is fully obvious that many call Christian faith a heavy burden; but is this the Christianity of the Bible? Is it true Christianity at all? No, it is slavery, legality, selfishness, death! Enough of it would make up the very essence of hell!

The real enjoyment of self-denial is the true criterion by which its character may and must be tested. If you do not enjoy self-denial, if it is not a real pleasure to you, that in which you delight and choose for its own sake, or if in any particular case it is not more desirable to you than any other course, it is no true self-denial, but only selfishness. Be sure to remember that self-denial consists in denying self from motives of disinterested benevolence. If, then, you deny yourself from such a motive, it must of necessity promote your happiness; since it is doing the thing you supremely love to do. Forever remember, then, that is not self-denial which does not promote your present happiness more than self-gratification would have done. But here again, notice that your own happiness must not be the object at which you aim, or else it is not self-denial, but self gratification, which you practice. There is a distinction as broad as the horizon between *pursuing* and *finding* your happiness in the duties of Christianity.

You can see from this subject that God *can* and *has* exercised self-denial in the great work of the Atonement, and probably in countless instances in the creation and government of the universe. You see from this subject the great self-denial of Christ in all His sufferings and labors for the glory of God and the good of mankind. We see that in all probability the holy angels have exercised and do continue to exercise great self-denial for the same object. The Apostle informs us that the angels are "ministering spirits, sent forth to minister for them who shall be heirs of salvation" (Heb. 1:14). Now in all their conflicts with the powers of darkness, in all their journeying to and fro, in all their watching over and laboring for the good of the saints, they are no doubt called to frequent acts of self-denial, to be absent from scenes in heaven that might greatly interest and benefit them, to forego many privileges and endure much toil that is real self-denial for the sake of saving men.

No one needs to pity those who are called to great self-denial for the glory of God and the good of others, for it is to them a real source of happiness. It is to them a greater good than any other course they could pursue. Christ is spoken of in the Bible as really enjoying the work of the Atonement. It is said ". . . who for the joy that was set before him endured the cross, despising the shame . . ." (Heb. 12:2). By this I do not suppose we are to understand that His personal enjoyment was the great end He had in view; but simply that as a matter of fact He counted it a pleasure and a joyful undertaking to deny himself and bear the pains of death for sinners. So in the case of the Apostles and primitive saints and martyrs: Their self-denial was to them a source of real and soul-satisfying enjoyment. Paul speaks of being exceedingly joyful in all his tribulations.

We are under great obligations of gratitude to those who exercise self-denial for our good, and under greater obligation by how much more happiness they experience in self-denial. If they did what they do grudgingly, and in such a temper as to find no happiness in it, just in that proportion we might be certain that they were not disinterested and did not aim with a single eye at promoting our good. They are happy precisely in proportion to their unselfishness. They are happy in denying themselves for our good only insofar as they are virtuous and really aim at our good instead of their own. Hence it follows that we are under obligations of gratitude precisely in proportion to the real happiness they experience in working for our good.

It is a great mistake to suppose that if God, the angels, and the saints really find a superlative pleasure in serving us, this diminishes our obligation to make what return we can for their labors of love. If a minister loves you well enough to labor for your good from disinterested motives, and really enjoys his labor even more than you do in receiving his instructions; if he is made supremely happy in laboring day and night for your good, insomuch that he asks nothing, expects nothing, and desires nothing for his labor, it by no means follows that you are under no obligations of gratitude. To bestow such temporal goods upon him as may add to his comfort or usefulness—or the usefulness or comfort of his family—is only to give him his due for the labor performed. Why? Because the Father freely gave up His Son for us all; because He did it joyfully and willingly; because He found an infinite satisfaction in it; because the blessed Son of God gave His back to those who lashed Him and His cheek to them that plucked off the hair; because He gave himself as an offering for sin, and found pleasure in becoming for your sake a man of sorrows and acquainted with grief; because He could delight to die for you, and drink of the bitter cup prepared for you, do you suppose you are relieved from the obligation to love and serve and glorify Him forever? Not at all, for who does not know that for these very reasons your obligations to gratitude are infinitely increased.

Do not hope for salvation if you do not live a life of daily self-denial. Observe what Christ says in the text: "If anyone would come after me, he must deny himself and take up his cross daily and follow me." It is not sufficient to practice occasional self-denial. Self must be set aside and crucified, and denied daily and continually. Your happiness must consist in unselfish endeavors to make others happy, or you never can be saved. I beg you to understand this. Denying yourself *daily*, taking up your cross *daily*, and following Christ *daily*, are indispensable conditions of salvation. And doing this *daily* is as indispensable as doing it at all. Christ does not say, if any person will come after me, let him deny himself occasionally, take up the cross occasionally, and occasionally—in seasons of special excitement and revival—follow me. Doing these things *daily* is here expressly made an indispensable condition of salvation.

Let me impress this upon you: It seems generally to be understood that if people go so far as *now and then* to practice what they call self-denial, now and then to take up the cross, and periodically, in seasons of special revival, follow Christ, that these are the conditions of salvation, and about as much as can be expected of Christians in this world. Now understand, this common opinion is a fatal error. The unalterable condition of salvation is that these things shall be done daily, that this shall be the state of the mind and the habitual course of life, that self-interest shall be rejected as the grand end of life, that self shall be *daily* denied, and that *daily* you shall bear the cross and follow Christ.

Notice that bearing the cross entails dying to our own reputation, and this is to be an habitual, *daily* abiding state of our hearts. Carrying the cross does not mean merely that once in a while we shall have a season of humiliation, breaking down before God, and make ourselves of no reputation; it presumes so thorough a death to our own reputation that this lack of regard to our own reputation shall be the *habitual state* of our minds. Observe that following after Christ must also be *daily*. You must daily aim at the same end from the same motives that He does. You must give up all your powers to the promotion of this end as He does. And this is to be done *daily* as an unalterable condition of salvation.

How infinitely different this is from the general notions of professing Christians in respect to the conditions of salvation! The general idea of those who profess Christianity seems to be that if they only once in a while "wake up" as they call it, if they are revived now and then, after long intervals, and once in a while bluster about, and "perform their duty" as they call it, this will suffice as a sufficient ground of hope for salvation. Living in this way, they expect to be saved. How amazing that with the express declaration of Christ before them, they can dare to hope in the face of His most solemn declarations. Why, these who profess Christianity, if you trust them, will land your soul in the depths of hell! I say again, remember that the *daily* doing of these things is just as expressly and indispensably a condition of salvation as that you should do them at all. Do you mean to dream of eternal life while you indulge your selfishness and lust, with only now and then a spasmodic effort, when conscience can remain no longer silent, and the Spirit of God forces upon you the conviction that you are one of the greatest sinners out of hell? Then you set to blustering about and seem to suppose yourself to be religious enough in a few weeks to offset years of selfishness and lust. Why, what do you mean?

How ridiculous it is for people to call such things as they often do, "self-denial and bearing the cross." Some will abandon the use of alcohol because its use has become disreputable, or because it is injurious to their health, or because their conscience torments them in the use of it, or because they fear they shall become alcoholics, disgrace and ruin themselves, and lose their souls. And this they call self-denial, when it is after all only refusing one form of selfishness for the sake of gratifying another form. In other words, they are denying one form of selfishness for the sake of promoting self-interest on a larger scale. "Verily they have their reward." Others will abandon the use of tea, coffee, tobacco, and many similar articles, for similar reasons, and call it self-denial. But who cannot see through this?

Others call it "taking up the cross" to pray in prayer meetings, to speak in public, or do anything that mortifies their pride. Now, it should be known that taking up the cross implies the death of pride, that pride or a regard to our own reputation is already dead. If this is not so, it is nonsense to talk of taking up the cross.

Our Lord Jesus Christ differed radically from multitudes of reformers. Reformers in general seem to aim at making as many proselytes to their peculiar views as possible, and are not likely to be so particular and searching as to render it very difficult for persons to fall in with and adopt their views. But Christ on the contrary, when multitudes seemed to be converted, professed to believe in Him, and followed Him, would turn upon them and cut to the very quick, informing them plainly that they could not be His disciples at all unless they forsook all that they had; unless they would deny themselves, take up their cross and follow Him. No person could be His disciple unless he would not only forsake all that he had, but would hate his dearest earthly relations—and even his own life—for Christ's sake. This certainly was a very different policy from that which is pursued by many ministers of the Gospel. Instead of insisting upon daily self-denial, the renunciation of selfishness, and a life of entire consecration to God as indispensable conditions of salvation, they seem to leave these conditions of Christ almost entirely out of view. For the sake of increasing the members of the church, practically at least, they hold out very different and almost infinitely lower conditions of salvation. Brethren, how dare you do this? I ask you solemnly before God and the Savior Jesus Christ, do you insist upon a life of *daily* self-denial, cross-bearing and following Christ? Do you insist that unless people forsake all that they have and renounce selfishness in their business transactions and in all their ways, and that unless they live a life of entire consecration to God, they can by no possibility be saved, and have no right to a standing in the church of God? What is the practical standard to which some of you, my brethren, as a matter of fact require persons to conform as conditions of church membership and of salvation? Do you not virtually plead for and allow sin? Do you not virtually deny or leave out of view the great truths upon which Christ so often insisted, that "except a man forsake all that he hath, deny himself and take up his cross daily, he cannot be my disciple"? Instead of making this a condition of salvation as Christ does, I ask you my brethren, and I ask the churches who hear you preach, do some of you not virtually maintain or make the impression that a state of entire consecration to God is so far from being an indispensable condition of salvation that it is actually never attained in this world; or at least, that it is never attained as a state in which people for any length of time continue?

Now my beloved brethren, if this is true, let me get down at your feet and plead with you in the name of the Lord Jesus Christ to consider what you are doing. How many of you are afraid to admit, avow, and maintain the doctrine of entire sanctification or consecration to God in this life? You are even afraid to allow that this state is ever attained and continued for any length of time by the best saints that ever lived on earth. But let me ask you, is not this state *as a state* made by the Lord Jesus Christ in these passages that I have so often quoted an express and indispensable condition of salvation? If it is not, I beg of you to show what these passages do mean. What does Christ mean when He says "except a man forsake all that he hath he cannot be my disciple"? When I say that this *as a state* is insisted on by the Lord Jesus Christ as an indispensable condition of salvation, I do not mean that the condition is that no occasional sin through the force of temptation is consistent with a state of real grace and with final salvation; but I do maintain that a state of entire consecration to God, or sanctification as a *habitual state* of mind is insisted upon in the Gospel as an indispensable condition of salvation. This state *as a state*, with only occasional interruptions through the force of temptation, is attained by the saints in this life. Under the Gospel, no one can be saved, nor ever has been saved, who has not attained and lived and died in this state; a state in which entire consecration or sanctification is the rule, and sin only the exception.

If this is not the doctrine of these texts, I ask what is? Do not understand me to affirm that a person's falling into occasional sins through the force of temptation is fatal to his salvation; but I do wish to be understood as affirming that regeneration itself is an act of entire consecration to God, that a state of entire consecration to God is the habitual state of every real saint; and that nothing less than entire consecration to God, as a *habitual state* of mind ought to be insisted on as a condition of salvation. To make the impression that anything less than this can ensure salvation is false, anti-Christian, and at war with every principle of the Gospel.

And now if this is so, how much blood is already in the skirts of the ministry? My brethren, I feel that I am compelled to look not only to some, but to all the conditions of salvation as laid down by Christ in the Gospel, and that as I value my own soul and the souls of my hearers—as I value the approbation, and dread the wrath of God, I am bound to lay down no other conditions of salvation, either in doctrine or practice, than this: Unless a person forsakes all that he has, except he deny himself and take up his cross and follow Christ *daily*, he cannot be saved. My brothers, dare any of us require in theory or in practice anything short of this? If we can, we are building wood, hay and stubble upon Christ's foundation, and in the day that shall try every person's work, the fruits of his labor shall be burned up.

What an infinitely terrible thing it is for ministers and professors of Christianity to be engaged in opposing the doctrine of entire sanctification or consecration to God in this life! I am amazed and distressed beyond measure to hear them speak of the dangerous tendencies of preaching this doctrine. I find it impossible to express the pain that sometimes comes over my mind when I see them hunting after and eagerly seizing upon every thing which they suppose exhibits the dangerous tendency of this doctrine, while at the same time overlooking the world of distressing and appalling facts that bring out with the force of a thousand demonstrations the dreadful tendency of the opposite doctrine. My brothers, would it not be well for us to look a little upon the other side of this question and see what is the actual tendency as developed in myriads of facts of preaching that a state of entire and continued consecration to God is not to be expected or attained in this life? Why is it that such great reaction follows revivals of Christianity? Why is it that the truth of the Gospel can bring people along so far as to effect their conversion and then leave them to backslide? I answer unhesitatingly that beyond that point the Gospel is not preached. Instead of holding up the perfect standard of the Gospel as a thing to be aimed at, actually attained and maintained, as an indispensable condition of salvation; instead of being encouraged to go right on to perfection until they stand and remain complete in all the will of God, no such end is presented to them, no such object of pursuit or of expectation is held up before them. But on the contrary, it is either expressly insisted or strongly intimated that no such state ever was or ever is expected to be attained in this life. And thus discouragement is thrown in their way. A stumbling block is laid before them that just as certainly results in their backsliding as any cause produces its effect.

My dear brothers in the ministry, who among you dare to quote and enforce with the expectation that it will take effect, the following language of Paul: "Know ye not that your body is the temple of the Holy Ghost which is in you, which ye have of God, and ye are not your own?" (1 Cor. 6:19). "As God hath said, I will dwell in them, and walk in them; and I will be their God, and they shall be my people. Wherefore come out from among them, and be ye separate, saith the Lord, and touch not the unclean thing; and I will receive you, and will be a Father unto you, and ye shall be my sons and daughters, saith the Lord Almighty. Having therefore these promises, dearly beloved, let us cleanse ourselves from all filthiness of the flesh and spirit, perfecting holiness in the fear of God" (2 Cor. 6:16–7:1). Clearly the Apostle expected them to do this in this world; for it was "from all filthiness of the flesh" as well as "spirit" that they were to cleanse themselves.

Now my beloved brothers, when you explain to church members what this and similar passages mean, do you make the impression that you expect them to do this, as you do upon sinners that you expect them to repent? How dare you, with this and multitudes of similar passages before you, stumble and talk as some of you do about the doctrine of Christian Perfection? Why, some of you seem to be horrified at the very idea of expecting Christians to perfect holiness out of reverence for God. The very term "Christian Perfection" seems to be an abomination to you, and a thing neither to be understood nor seriously insisted upon as a truth and a command of God. Oh, my brothers, I ask you how you dare to do this? How can you find it in your heart to do it? Will you consider these texts and tell your churches what they mean? Will you expound, enforce, and crowd them home, and expect your churches to receive and obey these truths? How can it be possible that so many of the professed ministers of Christ are stumbling at, opposing, and even ridiculing the doctrine of Christian Perfection? My soul trembles for you. It would seem as if your attention was so taken up with the fancied dangers of enforcing the doctrine and duty of Christian Perfection, that you count it an errant heresy for any person to teach or expect Christians to purify themselves from everything that contaminates body and spirit, perfecting holiness out of reverence for God, and this in the face of the church. My brothers, is this the work of the Gospel ministry?

About a year ago there was a powerful revival in a church not far from here. In the fullness of my heart I wrote to my brothers who were engaged in promoting it, imploring them to insist upon total abstinence from sin and to press the converts to a state of entire and continued consecration to God. I insisted upon this as the only course they could take to secure the revival against a reaction. At the time, I felt agonized with the thought that there should be a reaction in that place, and could have washed the feet of the brothers with my tears, if the act would have succeeded in persuading them to drive the converts to a habitual state of entire consecration so as to prevent backsliding. But all in vain. Within a few weeks or months, the pastor began to preach and allow others to preach in his pulpit against the doctrine of Christian Perfection. The result was just what might have been anticipated with as much certainty as any other event whatever. And now, although scarcely a year has elapsed since the revival was all in its glory, I have heard with unutterable pain that the pastor has confessed in public that out of the many converts that joined his church, only a comparatively small number of them are ever seen in his meetings. And yet this same dear brother seems to be still alarmed only at the tendency of preaching the doctrine of entire sanctification or consecration to God in this life. Strangely, he sees not, feels not, acknowledges not, the awful tendency of preaching as he has preached and maintains that it is a dangerous error to expect to live in a state of entire sanctification to the will of God in this life. "Tell it not in Gath, publish it not in the streets of Askelon; lest the daughters of the Philistines rejoice, lest the daughters of the uncircumcised triumph" (2 Sam. 1:20). Toward this brother, toward all of my ministerial brothers, I have none but feelings of the utmost tenderness. But yet I am grieved and pained, my soul is sick with the course that many of them are taking. Afraid to do as Paul did—pressing the church right to purifying themselves from everything that contaminates body and spirit, and perfecting holiness out of reverence for God—they merely satisfy themselves with saying it is a duty, it is naturally possible, but still not to be expected. Is this like Paul? Is this like Christ? Paul would say, "Since we have these promises, dear friends (for we can do it and must do it), let us purify ourselves from everything that contaminates body and spirit, perfecting holiness out of reverence for God." And Christ could say, "Be ye therefore perfect, even as your Father which is in heaven is perfect" (Matt.

5:48). And yet multitudes of ministers are opposing and even ridiculing the doctrine of Christian Perfection or entire consecration to God in this life, holding it up as a dangerous heresy, and even denying ministerial and Christian fellowship to those who believe it. Oh, what a state of things is this!

3

THE TRUE SERVICE OF GOD*

"And Joshua said unto the people, Ye cannot serve the Lord: for he is a holy God" (Joshua 24:19a).

In this sermon I will discuss the holiness of God and what constitutes acceptable service to Him. Then I will show that if you would truly serve the Lord, you must begin by making your heart holy.

The holiness of God consists of benevolence, love and good-willing: Willing the universal good of being. All of God's moral attributes are modifications of benevolence. His holiness consists in a disposition to do just that which is upon the whole best to be done under all circumstances, that which will most promote the general good, whatever self-denial and exertion this may cost.

Legal Service and Gospel Service

Legal service and gospel service are two different kinds of service that claim to be rendered to God. Legal service is a course of life which some pursue from considerations other than from a tremendous delight in the service of God for its own sake. Legal service sometimes originates merely in the constraints or restraints of conscience, or from hope or fear, or from a regard for reputation, personal safety, or a multitude of similar considerations. On the other hand, gospel service is a joyful compliance with convictions of duty from supreme love and delight in service for its own sake.

Legal service is regarded as basically only a choice between two evils, neither of which is absolutely lovely and desirable to the mind for its own sake. This is slavery, and this kind of service turns upon

---

The Oberlin Evangelist, lecture 29, March 31, 1841.

the very same principle on which the service of slaves is rendered. They prefer laboring for their masters to the evils which would result from their refusal. Therefore, upon the whole, slaves choose to work as they do; but it is only a choice between two evils. Since liberty is out of the question for them, they must labor or suffer worse consequences. They prefer labor to the consequences of refusing to work. But this is slavery. When this type of service is given to God, it is bondage and slavery.

Gospel service is regarded as supremely good, lovely and desirable for its own sake. This is true liberty. If left free to choose between all possible courses of life, gospel service is the very course of life which the person would prefer; and that solely on its own account or for the sake of its intrinsic value.

I do not know how to illustrate the difference between these two kinds of service more naturally than by referring to the conduct of children. Rather than be frowned upon by their parents, some will work instead of play. But they do not desire work for its own sake. Labor is chosen only as the lesser of two evils. If left wholly to themselves, they would prefer to play rather than labor. They love their amusements for their own sake.

True service of God is not submitted to as the lesser of two evils. Serving God is not regarded simply as something that must be done, however irksome the task. Gospel service is not an uphill business, a grievous chore in which there is no satisfaction. Like the playing of children, true service of God is delighted in and loved for its own sake.

Acceptable service of God consists in the total devotion of the heart to the same end to which God is devoted. God is love and He is above all devoted to the good of universal being. His heart is full of zeal. His mind is wholly bent in promoting universal good as far as it can possibly be accomplished. The true service of God consists primarily in a heart of supreme benevolence or supreme devotion to the glory of God and the interests of the universe.

True service of God consists in the complete devotion of the whole being to the same end to which God devotes all His attributes: To promote His own happiness and glory (not because it is His own, but because it is infinitely the greatest good in the universe), and to promote the holiness, happiness and universal good of moral and reasonable beings. God devotes His entire being to these things. Gospel service consists of commiting your whole being to the same end as God, for the same reasons He fully and freely gives himself to the promotion of this end.

Suppose you employ a servant who works only for his wages, and feels no interest in the goals which you are aiming to promote. He takes no interest in your business for its own sake. He has no disinterested desire to promote the end at which you aim. He simply labors for his wages. He begins as late in the morning as possible, rests as long at noon as conceivable, labors as sparingly as he can, and quits as early as possible, while trying not to threaten the reduction of his wages. You could say rightly that this man is serving himself and not you. He is a mere eye-servant. He is entirely selfish and has a completely different end in view from what you have. Now suppose the end you have in view is not selfish. Suppose your goal is not your own aggrandizement, the promotion of your own interests or happiness, but the promotion of the general good. Wouldn't you blame such a servant for not taking an interest in the end itself? Wouldn't you regard his selfishness with abhorrence? Wouldn't you regard him as engaged in self-service and as deserving reproach?

Suppose a king were entirely disinterested. Suppose he was engaging all his attributes, all his wealth and all his time in the unselfish promotion of public interests. Suppose he said to his subjects, "Here, take hold and help me to forward this great work. Since your individual interests are part of the public interest, I will see that you have your reward. But the thing I require of you is this: Take an interest in the end for its own sake. If you do not take an interest in the end for its own sake, your labor will all be selfishness and slavery. If you do not love the work on its own account, it will of course make you miserable. It will hang heavily on your hands and you will long for the going down of the sun. So, let your heart be deeply imbued with the spirit of doing good. Let doing good be the grand object of your life—love it for its own sake and your labor will be to you a continual feast."

Now suppose that the subjects took hold of the work as mere mercenaries, and cared for nothing but their wages, took no interest in public happiness and well-being, but simply served for reward. This would be a selfish eye-service and not heart-service. This would be serving self and not the king.

Therefore, true service of God consists in devoting your whole being to the promotion of the same end with the same motives or reasons that God has. Gospel service consists in serving from supreme benevolence, or having an absorbing disposition to do good for its own sake and because it is good.

True service of God consists in doing the above with the same feelings God has when engaged in this work. If your heart is fully devoted to this work, if your whole being is given up to service as God's being is fully given up to it, if this is done for the same reasons God has, if you have disinterested love for the work itself, the feelings with which you undertake this service will naturally and necessarily be the same in kind as those in God. The feelings with which you take up and pursue gospel service must depend upon your motives for engaging in it. If your motives are the same as God's, your feelings will be the same in kind as His.

Acceptable Service to God

Several things are implied in acceptable service to God. For sinners to render acceptable service to God they must have a radical change of heart from selfishness to disinterested benevolence. Please understand, by disinterested benevolence I do not mean that the mind feels no interest in the service; I mean the direct opposite of this. I mean that the mind does take the deepest, supreme interest possible in promoting the good of being *for its own sake and on its own account*.

Acceptable service to God implies a deep and efficient sympathy with Him in regard to the great end of life. By deep, I do not mean a mere superficial sympathy consisting in the emotions. I mean a sympathy of heart, a sympathy based on the deep foundations of moral action. People may have emotions and desires that consist merely in the effervescence of an excited mind, while their hearts—the deep fountains of moral action—are really utterly selfish. Therefore, by a deep sympathy I mean a sympathy of heart, of will, of preference and purpose. By an efficient sympathy, I mean an energetic, active sympathy; one that produces active and vigorous effort to glorify God, to save souls and to promote universal good.

Acceptable service to God necessarily involves a continual manifestation of benevolence by the most strenuous and self-denying efforts to promote the universal good of being. Acceptable service also requires the same feelings in kind toward whatever hinders or promotes the work that God has. For example, because God always performs acceptable service, He has absolute sureness or peace of mind in himself. God, knowing himself to be infinitely benevolent, has a supreme contentment in himself. Every benevolent being in the universe should feel a perfect serenity in God, because He is benevolent. We naturally and necessarily feel delight in a being whose character is in all respects just as we would wish it to be. We should also have delight in the character of Christians, as far as benevolence is discernible in them. We should have grief and indignation at sin and sinners, and at whatever is inconsistent with the highest good of the universe.

Difficulty in Passing Judgment on Others

Sometimes legal service and gospel service can be distinguished from each other; but they are not always distinguishable from each other in their *outward* manifestations or in the visible conduct of people. The servant who labors merely for his wages, *may* to most human eyes appear just as good as one who is truly unselfish in his labors. A mere legal religion *may* be strictly punctilious in all the outward duties of life. The Pharisees were like this to a very great extent, and great multitudes in every age of the church have been this way as well.

People rendering legal service cannot always be distinguished from others by the amount of zeal they have concerning religious subjects. The Pharisees were very zealous. They would compass sea and land to make one proselyte. Paul testifies that the Jews had a "zeal of God, but not according to knowledge." Paul seems to have been as zealous before his conversion as afterward; therefore, his legal and his gospel religion could not be distinguished from each other in the amount of zeal which he manifested while under the dominion of each.

Legal and gospel service cannot always be distinguished in their visible results and effects. A legal zeal may be very punctilious in the discharge of outward duty, may make many proselytes, and may bring multitudes under conviction so they can embrace a legal religion. Legal zeal may bring multitudes under the dominion of a religion of resolutions and self-dependent efforts to serve the Lord. The law has its converts as well as the Gospel. People may be baptized unto Moses as well as unto Christ.

For example, thorough legal laborers may promote extensive apparent revivals. And indeed, they may be real revivals, so far as they go: a revival of conviction in the church; a revival of confession; a revival of zeal; a revival of resolutions; a revival of conviction among sinners; a general awakening to religious subjects; and a revival of obtaining hopes and engaging in the legal service of God. But all this can take place without a solitary conversion to Christ and His Gospel; with scarcely an instance of bringing a person into the liberty of the blessed Gospel.

As far as the *number* of converts is concerned, and as far as most visible appearances go, these two kinds of service may resemble each other to the extent that one is not distinguished from the other.

How to Distinguish Legal From Gospel Service

Legal and gospel service may be distinguished by the *kind* of zeal. The kind, not the degree, of Paul's zeal set apart his Christian character from his legal character. His Christian zeal was benevolent, kind, compassionate, heavenly. His legal zeal was boisterous, denunciatory, censorious, hard-hearted, fiery, earthly, sensual, devilish. Therefore, a truly Christian zeal may always be differentiated from a legal zeal in the manifestation of deep benevolence and compassion; a sensitive, chastened, heavenly sensibility to the wants and woes of men.

Gospel service may be distinguished from legal service by the fact that it affords to our minds the fullness of a present satisfaction and happiness. Gospel service is the mind's present solace and joy, its own present reward and happiness. From the very nature of the case this must be so. Acceptable service to God is doing just what the mind views in its own nature as supremely desirable and agreeable. It is that which the mind loves for its own sake, and therefore it naturally and necessarily makes the mind happy. From the laws of its own being, the more intently the mind actively participates in this employment, the more full and perfect is its joy.

Here I must remark that a very extraordinary objection has been stated to this view of the subject: *If the mind loves the service of God for its own sake, there is no more virtue in that state than there is in eating our food because we love it.* To this I reply: Our appetite for food is constitutional and not something in which we are voluntary; therefore, partaking of our food because we love it is not virtuous. If our love of the service of God were involuntary and constitutional, as our appetite for food is, the service of God would not be virtuous. But remember, the appetite or disposition to serve God consists of benevolence or good-willing; therefore, it is entirely voluntary. Indeed the very appetite is itself a choice. It is therefore virtuous in the highest degree. If our appetite for food were voluntary and depended upon our own voluntary choice, both the exercise and the gratification of our appetite from correct motives would be virtuous. Therefore, the virtue of serving God lies in the exercise of benevolence or in choosing to do good for its own sake.

The very exercising and carrying out of benevolence in the active service of God necessarily brings with it a present and essential happiness. God's happiness consists in His benevolence. God has always found His happiness in the exercise of benevolence. He does not need to wait until He has done His work before He enjoys it. He is not waiting to complete His toils, expecting happiness only when He can sit down in supineness and inactivity. The more glowing and deep His benevolence, the greater is His happiness. Just so with a gospel service. The mind engaged in this service feels that "an excellent oil is distilled" upon it in the very exercise itself. It feels itself fanned by the breezes and moistened by the dew of heaven. It feels itself to be in an atmosphere of love. Its very labors are essential sweetness, and it drinks from the river of life while it pushes its efforts to promote universal happiness.

Gospel service is a course of life in which all the powers of the mind harmonize. This harmony of the soul brings necessary and essential happiness. Why? Because gospel service is love. It is the love of God. It is the temper and spirit of God. It inherently produces the very happiness of God in kind. Except for outward trying circumstances, it would be as perfect as that which God experiences amid His own labors of love.

In proof of the position I have taken, I will quote from the Bible. "Will he delight himself in the Almighty? Will he always call upon God?" (Job 27:10). Here we see one of the marks of the hypocrite; he does not *delight* himself in the Almighty. It is truly remarkable to what an extent the Bible exhibits true Christianity as affording present joy and delight. I will only quote a few other passages out of the great multitude of passages upon this subject which may serve as specimens of the light in which the Holy Scripture presents this subject.

The work of righteousness shall be peace, and the effect of righteousness, quietness and assurance for ever. (Isa. 32:17)

All thy children shall be taught of the Lord; and great shall be the peace of thy children. (Isa. 54:13)

Thus saith the Lord, Behold, I will extend peace to her like a river, and the glory of the Gentiles like a flowing stream. (Isa. 66:12)

Thou wilt keep him in perfect peace, whose mind is stayed on thee: because he trusteth in thee. (Isa. 26:3)

Delight thyself also in the Lord; and he shall give thee the desires of thine heart. (Ps. 37:4)

I delight to do thy will, O my God; yea, thy law is within my heart. (Ps. 40:8)

When he cometh into the world, he saith, Sacrifice and offering thou wouldest not, but a body hast thou prepared me. (Heb. 10:5)

I have rejoiced in the way of thy testimonies, as much as in all riches. I will delight myself in thy statutes: I will not forget thy word. Make me to go in the path of thy commandments; for therein do I delight. I will delight myself in thy commandments, which I have loved. Their heart is as fat as grease: but I delight in thy law. Unless thy law had been my delights, I should then have perished in mine affliction. O how love I thy law! It is my meditation all the day. Thy testimonies have I taken as a heritage for ever: for they are the rejoicing of my heart. I love thy commandments above gold; yea, above fine gold. (Ps. 119:14, 16, 35, 47, 70, 92, 97, 111, 127)

Blessed is the man that feareth the Lord, that delighteth greatly in his commandments. (Ps. 112:1)

Are the consolations of God small with thee? Is there any secret thing with thee? (Job 15:11)

The statutes of the Lord are right, rejoicing the heart: the commandment of the Lord is pure, enlightening the eyes. The fear of the Lord is clean, enduring for ever: the judgments of the Lord are true and righteous altogether. More to be desired are they than gold, yea, than much fine gold: sweeter also than honey and the honeycomb. Moreover, by them is thy servant warned; and in keeping of them there is great reward. (Ps. 19:8–11)

The disciples were filled with joy, and with the Holy Ghost. (Acts 13:52)

The kingdom of God is not meat and drink; but righteousness, and peace, and joy in the Holy Ghost. (Rom. 14:17)

Now the God of hope fill you with all joy and peace in believing, that ye may abound in hope, through the power of the Holy Ghost. (Rom. 15:13, 29)

Not for that we have dominion over your faith, but are helpers of your joy: for by faith ye stand. (2 Cor. 1:24)

I wrote this same unto you, lest, when I came, I should have sorrow from them of whom I ought to rejoice; having confidence in you all, that my joy is the joy of you all. (2 Cor. 2:3)

In a great trial of affliction, the abundance of their joy and their deep poverty abounded unto the riches of their liberality. (2 Cor. 8:2)

The fruit of the Spirit is love, joy, peace, long-suffering, gentleness, goodness, faith, meekness, temperance. (Gal. 5:22)

I thank my God upon every remembrance of you, always in every prayer of mine for you all making request with joy. (Phil. 1:3, 4)

Looking unto Jesus, the author and finisher of our faith; who for the joy that was set before him endured the cross, despising the shame, and is set down at the right hand of the throne of God. (Heb. 12:2)

Whom having not seen, ye love; in whom, though now ye see him not, yet believing, ye rejoice with joy unspeakable and full of glory. (1 Peter 1:8)

These things write we unto you, that our joy may be full. (1 John 1:4)

I am filled with comfort, I am exceeding joyful in all our tribulation. (2 Cor. 7:4)

Ye had compassion of me in my bonds, and took joyfully the spoiling of your goods, knowing in yourselves that ye have in heaven a better and an enduring substance. (Heb. 10:34)

All these curses shall come upon thee, and shall pursue thee, and overtake thee, till thou be destroyed; because thou hearkenedst not unto the voice of the Lord thy God, to keep his commandments and his statutes which he commanded thee. And they shall be upon thee for a sign and for a wonder, and upon thy seed for ever. Because thou servedst not the Lord thy God with joyfulness, and with gladness of heart, for the abundance of all things. (Deut. 28:45–47)

In this last passage the terrible curses of the law are represented as coming upon the children of Israel because they had not given that service to God which made them happy. They had not enjoyed and delighted in the service of God.

Finally, my brethren, rejoice in the Lord. (Phil. 3:1)

Rejoice in the Lord alway: and again I say, Rejoice. I rejoiced in the Lord greatly, that now at the last your care of me hath flourished again; wherein ye were also careful, but ye lacked opportunity. (Phil. 4:4, 10)

Hannah prayed, and said, My heart rejoiceth in the Lord; mine horn is exalted in the Lord; my mouth is enlarged over mine enemies; because I rejoice in thy salvation. (1 Sam. 2:1)

My heart is glad, and my glory rejoiceth; my flesh also shall rest in hope. (Ps. 16:9)

They departed from the presence of the council, rejoicing that they were counted worthy to suffer shame for his name. (Acts 5:41)

Obviously, from these and multitudes of other passages as well as from the very nature of the case, the acceptable service of God must constitute the present happiness of the soul.

Legal service and gospel service may be differentiated from each other in the fact that a legal service affords very little present satisfaction since it consists of a self-righteous peace. The very nature of the case shows this must be so. Since legal service is not chosen for its own sake, it is often a laborious and bothersome business. It is something submitted to, which is not pleasant in itself, but on account of an anticipated reward. Such a man is religious for the same reason that some people take bitter medicine. The medicine is disagreeable in itself; but submitted to for the sake of an anticipated good. It is taken as the lesser of two evils. Therefore, a person may toil hard for the sake of his wages; but toil is not desired for its own sake, but only submitted to for the sake of the end. Just so with a legal religion. It is an uphill business. It is regarded as the lesser of two evils. It is something that must not be omitted, but attended to from the dire necessity of the case. Since it does not consist in benevolence, and is not disinterestedly loved for its own sake, in the very nature of the case it cannot compose the mind's present happiness. The principal happiness which the mind can feel in it is just that kind of satisfaction which a man may take in labor for the sake of the end he has in view. If the end could be obtained without it, he would gladly forego the labor; but since it cannot, he submits to the labor just in proportion as he regards the end. So when a man's convictions of the validity of religion, the danger of hell, and the desirableness of heaven, are vivid in his own mind, he engages in the duties of religion with a good degree of alacrity, feeling, and sensible satisfaction. Just as a man who had a prospect of a great reward would feel a kind of satisfaction in his work. But as soon as his convictions of sin and danger subside, in the same proportion his religion becomes an irksome business. His prayers are short and far between, and the whole round of what he calls his religious duties drags heavily as a sad weight upon his shoulders. In short, his religion is slavery. It is more tolerable than hell; but it does not have the comforting sweetness of heaven.

Holiness of Heart

If anyone would serve the Lord, he must begin by making his heart holy. God says to the wicked, "Make to yourself a new heart and a new spirit." From Ezekiel we read, "Cast away from you all your transgressions, whereby ye have transgressed; and make you a new heart and a new spirit: for why will ye die, O house of Israel?" (Ezek. 18:31). The very beginning of true religion is to give up selfishness and become supremely, disinterestedly benevolent.

Since a holy heart consists of this, it is impossible that any other service can be acceptable to God. Indeed it is the only service that is really offered to God. A legal service is self service. It is laboring for wages. It is not doing good for the love of doing good, and for the sake of the good, but merely for the sake of the wages; therefore it is not the service of God but of self. Those, therefore, who have unholy hearts "cannot serve the Lord, because He is a holy God." Until they are holy, they cannot engage in a holy service. When Joshua told the people they could not serve the Lord, because He is a holy God, he did not intend to tell them that they could not become holy, but that remaining unholy, they could not serve the Lord. You, therefore, who are unholy, must not think to set about the acceptable service of God without first becoming holy. This is your first work.

Holy service is the only service that can do you any good. God cannot *honestly* reward a legal service with the gift of eternal life, because there is not a particle of real virtue in it. Nor can He *possibly* reward a legal service with eternal life; for eternal life is holiness and its indispensable results. It is absurd, therefore, to suppose that God can give you eternal life as the reward of legal service. Nor can you receive eternal life as the gift of grace while your heart is not holy and you are not rendering to God a holy and acceptable service. Remember, if a man does not find his happiness in benevolence and in that course of life which God requires, he neither deserves to be happy nor is it possible for God to make him happy. If he does not love his work, he does not deserve any reward for it, because his heart is not in it. Nor is it possible that he should be acknowledged for his labor, unless he finds a sweetness and an enjoyment in the labor itself. Heaven will not consist in laziness and inactivity, or in giving yourself up to the practice of sweet emotions and ecstacies without benevolence and effort, but must consist in the service of God. If you are not engaged in that kind of service here which makes you happy, the same kind of service will not make you happy in heaven.

If your legal service does good to others, it is no thanks to you. If through your legal and selfish efforts others are blessed, really converted and saved, it is not because you have had this end ultimately in view, as one desired and chosen for its own sake. Therefore, whoever may be blessed, you are not blessed and do not deserve to be. The conversion of souls does not fill you with joy and satisfaction, because it is not the end which you have chosen for its own sake. If you do not find your reward in the very luxury of promoting the good of others, then you are deceiving yourself in the anticipation of a future reward for mere legal services. This is a horrible delusion.

In all probability you will do no good in a legal state of mind; for it seems to be a universal law that "like shall beget like"—slaves shall beget slaves. Being a legalist yourself, you will beget proselytes in your own likeness. Christ said of the Pharisees, "ye compass sea and land to make one proselyte; and when he is made, ye make him two fold more the child of hell than yourselves" (Matt. 23:15). If you have not in your own experience gone any further than a legal religion, your spiritual children will be legalists. You may make converts, but they will not be Christians. They may be zealous, a great change may occur in them; but they will not be converts to Jesus Christ. They will not know what the true mind of God is, because you have never really and fully exhibited it to them, either in your preaching or in your temper and life. As a general thing, your converts will fall even below you, and be twofold more the children of legality and of hell than yourself.

If your religion does not afford you present happiness, if you do not feel that there is real salvation in it, it is a legal and not a gospel religion. Beloved, there is a sad mistake upon this subject among professing Christians. Instead of finding their religion a peace-giving, soul-satisfying employment, they think themselves to be engaged in what they call Christian warfare, and expect to be happy when they get to heaven and can cease their troublesome labors. They drag on against their feelings, and elaborate a most distressing religion. The more they have of it, the more miserable they are. They keep up a continual controversy between their conscience and their hearts, supposing this inward struggle to constitute Christian warfare. They please themselves with the idea that their painful service will soon be over, and they shall have nothing to do but sit down in the midst of the joys of heaven.

Now Christian warfare consists of conflicts with those temptations, persecutions and besetments that endeavor to draw us aside from the labor in which we take so much delight. The true Christian's religion is his life. When he is left to pursue his course of doing good without opposition or temptation, he finds the service itself to be the delight and satisfaction of his soul. He knows full well that the grand difference between heaven and this state of existence lies in the fact that there he will have less interruption, temptation and resistance, and therefore can give himself up uninterruptedly and without fighting Satan to that service in which he has had such supreme delight. Is this your religion?

True Service of God and Revivals

There is reason to believe that many of what are called revivals of religion go no further than to make the converts mere legalists, and that the converts never get fairly into the kingdom of God. They are awakened and more or less deeply convicted, but never come to possess the idea that religion is love since their hearts remain entirely selfish. They are deceived by the vividness of their emotions and the excitement of their minds into a belief that they are truly converted to God.

To prove this position, observe the spirit in which what claim to be revivals are often conducted; the class of motives presented are merely legal. The spirit in which they are preached is merely legal. The whole tendency of the sermon and the manner of the preaching (together with the illustrations used in endeavoring to impress the minds of inquirers with the true nature of religion, submission and conversion), are altogether calculated to induce only a selfish religion, to bring the converts under bondage to law and to sin, instead of bringing them into the glorious liberty of the children of God. I could give multitudes of illustrations of this method of conducting revivals that would naturally lead a reflecting mind to the conclusion that such partial exhibitions of truth, and the exhibition of such a legal spirit and zeal as are constantly presented to the minds of inquirers, would have a tendency only to a legal, selfish, self-righteous religion.

Another example is the spirit of the converts of such revivals. They often manifest nothing more than a legal spirit. As a matter of fact, they are not brought into the glorious liberty of the children of God. Instead of gospel liberty, they are brought into legal bondage. By a little conversation with them, it appears that their religion is not love; it is not holy, heavenly, meek, humble and broken-hearted, but selfish, constrained, severe, unkind, sectarian and censorious.

Sometimes inquirers are told not to expect happiness in Christianity. They are told they must be willing to wait for happiness until they get to heaven. When those who have professed submission begin to suspect that their submission is not the right kind, and to complain that they don't feel right, that their hearts are hard, that they have little or no enjoyment in the duties of Christianity, that they are very little inclined to labor and to pray for the conversion of souls, and that as a matter of fact they do not enjoy or find themselves blessed and happy in the service of God, they are flatly told (when thus convicted by the Holy Ghost of being wrong) that they are not to expect to be happy in this world. They are told that labor is their great business (whether they enjoy it or not), that they must not regard the feelings with which they work, but live up to their convictions of duty (whether they enjoy this service or not). Sometimes they are even told that the less enjoyment they have in Christianity, the more virtue there is in it, since in that case their faith is not selfish but disinterested.

Now I do not hesitate to say, and I say it with grief, that in this kind of instruction there is a radical and most ruinous error. Such teaching, from its very nature, is calculated to fatally mislead the soul just as universalism does or even more so; for while this teaching is equally false, it is much more plausible than universalism. It entirely overlooks the nature of true Christianity. It completely sets aside the idea that Christianity is love, and that nothing but love and its resultant fruits are true Christianity. It holds up the idea that Christianity consists of a mere legal conformity to convictions of duty.

It is true that people are not to wait for particular emotions of any kind, nor to be stumbled in the discharge of their religious duties, because they do not at all times experience the same inward emotions in the discharge of duty. But it is also true that all Christianity is love or benevolence, and that the exercise of benevolence naturally and necessarily produces happiness, and that there is a divine sweetness, peace and soul-satisfying happiness in the very exercise of benevolence itself. Therefore, when a professed convert finds that his religion hangs heavily and that his religious duties lay as a weight upon his hands, if you tell him this is just what he may expect and that this is no evidence that he is wrong, that this laborious and annoying business may after all be true faith, you will inculcate upon him an abominable delusion and fatally deceive him as much as if he were taught that he could go to heaven without a change of heart.

In all such cases, it is of fundamental importance to discriminate clearly between *seeking* happiness in religion and actually *finding* it. The Bible most clearly teaches us (and we may learn the same from common sense and from the nature of the case) that if permanent happiness is the object of pursuit and the grand motive which leads the mind to become involved in religion, this is self-righteousness, self-service, and not the true service of God. But it is also true that if the heart is truly benevolent, if the service of God is chosen and loved for its own sake, if to do good for the sake of the good and from a desire to promote the holiness and happiness of being for its own sake is what the mind desires above all and chooses on its own account, it is impossible that the duties of religion should not afford an exquisite relish in themselves and a permanent and blessed happiness.

If a convert complains that he does not enjoy the service of the Lord, he should be instantly and plainly told that he is not performing the service of the Lord, that "wisdom's ways are ways of pleasantness and all her paths are peace," that "the path of the just is as the shining light that shineth more and more unto the perfect day," and that if these are not conscious realities in his own experience, he is deceiving himself. He needs to be told that there is a divine sweetness and relish in benevolence and that if he does not find this in the service he proffers to God, it is because he does not keep God's commandments. For "in the keeping of [God's commandments] there is great reward" (Ps. 19:11). Nothing can be of greater importance than to make the impression at once that he is a legalist and has not been born again. But instead of this, professed converts are often encouraged to rest in a legal religion as though it were true Christianity, and are only exhorted to persevere, be faithful in the discharge of duty, binding and supporting themselves by oaths and promises and resolutions, and not to expect happiness in religion until they get to heaven. What a terrible delusion is this! And yet this is, as a matter of fact, the real history of many in revivals.

Another consideration that establishes the fact that multitudes of professed converts have only a legal religion is they so suddenly backslide and, as it is commonly expressed, "grow cold in religion" as soon as the effervescence of excited emotion subsides. Now whether their religion is of the heart or merely of the emotions can only be known as the greatness of the excitement subsides. Strong feelings or very highly excited emotions may induce volition or a series of volitions at variance with the state or permanent preference of the will or heart. A miser may be so affected in view of some spectacle of wretchedness as to exert a temporary influence over his will, so that by a single choice he will relieve the sufferings before him in view of which he is so greatly excited. But his volition has been induced by an excitement of feeling in opposition to the permanent state of the will. Now as soon as the excitement has subsided, he calls himself a fool for having been thus induced to part with his money and almost curses himself for his folly.

In revivals of religion it often happens that strongly excited feelings will induce for the time being a series of volitions that will so shape the life as to really lead us and the subject of them to believe that the heart is truly changed, that the deep moral preferences of the soul are reversed, that selfishness is given up, and that benevolence has taken its place. But let excitement fully subside, and then you will be able to discern clearly and distinctly whether the heart is changed or whether the choices of the mind were only induced by temporary excitement. If it is found that the deep currents of the soul are benevolent, that selfishness in heart, life, business, and social relations is abandoned, and that love and a supreme disposition to do good to all around is the real state of the heart, then you may be certain that there is true conversion. Only then has the soul truly entered into the service of God, rather than a mere legalist serving for wages.

Converts should always be made to see that the more unselfish they are in religion the more happy they will be. Of course the less they seek happiness the more they will find it. The less regard they have to their own happiness, the more self-sacrificing and disinterested they are, the greater will be their joy and the fuller the tide of their blessedness.

Suppose a man comes across a person in deep distress sitting in the street. Being touched to the very quick with the spectacle before him and from unmingled benevolence, he steps into a store and purchases a basket of provisions and sets it at the feet of this object of poverty and distress. The fainting, starving person lifts up his streaming eyes of gratitude, speaks not, but gives a look of unutterable thanks. Now the happiness of this benefactor would be precisely in proportion to the strength of his benevolence and disposition to do him good. If his benevolence was strong and unselfish, and he longed to do him good for its own sake, his happiness would be full in compassion and he would find his happiness to be in proportion to his unselfishness. In this thing he would find the most exquisite happiness simply because he sought it not, upon the principle that he who would lose his life for the sake of doing good shall find it and keep it unto eternal life.

Perseverance and Apostasy

The secret of the perseverance of the saints in Christian faith is that they love it for its own sake. On the other hand, the secret of the apostasy of legalists is that when their excitement subsides, their religion becomes too irksome a business for them. They abandon it because they have no heart in it. "They went out from us," says John, "but they were not of us; for if they had been of us, they would no doubt have continued with us: but they went out, that they might be made manifest that they were not all of us" (1 John 2:19). Now the same apostle affirms that "Whosoever is born of God doth not commit sin; for his seed remaineth in him: and he cannot sin, because he is born of God" (1 John 3:9). The seed which remains in him is the love of God, the same benevolence that is in the heart of God. This has taken the place of selfishness, has come to be the supreme ruling disposition of his soul. And because his seed *remaineth* in him he cannot live in sin. And if it is found that he can live in sin, it is certain that he is not born of God.

Whether your religion is of the right kind or a mere legal religion will be attested by your own consciousness. You cannot help but know, if you will be honest with yourself, whether your religion is liberty of slavery. Would enough of the same kind make heaven? Or if you should multiply it a thousand fold would it increase your wretchedness?

The legality of professing Christians is a great stumbling block to sinners. Seeing as they do that there is little or nothing of enjoyment in the religion which they observe in some people, they conceive of God as a hard master, of religion as a hard and cruel service, as destitute of everything that is pleasant and sweet and soul satisfying, infinitely less delightful than the pleasures of sin. Therefore they think religion is to be postponed as long as possible, and yielded to only when dire necessity forces it upon the soul. It is obvious that they look upon religion as only the lesser of two evils. It is better than to go to hell, but much less valuable in itself than the pleasures of the world. Now where do they get this idea? How can it be so almost universally prevalent among the unrepentant? The fact is, they receive their notions of what Christianity is from what they observe among those who profess to be Christians, those characteristics they behold in their parents and relations and friends around them who claim to be in the service of God.

Can you see why sinners are so reluctant to give up the pleasures of sin, and why young persons are apt to conclude that Christianity would set aside all their happiness? Why, because this is the very idea of some who claim to be Christians themselves! A few years ago, a mother (who professed to be a Christian) was distressed that her daughter, a light-hearted young lady, had become convicted and hopefully converted in a revival of religion. "Oh," she said, "what a pity that such a charming girl should be so early cut off from all the pleasures of the ballroom, and secluded from the gaiety of her young friends, and shut up to the sameness and solemn performance of religious duties." I trust there are not many professedly religious mothers who would say as much as this or even think it. And yet, if they did not, it might be that a mere natural fear of the loss of the soul, rather than a rich experience of the joys of God's salvation, would prevent their saying it. The fact is, multitudes of professing Christians know not what enjoyment in religion is. To them it is, after all, a naked reality that God is a hard master, that they have short keeping and hard labor, that they live on husks, and their Father does not feed them. But this is not the religion of the Gospel. It is not the religion of love. It is self-righteousness and ruin.

Do you see how some who profess to be Christians have not truly embraced the Gospel? Do you see why there are so few who truly enjoy the service of God, and feel constrained to speak of the joys of God's salvation? Those who do seem to enjoy the service of God, and who speak of the joy they find in serving God, are looked upon as a wonder, as having a great deal of animal feelings, and as being well nigh deranged. They are frequently rebuked and even despised for talking so much about their enjoyment in Christianity. They are suspected and publicly accused of selfishness, and of serving God for the loaves and fishes, without considering at all that it is their disinterested benevolence and labors of love that constitute their happiness.

There is a kind of happiness that is not Christian. And wherever it appears, it needs and deserves rebuke. It is the opposite extreme of a legal religion. It is antinomianism—the religion and happiness of emotions, ecstacies, and a false peace—amounting to a kind of quietism that does little or nothing to glorify God or benefit humanity. Now between this state of feeling and the happiness of true Christianity there is a distinction as broad and palpable as the noonday light. The one consists of the emotion and effervescence of excited feelings which does nothing, and the other consists in the exercise of good-willing, of benevolence, and labors of love, together with those states of emotion that naturally and inevitably result from this state of will. The happiness of one lies in doing nothing for the glory of God and the good of others, but rather giving up the mind to the influence of imagination and excited emotion. The happiness of the other is in giving up the whole being to active exertions for the promotion of the glory of God and the salvation of others.

Do you see the necessity of a class of ministers who know and continually experience the joys and the power of God's salvation? It is evident that ministers and all Christians must have such an experience if they are going to promote true Christianity. How shall a person describe what true Christianity is unless he has it in his own experience? How shall a man preach Christ, who does not know Christ? How shall a man preach a religion of love, and make people understand it, who is not himself in the enjoyment of it? Isaiah says: "Therefore the redeemed of the Lord shall return, and come with singing unto Zion; and everlasting joy shall be upon their head: they shall obtain gladness and joy; and sorrow and mourning shall flee away" (Isa. 51:11). The Psalmist says: "Create in me a clean heart, O God; and renew a right spirit within me. Cast me not away from thy presence; and take not thy Holy Spirit from me. Restore unto me the joy of thy salvation; and uphold me with thy free spirit. Then will I teach transgressors thy ways; and sinners shall be converted unto thee" (Ps. 51:10–13).

The grand reason ministers promote a legal religion is that they are themselves legalists. They preach as far as they know, and having only the baptism of John, they need someone to expound to them the way of God more perfectly. They testify and persistantly impress upon others what they have seen and experienced, and this they consider to be true Christianity. Nothing is more alarming to them than the idea of overcoming their sins. They would even show indignation at the profession of sanctification on the part of anyone. They would think that surely he knows little or nothing of the evils of a wicked heart, and would look upon him as in a most deluded and self-righteous state. They have never so much as conceived of gospel liberty. A religion of love, joy, peace, long-suffering, gentleness, goodness, faith, temperance, meekness, and all the graces of the Holy Spirit—what do they know of these? "That Christ may dwell in your hearts by faith; that ye, being rooted and grounded in love, may be able to comprehend with all saints what is the breadth, and length, and depth, and height; and to know the love of Christ, which passeth knowledge, that ye might be filled with all the fulness of God" (see Eph. 3:17–19). What do they know of this? Alas, the poor slaves! They regard the doctrine of entire sanctification in this life as a most dangerous heresy. It is so infinitely at variance with their own experience, and with all that they call and suppose to be Christianity, that they look upon such a sentiment as ridiculous and dangerous. I say then, we must have a class of ministers who will imperiously demand sanctification, and who know what gospel liberty is.

Look at Wesley and his coadjutors—or at Luther and his coadjutors. Read their writings. Look into Luther's Commentary on the epistle to the Galatians. Read the history of the life and times of those holy men. Witness the effect of their labors. What was the secret of all their success? The fact that they walked with God, that they were in the liberty of the Gospel, that they distinguished between the righteousness which is by faith and the righteousness of the law. In short, they pressed upon their hearers the great idea that God is love, that religion is love (not emotions or complacency), that benevolence is love, and under God this succeeded in kindling up among mankind the very fire that lives in the heart of God.

The truly Christian person need not and does not want to get to heaven in order to be happy. He is happy here. He finds that to be true in his own experience which James declares: "But whoso looketh into the perfect law of liberty, and continueth therein, he being not a forgetful hearer, but a doer of the work, this man shall be blessed in his deed" (James 1:25). Unless self-denial and the carrying out of your benevolence work in you a soul-satisfying happiness, you are not truly converted.

Great multitudes make up their minds to serve God without understanding definitely what it is to serve God. Many ministers preach on such texts as this when pressing sinners to the point of decision: "Choose you this day whom you will serve." But in respect to whose service they will choose, these ministers fail to accurately discriminate between a Gospel and a legal service. People today are in the habit of seeing themselves and others serve for reward. Because all their notions of service on every subject are selfish and they have little or no idea of any other service than this, it is fundamental to their salvation that a demarcation as clear as light be made between a selfish and a disinterested service. And as their notions are all selfish, no pains should be spared to fully clarify the true idea of a gospel service as distinguished from a legal service. They should be shown that one is holiness and the other is sin; one is serving God and the other is serving self; one is true Christianity and the other errant wickedness.

And now, dearly beloved, as I have spread out this subject before you, let me ask you where you are. What is your true character? What is your religion? Are you a real servant of God, or are you serving yourself? Are you a legalist, or are you a Christian? Are you converted, or are you unconverted? Are you free, or are you a slave? Do you walk with God in the liberty of the Gospel, or are you wearing the galling yoke of the law and living in bondage to sin? Oh, beloved, come to an honest answering of these questions. Remember that God has said, "For sin shall not have dominion over you: for ye are not under the law, but under grace" (Rom. 6:14). Does your experience test the truth of this? Can you honestly say "the law of the Spirit of life in Christ has made me free from the law of sin and death," or are you still crying out from the legal experience portrayed in the seventh chapter of Romans: "What a wretched man I am! Who will rescue me from this body of death?" My perishing and beloved souls, do not rest a moment in such a state as this. The whole matter of a legal experience is full of death, and the rottenness of a legal religion will lead you down to the gates of hell. Remember that "there is therefore now no condemnation for those who are in Christ Jesus. For the law of the Spirit of life in Christ Jesus has set me free from the law of sin and death."

If then your own heart condemns you, remember that God is greater than your heart and will also condemn you. Can a mortal be more righteous than God? Escape for your life, and rest not till you are rooted and grounded in love.[1]

---

[1]For more help in moving from a legal religion to gospel liberty in Christian faith, see especially Finney's sermons on Romans in *Principles of Victory* and *Principles of Liberty*.

4

ENTIRE CONSECRATION: A CONDITION OF DISCIPLESHIP*

"Whosoever he be of you that forsaketh not all that he hath, he cannot be my disciple" (Luke 14:33).

In this discussion I will show what is and what is not implied in forsaking all for Christ. I will discuss what is intended by being a disciple of Christ, and that being His disciple is an indispensable condition of salvation. We have a right to lay claim to discipleship and ask for divine teaching only insofar as we live in a state of entire consecration to God.

Forsaking all for Christ does not mean abandoning our possessions and friends to go on a pilgrimage. It does not suggest that we must actually part with all our possessions to be a disciple of Christ. Nor is forsaking all simply a barter or exchange—giving up worldly things in exchange for eternal life. Unfortunately, many people seem to think that forsaking all for Christ is merely giving up worldly things for the sake of getting heavenly things. This would be no more than speculation in the sense of gambling and is by no means the thing intended in the text.

What Does Forsaking All Really Mean?

Forsaking all for Christ implies a radical change of heart from selfishness to benevolence. In other words, "forsaking all" means abandoning self-interest as the chief end of your pursuit. Forsaking all is an absolute and everlasting giving up of self-interest and self-gratification as the goal of life. Forsaking all for Christ means entering into the views,

---

*The Oberlin Evangelist, lecture 30, April 14, 1841.

sympathies, and designs of Christ in promoting the glory of God and the interests of His kingdom.

Forsaking all for Christ unavoidably calls for abandoning the principle of self-ownership. Sinners are continually acting upon the principle of self-ownership, and practically insisting upon their right to dispose of themselves as they please without being accountable to God or man. Christ abhors this course of conduct. He denies their right to dispose of themselves, and claims them as His own because they were first created by Him and afterwards redeemed by His blood. Christ therefore insists that sinners cease to contend, in theory and in practice, that they are their own and have a right to dispose of themselves as they please.

Forsaking all for Christ also implies renouncing the claim of absolute proprietorship in anything. This means that you recognize the truth that you have nothing to properly call your own—that everything is God's and that you are His steward.

Forsaking all entails the hearty and practical recognition of universal stewardship—that everything you have and are, your being, life, health, body, soul, time, possessions and friends, are all regarded and treated by you in the highest possible sense as belonging to God. In everything, as His steward, you give Him a strict and impartial account. This implies that you really feel all your possessions are God's, and that you have no right to dispose of them except by His order. You should feel this way in regard to a farm, a house, or any piece of property for which you have title deeds. You should see yourself remaining in possession of these only as a tenant at will.

Suppose you had sold your farm or your house; title deeds had been executed, delivered, recorded, and you were only allowed to retain them till the owner came or sent someone to take possession. In such a case, you understand very well in what light you would regard his property. If you are an honest man, you would not think of selling it or making any disposition of it, except to maintain it to the best advantage for the owner—and whenever he should appear or send to take possession, you would have no thought of demurring to his right to take possession. You would feel all the time, "This is not mine." This would have a practical bearing upon all your conduct. You would naturally expect, at any time, to deliver possession at the call of the owner without gainsaying or resistance.

Forsaking all for Christ intrinsically implies a course of conduct in all respects corresponding to the state of mind of which I have just spoken. It is a state of mind in which you would no more think of disposing of the things in your possession without consulting God, and being satisfied in respect to His will upon the subject, than you would think of going and disposing of your neighbor's goods without consulting him. The man who forsakes *all*, in the sense of the text, feels that with respect to his fellow man his possessions are his own in reference to them; but in reference to God, his conscious and practical feeling is that these things are no more his—that he has no more right to discard them except at the bidding of God, than he has to discard of his neighbor's things.

Forsaking all means doing all this out of love for God, and not, as I have said, upon the principle of barter and exchange. It is to be done on the same principle which an affectionate wife would forsake all that she has and go into banishment with her husband from affection for him, and not because she expected an honor or prize.

Forsaking all must be joyful and not coerced. You must not consider forsaking all as the least of two evils, but as that which is right, just, useful, and loved for its own sake. It really is strictly just, for as a matter of fact you are not your own, but are mere tenants at will, with respect to all your possessions. It is therefore really a matter of strict justice that you should forsake all that you have in the sense explained. It should be done by you, because it is just and right, and from a love for right (not from fear of punishment if you do not do it). It implies your entire consecration to God and of all that you have and are: Nothing short of this is implied in forsaking all for Christ.

Who Is a Disciple of Christ?

A disciple is a pupil. To be a disciple of Christ is to be His pupil and have Him for a teacher. To be a disciple of Christ is to be a Christian, a follower of Christ, one devoted to His interest, one who embraces His principles, who believes His doctrine and follows His example.

Being Christ's disciple and receiving divine teaching is an express and indispensable condition of salvation. The doctrine of the indispensable necessity of the teaching of the Holy Spirit to the salvation of the soul is abundantly taught in the Bible, so abundantly that I need not take up your time in quoting proof texts.

Words are only signs of ideas. They give us no ideas where we have no experience. Unless we have the idea in our mind which they are designed to represent, or unless we have some experience that shall enable us to understand the meaning of the words used, they are a foreign language. Words that express spiritual truth are figurative, and except for the influence of the Holy Spirit, we would not grasp the real meaning of words any further than our natural experience of things would place us in circumstances to understand them. A selfish mind may and does understand enough to convict and condemn it, and enough to enable the mind to acceptably obey God. But since the unregenerate man is wholly indisposed to obey God, he does not and will not understand enough of divine truth to induce him to change his heart without the teachings of the Holy Spirit. Hence, the necessity of being taught by Christ.

Why Is Forsaking All a Condition of Discipleship?

The Bible plainly teaches that forsaking all is an indispensable condition of discipleship. Study the text, "Whosoever he be of you that forsaketh not all that he hath, he cannot be my disciple." Look at the nature of the case: Nothing short of this is conversion or regeneration. Regeneration consists in renouncing selfishness and becoming supremely benevolent. Regeneration is a change of heart. Nothing short of this is virtue, because nothing short of this is right. A man has not done right until he has done all that justice requires. Justice requires entire renunciation of self-interest as the great goal of life, and a cordial and universal consecration of self and all that we have to God. Until a person has done this, he has in no sense done right; he is dishonest; a defrauder and robber of God; and there is not and cannot be a particle of virtue in him.

Forsaking all is naturally indispensable to salvation. The prime idea of salvation is holiness. A man can neither be holy nor happy without forsaking all he has in the sense in which I have explained it above. Without this, he cannot be at peace either with God or with himself. It is just what God demands, what his own conscience demands, and what the universe demands of him. Until he does this, it is impossible that he should have peace.

Forsaking all is indispensable to understanding divine teaching. Renouncing selfishness as the rule of life, and entering a state of entire consecration to God's service are naturally indispensable to a right understanding of Christ's views, sentiments and instructions. There must be a similarity of views, feelings and experience between two persons, or they cannot satisfactorily understand each other.

If you are selfish and God is supremely benevolent, your views, feelings, and state of mind are so contrary to His that it is impossible for you to understand Him. All your habits of thinking and reasoning, and all of your understanding of language, is in accordance with the totally selfish state of your heart. How, then, will you understand the language of one whose state of mind is in all respects the exact opposite of your own?

Don't you find it remarkable that as soon as a person becomes thoroughly converted, the Bible (which had before been to him a dead letter), becomes at once so plain and simple? That which he read before without any interest or understanding now appears all new, plain, and glorious. His mind is filled with wonder that the Bible has never appeared so before. This is the natural result of being in a state of mind similar to that of the writers of the Bible. When people speak to us in our own language, and upon a subject in which we strongly sympathize with them, we understand them with the utmost ease. But if we are in the opposite state of mind, we almost invariably misunderstand them.

Without this state of mind, Christ cannot teach you; because you will not study. It is in vain for anyone to attempt to teach another, if he will not yield up his mind to the investigation and consideration of the subject. Therefore, unless you forsake your selfishness and become truly benevolent and engage your heart and soul with Christ in building up His kingdom, you will have no such interest in His purpose to motivate you to give your mind to the study and understanding of the means by which His end is to be obtained.

Unless you forsake all that you have, Christ cannot teach you, because you will not be sincere. What He says will not be received by you with honesty, candor and a disposition to know the truth. Without this state of mind, you will not be diligent in searching out His meaning. Nor will you understand the doctrines of self-denial which He teaches. Without a self-denying state of mind, without that state of mind which forsakes all that we have and abandons selfishness in every form and degree, we naturally shall not understand the doctrines of self-denial as taught by Christ. Without this state of mind, you will resist when He rebukes your prejudices, selfishness and lust. The doctrines of the cross cannot be received without the spirit of cross-bearing. Hence, cross-bearing is forever indispensable to discipleship.

Entire Consecration

We have no right to profess discipleship, nor to ask for divine teaching, unless we live in a state of entire consecration to God. This is the express condition of discipleship. The Bible invariably presents the beginning of true Christian faith as an act of entire consecration. It is, in the Bible, spoken of as a radical change of moral character, as a change of heart, as a new birth. The nature of the case shows that nothing short of this can be either virtue or obedience to God.

You are tempting God when you profess discipleship without possessing that state of mind which is the expressed and indispensable condition of discipleship. You tempt God to ask for divine teaching, or to ask Christ to be your teacher, unless you fulfill the condition upon which you can become His disciple.

Certainly Christ has a right to impose such conditions upon us. He is absolutely bound to do so. Both justice and the nature of the case render such a condition indispensable. It would insult Him to ask for divine teaching and claim to be His disciple, while as a matter of fact you do not fulfill the expressed condition of discipleship. Have we a right to retain our selfishness, to live in any form of sin, to reject the conditions and yet claim to be His disciples and come to Him for instruction, as if we fulfilled the conditions? Surely we have no such right and every such expectation is vain.

Christ regards all professions of discipleship without the spirit of entire consecration as highly abominable and dishonorable to Him. To all such persons He says, "I would thou wert cold or hot. So then because thou art lukewarm, and neither cold nor hot, I will spew thee out of my mouth" (Rev. 3:15–16).

Entire consecration and entire sanctification are the same thing. Recently, I have been amazed on many occassions to hear people contending for the doctrine of entire consecration to God in this life, who pretend to reject the doctrine of entire sanctification, as if they were two different things. Now the very meaning of the term *sanctification* is consecration. This is the meaning of the term as used both in the Old and New Testaments. It is really astonishing to see how much play there can be upon a word among professedly good men. They dare not deny the doctrine of entire consecration to God in this life, but having committed themselves against the doctrine of entire sanctification, they try to preserve their consistency in holding to the one and rejecting the other, thus assuming what is certainly contrary to fact, that they are different things.

Curiously, some writers in the religious periodicals are opposing the doctrine of entire sanctification, while they profess that all ought to preach the doctrine of entire consecration, not only as a thing attainable, but as something which we are to expect to attain in this life. I say again, to sanctify means to set apart, to consecrate to the service of God. Consecration and sanctification to God are words of precisely similar significance.

Entire sanctification is the very beginning of true Christianity in all saints. It is the very first act of obedience. This has been substantially insisted upon by all the leading orthodox writers for ages. President Jonathan Edwards says on this subject, in his treatise titled "Religious Affections," (Vol. 5 of his works, pp. 261–5):

> And this point may be further illustrated and confirmed, if it be considered, that the holy Scriptures abundantly place sincerity and soundness in religion, in making a *full choice* of God as our only Lord and portion, *forsaking all* for Him, and in a *full determination* of the will for God and Christ, on counting the cost; in our hearts closing and complying with the religion of Jesus Christ, with all that belongs to it, embracing it with all its difficulties, as it were

hating our dearest earthly enjoyments, and even our own lives, for Christ; giving up ourselves with *all that we have, wholly and for ever* unto Christ, without keeping back *anything* or making *any reserve*. In one word, sincerity consists in the great duty of *self-denial* for Christ; or in denying, that is, as it were disowning and renouncing ourselves for Him, making ourselves *nothing that He may be all*. Matt. 5:29, 30: "If thy right eye offend thee: pluck it out, and cast it from thee; for it is profitable for thee that one of thy members should perish, and not that thy whole body should be cast into hell. And if thy right hand offend thee, cut it off, and cast it from thee: for it is profitable for thee that one of thy members should perish, and not that thy whole body should be cast into hell." Matt. 6:24: "No man can serve two masters: for either he will hate the one, and love the other; or else he will hold to the one, and despise the other. Ye cannot serve God and mammon." Matt. 10:37–39: "He that loveth father or mother more than me is not worthy of me. . . . He that findeth his life shall lose it; and he that loseth his life for my sake, shall find it." Matt. 13:44–46. Luke 14:16–20, 25–33, and 16:13. Rom. 6:3–8. Gal. 2:20 and 6:14. Phil. 3:7–10. 1 John 2:15. Rev. 14:4. Gen. 12:1–4, with Heb. 11:8–10. Gen. 22:12 and Heb. 11:17, 24–27. Deut. 13:6 and 33:9. Now surely having a heart to forsake all for Christ, tends to *actually forsaking all* for Him, so far as there is occasion, and we have the trial. Having a heart to deny ourselves for Christ tends to *denying ourselves in deed*, when Christ and self-interest stand in competition. A giving up of ourselves universally as His, as subject to His will, and devoted to His ends. Our hearts *entirely closing* with the religion of Jesus, with all that belongs to it, and as attended with all its difficulties, upon a deliberate counting of the cost, tends to a universal closing with the same in *act and deed*, and actually going through all the difficulties we meet with in the way of religion, and so holding out with patience and perseverance.

Now here President Edwards expressly maintains all that is asserted in this discourse in respect to the real meaning of this text, and fully confirms the idea that entire consecration in the sense explained here is implied in "sincerity" in Christianity, and that it is indispensable to the existence of true Christianity in the soul. Indeed, President Edwards fully asserts all that any of us at Oberlin have ever pretended to teach on the subject of entire sanctification; for observe that he teaches in this paragraph (where he is discoursing particularly upon the nature or attributes of true Christianity), not only entire, but also continued sanctification. This, President Edwards says, is indispensable to the existence of "sincerity or soundness in religion at all."

Now let me ask, suppose someone were just what President Edwards here asserts is implied in the very existence of Christianity in the soul. What more does God require of him? Just read over the paragraph again, and see if he does not teach the very doctrine, in all its length and breadth, for which we have contended. President Edwards is not speaking of some rare attainment in religion, but of that which is indispensable to the very beginning of religion, as that without which there is no "sincerity or soundness in religion."

President Edwards, then, with all his fears of the doctrine of Christian Perfection, when describing true religion, asserts and maintains the very sentiment for which we contend, only changing the phraseology but manifestly meaning the same thing. What a deplorable state of things, when the church and its ministers, many of them, seriously call in question the practical attainability in this life of that which constitutes the very beginning of true Christianity.

The fact that Christianity consists in entire consecration is not at all inconsistent with growth in grace. To grow in grace is to grow in favor with God, for this is the meaning of the language. A child may consecrate all his little powers to God, and yet continue to grow in grace; that is, in the favor of God. This was actually the case with the Lord Jesus Christ himself. The word rendered *in favor* in the case of Christ is elsewhere rendered *grace*. As knowledge extends, holiness will extend; thus, the saints will grow in grace to all eternity.

You can see why Christ found fault with the members of one of the churches for having left its "first love." Their first love was right. It was entire consecration. And He regarded their having left their first love as an act of apostasy, for which He threatened them with destruction.

Since regeneration consists in entire sanctification, or consecration to God, the only question that can reasonably be incited is in respect to its permanency—whether, as a matter of fact, we may expect to continue in our first love—whether we may expect to abide in a state of entire consecration, or whether backsliding is a thing to be naturally expected. After all, who can really doubt that by the grace of God, a convert may avoid backsliding! Who can really doubt, if he be properly instructed, that he may continue to grow in grace, as he grows in the knowledge of our Lord Jesus Christ, until he becomes rooted and grounded in love? But this would be a state of permanent or continued sanctification.

To my mind, it is really shocking that the church should be alarmed when people are taught that they are to expect to attain a state of entire sanctification in this life. It is certainly a monstrous error to maintain that anything short of entire consecration to God is regeneration. If anything short of this is admitted by the teachers of religion to be true Christianity, it will inevitably lead the church into a fatal error. And here I could inquire of my brothers upon my knees in agony, whether it is not true that the preaching of the present day often makes the impression that entire consecration to God is a rare attainment—something to be aimed at indeed—but seldom if ever reached in this life—that the best services of the saints, and the best states of mind in which they are, are mingled with much that is wrong—and that they hourly, continually offend and even sin in their most holy performances. How infinitely dangerous is such teaching as this! How many thousands of souls have gone to hell because they have been led to believe they could be true Christians and yet be conscious of sin all the time. They have been convicted and conscious indeed that their best performances were sinful. And they have been taught that this is the case with all true saints, and that a consciousness of present sin is not at all inconsistent with their being saints. Worse still, that the more deeply conscious they are of sinning daily, in word, thought, and deed, the greater is the evidence of their humility, of the knowledge of their own hearts, and of the soundness of their piety.

Now I humbly ask, is this the standard God has set in this and many similar texts? Is this daily living in sin consistent with being a disciple of Christ? I implore you, my brothers, look to this, and see whether the blood of deceived professing Christians is not to be found on your skirts. Why, some of you talk about the dangerous tendency of preaching the doctrine of entire sanctification in this life. What can it mean, my brothers, that you do not perceive the dangerous tendency of preaching the opposite doctrine—the absolutely disastrous tendency of admitting, for one moment, that anything less than a state of entire consecration is at all acceptable to God or at all consistent with the existence of true Christianity? Here I wish to be carefully understood: I do not mean that a person's occasionally falling into sin is entirely inconsistent with his ever having been converted or with his being a true Christian. But I do mean and I solemnly believe that Christ meant to teach that nothing is acceptable to God short of entire obedience; and that every act which is really acceptable to God implies entire consecration to God. I have so recently addressed you upon this subject that I need not enlarge upon these thoughts.

Continuance in your first love, or in your state of entire consecration or sanctification to God, is indispensable to the enjoyment of divine teaching. Remember, I entreat you, that this alone is the express condition upon which you are to expect the teachings of Christ. Unless, therefore, you continue in this state, daily and hourly fulfilling this condition, you have no right to come to Christ expecting to be taught of Him. If you do expect it, you will not receive it. If you pray for the teachings of the Holy Spirit, you will not receive His influences unless you live up to His divine instructions, obey all the light you have, and thus live in a state of entire consecration.

Do you understand why so few really enjoy the continual teachings of the Holy Spirit—why they so often pray for the Spirit to teach them and are not taught by Him? Why is it that you, my brothers, so often ask for the Holy Spirit, and pray for divine guidance and teaching, and do not receive what you ask? I can tell you. It is because you do not fulfill the condition upon which alone you will receive His influences. You are indulging in some form of selfishness. You do not literally forsake all that you have. If you did, you might approach Christ, at any time, with the assurance that He will teach you. But as it is, He says to you, "Why call ye me Lord, Lord, and do not the things I say?" "Why do you claim me as your teacher, and come to me for instruction, when you do not comply with the expressed conditions upon which alone I have promised to teach you?"

You see, whenever you go to pray for divine teaching, this question must be distinctly before you: Do you so live in the fulfillment of the condition that you have a right to ask for His instruction? Many live in selfishness. They are as conscious that they do not live in a state of entire consecration as they are that they live at all. And yet, they continue to pray for divine teaching as if they fulfilled the condition. Sometimes they deceive themselves by thinking they are taught of Christ, when they are only amusing themselves with their own delusions or following the suggestions of Satan. At other times, they pray so often for divine teaching with a consciousness that they do not receive it, that they become discouraged and feel as if praying was of very little use. They really doubt whether the promises of Christ mean what they say. In all this they overlook the fact that there is an express condition to these promises, although not in all cases immediately connected with them. In our text, and in multitudes of similar passages, this is expressed in the plainest language; but they do not comply.

Do you see why the Bible is so little understood, even by the Christian Church? While the Church is in such a state that it doubts whether Christians are expected to live one single day without sin, it is no wonder they do not enjoy divine teaching. How can they understand the Bible without the Spirit of God? And how can they have the Holy Spirit without being in a state of entire consecration? In other words, without living in all respects up to the best light they have. When you obey one truth, Christ will teach you another. Of what use is it for Him to continue to teach you, if you refuse to obey what He teaches?

You can see why so few become thoroughly proficient in theological study. If young people studying theology, or ministers of any age neglect to fulfill the conditions, and refuse to live in a state of entire consecration to God, they will not and cannot enjoy divine teaching, and of course, will make very little progress in theological study.

You can see why ministers are so often at a loss to know what to preach. They seem to be very dull and dark, and feel it difficult to prepare for the pulpit. If they lived in a state of entire consecration, their feelings would be the very reverse of all this. They would enjoy the continual teaching of Christ. They would continually feed the church with knowledge and understanding. Out of their belly, as Christ has said, would flow rivers of living water.

You can see from this subject what great injustice a minister does to Christ, and to the church to which he ministers, if he does not live in a state of entire consecration to God. Why, suppose a church employed a minister, and instead of his living in such a manner as to enjoy divine teaching, he indulged in selfishness, appetites and lust, and thus deprived himself of the teaching of Christ. How infinitely does it endanger souls! How greatly does it dishonor God!

How much does praying for the influence of the Holy Spirit really mock and tempt God? Look at a band of selfish people professing to be Christians. They are assembled for a prayer meeting. Everyone of them, perhaps, is as conscious that he does not live up to the best light he has, that he does not forsake all that he has and live in a state of entire consecration to God, as he is of his own existence. Now what are they assembled for? Why, to pray for divine teaching, for the outpouring of the Holy Spirit upon them and upon others. Indeed! And is this not tempting God? You ought to remember the word of the Lord in Ezekiel 14:3: "Son of man, these men have set up their idols in their heart, and put the stumblingblock of their iniquity before their face: should I be inquired of at all by them?"

Now watch these same who profess to be Christians, praying daily around the family altar for divine teaching, without so much as seriously intending to live for a single day in a state of entire consecration to God. Why do they make such prayers? Why do they indulge the expectation of mercy, the influence of Christ's Spirit to instruct them? I answer, because they are not themselves thoroughly and continually taught that a state of entire consecration is the indispensable condition of being a disciple of Christ. Why, instead of this, the impression is made upon them that a state of entire consecration is rarely attained during one's earthly existence. And thus they live on, dragging their way down to death and hell, afraid of the doctrine of entire consecration to God in this life—for surely this is something entirely inconsistent with their experience. And how shall they ever have a different experience, unless the teachers of religion thoroughly awake to a state of entire consecration themselves, and to the duty of insisting universally upon entire consecration as the indispensable condition of discipleship?

Now, beloved, is it not one of the most astonishing things in the world, that with this and so many similar texts upon this subject in the hands of the church, a state of entire consecration should be so little insisted upon as indispensable to any degree of true Christian faith?

Forsaking all that you have and dying to selfishness is indispensable to the enjoyment of God and of Christ. A wife enjoys the society of her husband just in proportion as her heart is swallowed up in him. His presence is no satisfaction to her if she does not love him. If she has other lovers, the presence of her husband is but an annoyance to her. Just so with you. Unless you are supremely devoted to Christ, His presence would be but an annoyance to you.

Do you see why He so often cuts off every dependence on an idol? He is jealous over you with a godly jealousy. If He sees you going after idols and other desires, He will often interfere and remove them out of the way.

The doctrine of entire consecration or entire sanctification in this life is no new doctrine. It is as old as the Bible and as old as true religion. And as I said before, the only question is in respect to the continuance and permanency of this state in this life, and not at all whether a state of entire consecration is attained in the present life.

Sinners can see what they have to do to become Christians. You must renounce your selfishness and become supremely and disinterestedly benevolent. You must change your heart, forsake all that you have and consecrate your all to Christ.

To refuse or neglect to do this is to continue in a state of high-handed injustice and rebellion against God. It is refusing to render to God that which belongs to Him. It is to refuse to become an honest man, to do what is right because it is right. Until you do this, God cannot and ought not to forgive you.

And let me remind you all once more, that when you go to God in prayer, if you would be heard, you must go with the consciousness that you fulfill the condition; and remember, that "For if our heart condemn us, God is greater than our heart, and knoweth all things. Beloved, if our heart condemn us not, then have we confidence toward God. And whatsoever we ask, we receive of him, because we keep his commandments, and do those things that are pleasing in his sight. And this is his commandment, That we should believe on the name of his Son Jesus Christ, and love one another, as he gave us commandment" (1 John 3:20–23).

Now, therefore, I beseech you, remember to fulfill the condition that you may enjoy the teaching of Christ. Unless you are His disciple, you cannot be saved. And you cannot be His disciple, unless you "forsake all that you have."

5

A SEARED CONSCIENCE*

"Having their conscience seared with a hot iron" (1 Timothy 4:2).

In this sermon I will show what the conscience is and what it is not. I will explain what the Bible intends by a *seared conscience* and its evidences. I will also explain how a conscience becomes seared and the consequences of this.

The conscience is not the mere knowledge of right and wrong. Nor is it the mere knowledge of whether we do or do not, have or have not done, or been, or said, or felt right or wrong. The conscience may be regarded either as a power or as an act of the mind. In the former case, it is that power of the mind that affirms and enforces moral obligation, and that pronounces judgment upon obedience or disobedience. Conscience is not a legislator that makes law, but a judge that convicts of guilt and passes sentence in respect to the past. Conscience decrees and enforces moral obligation to obey law in regard to the future.

As a judge, conscience smiles upon obedience and frowns upon disobedience.

As an act of the mind, conscience is an affirmation or testifying state of reason in respect to the agreement or disagreement of the will with the law of God. Conscience testifies to the *moral character* of this agreement or disagreement of the will with the law of God; it testifies to the good or ill we deserve; and testifies to *our moral obligation* to obey in the future.

In short, conscience is the conscious affirmation or felt testimony of the reason upon these points. Sometimes conscience seems to be used in the Bible as including that state of the sensibility, compunction,

The Oberlin Evangelist, lectures 31 and 32, April 28 and May 12, 1841, are combined in this sermon.

and distress of the mind on the one hand, or the consciousness of peace and happiness on the other that is naturally connected with the emphatic affirmations of reason. The Bible is written in philosophical language, but for the most part in popular language. And I am persuaded that the modern understanding of the term conscience often, if not always, includes that state of the sensibility which we call remorse or approbation. In this definition, I do not intend to speak in strictly scientific language, but what I have said is sufficiently accurate for the purpose of explaining the conscience to those who do not study metaphysics.

A Seared Conscience

A seared conscience is the refusal or neglect of the reason, or that power of the mind (whatever you may please to call it), to make emphatic representations of moral obligation or of guilt. A person may know his duty without feeling impelled by an emphatic affirmation of moral obligation to do it. He may know that he is or has been wrong without the consciousness of being arraigned, convicted of guilt and condemned. When a person does not feel obligated to do his duty, his state of mind clearly indicates a seared conscience.

The conscience must be seared with a hot iron when questions that respect our own usefulness, or the usefulness of others, are not treated as moral questions. Conscience must be seared with a hot iron when the choice of a profession, companion for life, or anything else that must increase or diminish or in any way have a bearing upon the moral influence we are to exert upon the world, fails to be regarded and treated as a moral question of deeply solemn importance and an imposing moral obligation of awesome magnitude.

If you can neglect to inform yourself on such subjects as those above without a sense of guilt (especially when the means of information are within your reach, and still more especially if the subject is presented to your consideration), if you can remain quietly ignorant in respect to questions of usefulness or duty without a deep sense of guilt, it demonstrates that your conscience is seared with a hot iron.

When you can neglect any known duty without the bitterness of remorse, your conscience is seared with a hot iron. When you can trifle with your health; go out in the cold in any way inappropriately clothed (unless you are under the necessity of doing so) your conscience must be seared with a hot iron. When you can neglect to ventilate your room, see that you have not too little or too much heat; in short, when you can in any way trifle with your health (that precious gift of God) without conviction of guilt, your conscience is alarmingly seared.

When you can trifle with your time; spend it reading plays and novels, slang in newspapers, or in any other way squander an hour or a moment of your precious time, without compunction, your conscience is already seared.

When you can hinder others and trifle with their precious time, without remorse, your conscience is seared. Suppose you have an appointment to meet others on business and are behind your time and hinder them; what an evil this is. If you can be guilty of it without remorse, your conscience is seared as with a hot iron. If you have boarders and do not prepare their meals punctually, but hinder them by not having their meals in readiness at the specified moment; you have done them and the cause of God an injury. And if you do not feel condemned for this, it is because your conscience is seared.

If you do not feel condemned for coming late to church and disturbing the worship of God's house, it is because your conscience is seared with a hot iron. This is especially true if you are a minister and are in the habit of being late.

If you can stand and talk with and hinder a man while at work, or in any way cause him to spend a moment's time in vain, without remorse, it is an evidence that your conscience is seared. When you can in any way disregard the rights of others, in things ever so trifling, it indicates a seared conscience.

When you can squander your possessions in any way, and consume them upon your lusts, without remorse, your conscience is seared as with a hot iron. If you can spend God's money for tobacco or any unnecessary and unwholesome articles of luxury or dress without deep compunction, it shows conclusively that upon those subjects your conscience is seared with a hot iron.

When you do not feel that you are stewards and absolutely and practically regard yourselves in this light in respect to all the possessions you have, it is because your conscience is seared with a hot iron.

When you can neglect to pay your honest debts, or when you can consider yourself as not to blame for being in debt, especially when your debts were not contracted under the pressure of an absolute necessity, it is because your conscience is seared with a hot iron.

When you can lay a stumbling block before a brother without compunction or remorse; when you can indulge in any course of life that has a tendency to mislead him; when you can unnecessarily try his temper, say or do anything that has a tendency to mislead him or guide him into sin, it indicates a seared conscience.

When you can allow difficulties between yourself and others to remain unsettled, without using every Christian means to adjust them, it proves that your conscience is seared as with a hot iron.

When you can be in the habit of borrowing and using your neighbor's tools without perceiving and feeling the injurious tendency of such conduct and without realizing the pernicious principle on which such a practice turns, it is because you have a seared conscience. Many people act as if conscience had to do with but one side of this question; that it is the lender exclusively, and not the borrower, who is to look to his conscience and see that he does not violate the principles of benevolence. But let us look at the principle contained in this. If you borrow money from a person, you expect to pay him interest or at least repay the same amount you borrowed. But if you borrow a man's coat or tools that are injured by wear, the lender and not the borrower has to pay the interest, and often a very high rate of interest too. Many have lost their tools and have paid at the rate of twenty-five percent for the privilege of lending them.

Suppose a man has a hundred dollars in dollar bills. Suppose money is scarce, so a hundred men desire to borrow it, every one in his turn. Suppose each one should wear out a dollar of it. The man's hundred dollars are used up. Now, suppose a man asked you to lend him money and also pay him the interest on the money he borrowed from you. Since he was asking you to pay the interest instead of him paying the interest, wouldn't you exclaim, "Why, I never heard of such a request! Do you ask me to lend you money and pay you the interest besides?" Now anyone should be ashamed, and have reason to be ashamed, to make such a request. His naked selfishness would in such a case be obvious to everyone. And who would think of accusing the lender of selfishness in such a case, if he should refuse to lend his money for nothing *and* pay interest besides *and* finally take the trouble to go after it. And yet, this involves precisely the same principle upon which many conduct themselves in the neighborhoods where they live by continually borrowing and using up their neighbors' tools and perhaps compelling them to go after them, and that too without compunction or remorse. They are far from feeling compunction or remorse and perceiving that they are actuated by the most unpardonable selfishness. Sometimes they complain and suppose themselves to have a right to complain of the selfishness of a neighbor who should refuse to indulge them in acting upon such principles.

By this I do not mean to say or intimate that in certain cases it is not proper and a duty for neighbors to borrow and use each other's tools. But this I do say, the practice *as practiced* is unjustifiable. Borrowing should not be resorted to except in cases where a man might, without any cause for blushing, ask a man to lend him money not only without interest, but also with him paying the interest as well.

When you can neglect secret prayer without feeling condemned or without feeling a great sense of guilt resting upon you, it is because you have a seared conscience. The same is true when you can perform secret prayer slightly, with little or no feeling, faith or earnestness. Or when you can indulge wandering thoughts and use words in prayer scarcely knowing what you say, and all this without deep compunction and remorse. This state of mind is a certain indication of a seared conscience.

When any duty is urged upon you, without your feeling the force of moral obligation to perform it; when truth and argument do not take hold of your mind and deeply impress you with a sense of responsibility; and when, in such a case, you do not feel the impressive affirmations of conscience impelling you to the discharge of duty, it indicates a seared conscience. When you can satisfy yourself with the outward performance of duty, while your heart is not right; when you can satisfy yourself with the mere form of religion and duty, while your heart is not deeply engaged in it and this without a deep sense of guilt, it indicates a seared conscience. When you can neglect the means of grace, or attend upon them carelessly, in a prayerless, heartless manner; when you can indulge wandering thoughts under preaching or in reading your Bible; when you can go to and return from a meeting without earnest prayer that the word may be blessed to you; when you can hear and soon forget what you hear, without solemnly laying it to heart with a fixed purpose of entire obedience; when these things can be without deep compunction, it is because your conscience is seared with a hot iron.

When you are satisfied with anything as a performance of duty, knowing that you are not actuated by love, it is because your conscience is seared and has become very superficial in its affirmations.

When light upon any subject does not cause your conscience to enter into judgment, strongly affirming moral obligation and pronouncing its sentence upon you if you neglect your duty, it is because your conscience is seared with a hot iron. When evidence makes but little impression upon you; when it does but little good to reason with you; when light, truth and argument seem to pass over your mind without lodging in it; when you are not convicted and converted by a reasonable degree of evidence; when you do not feel yourself shut up to the necessity of yielding to a preponderance of evidence or falling under deep condemnation, it is because your conscience is seared.

When the discussion of any important practical question can be postponed and place given to matters of less importance; when you can lay up such a question for future consideration and go on in courses that are at least questionable, merely designing at some future time to examine and settle the question; when this can be done without a deep sense of guilt, it shows that the conscience is seared with a hot iron.

When any form of selfishness can be indulged without shame, it is because you have a seared conscience. When you can transact business upon selfish principles, take advantages in business that put money in your own pocket at the expense of another; when you can enrich yourself by any employment without regarding the interests of those with whom you deal as you do your own, your conscience is seared with a hot iron.

When you can complain of a lack of conviction of sin, this is evidence of a seared conscience. When you can neglect to make confession of your sins to those who have been injured by you, and thus persist in your injustice and wickedness without remorse, your conscience is seared with a hot iron. When you can make excuses for not confessing; when you do not feel impelled by a sense of duty to make *full* confession; when you can satisfy yourself with a heartless, constrained or partial confession; when you can be satisfied with a private confession when it ought to be public; when you can be satisfied with confession without repentance, your conscience is seared with a hot iron.

When you can neglect to make restitution to the extent of your ability; when you can retain in your possession that which in equity belongs to another (in short, when you can hold on to possessions that were obtained by a violation of the great law that requires you to love your neighbor as yourself); when you can hold on to them without restoring them to their rightful owners when it is in your power, it is a demonstration of a seared conscience.

When you have no sense of moral obligation in respect to those habits of life that have an influence upon your brothers, your family, the community in which you dwell, and upon the world at large, it is because your conscience is seared. For example, if you have no conscience on the subject of retiring to rest in due season, and rising in the morning also at such an hour as best consists with health; if you can habitually allow yourself on any occasion without necessity to sit up late at night and rise late in the morning; if you can have no system in this respect, no principle, no conscience about it; if these things are left without consideration or reflection to the neglect and injury of your own health, the injury of your family, and of course to the injury of the church and the world, your conscience must be seared with a hot iron. If you have no conscience in respect to observing these things for your family's sake; if you do not require them and everyone under your control to have a system, principle and conscience upon these subjects from which they will no more depart without imperative necessity than they would go without their necessary food, it is because your conscience is seared.

When you have no conscience in regard to your mode of dress; if you can compress your chest with tight lacing or in any other way jeopardize your health for the sake of personal appearance without compunction of conscience, it is because it is seared with a hot iron.

When you can wear ornamental dress and consult appearance rather than utility in your dress and equipage; when you can have regard to fashion rather than to health, without hesitation, your conscience is seared.

When you can neglect cleanliness in respect to your person, your dress, your house or your furniture, your conscience is seared. When you can neglect to attend to things in their proper season, or only transact your business in a careless and slovenly manner; when you can leave your tools where you use them without putting them in their place; when you can leave your tools exposed to the weather, leave your barn doors open, and things around you in a state of confusion and disorder; when you can waste anything (in short, whenever you can neglect to attend to every duty that belongs to you, at the right time, in the right manner, and in all respects as it ought to be attended to) without feeling condemned for this neglect, it is because your conscience is seared with a hot iron.

Whenever you can without compunction and through any neglect or carelessness break anything, injure the tools, furniture, or anything else with which you are entrusted, whether it belongs to yourself or anyone else, your conscience is seared.

When you can neglect without a sense of guilt and condemnation to ventilate your rooms, air your beds and clothing, neglect to exercise, labor, or rest, or to attend to anything else that your health and highest usefulness demand, your conscience is seared.

When you can neglect, to the extent of your ability, to support the institutions of the Gospel, to pay your minister's salary, to aid in the support of the expenses of the church; when you can see the house of God lie waste, the doors and windows out of repair, the house in a filthy state, and things at loose ends; when you can allow these things to be, without deep compunction of conscience, your conscience is seared with a hot iron. When a church is in a state to allow such things without deep remorse and self-condemnation the conscience of the church is seared.

But to notice again personal habits, if you have no system, no conscience, no principles in respect to the hours of eating and drinking, but allow yourself to consult convenience rather than physiological law, taking your meals at one time many hours apart, and at other times within three or four hours of each other, thus recklessly violating the laws of God established in your own constitution, your conscience is seared.

If you have no conscience respecting the kinds of food and clothing with which you attempt to supply the physiological needs of your system; if you can neglect to inform yourself in respect to what your habits ought to be in order to secure your highest health and usefulness; if you can make your depraved appetites the guide and measure of indulgence without deep remorse, it is because your conscience is seared with a hot iron.

When you can waste God's money in administering your lusts, when you can buy tobacco, tea, coffee, and similar fashionable but pernicious articles without deep compunction and remorse, your conscience is seared with a hot iron. When you can say you have no conscience on these subjects; when you can give countenance to these practices and to the use of these articles at home or abroad; when you can use them yourselves, or furnish them for your friends, and thus countenance the gratification of depraved artificial appetites, rather than use your resources for building up the cause of Christ and saving deathless souls from hell; when you can hear the wail of hundreds of millions of immortal beings coming upon every wind of heaven and crying out for the bread of life, and still have no conscience on the subject of the use of these pernicious articles by which the church is poisoned and the heathen robbed of the everlasting Gospel of the blessed God; if you have no conscience on such subjects as these, it is because your conscience is seared with a hot iron.

When you can see the church indulging in such things and not reprove them at home or abroad, especially by the impressible lesson of your own example, you must be extremely hardened and your conscience seared as with a hot iron.

When you can neglect to scrutinize your motives of action and go on day after day without self-examination in this respect; when you can neglect to exercise a godly jealousy over yourself without remorse, your conscience is seared.

When you can speak evil of a neighbor; when you can publish his real or supposed faults without necessity and do this without remorse, your conscience is seared.

When you can allow sin upon a brother without faithfully reproving him and yet not feel compunction of conscience, it is because it is seared.

When you can feel contempt for the person or talents of anyone without deep remorse, it is because your conscience is seared.

When you can think of sin without horror, something they would feel at such a thought in heaven, it is because your conscience is seared. How do you think an angel would feel if he thought he should sin against God? How would a saint in heaven feel under the same impression? Why, it would come over all heaven like the shock of an earthquake. They would all stand aghast and grow pale, would hang up their harps, and wail out with pain at the thought that one of their inhabitants should sin against God. Now what state of mind must that be when you can expect to sin without the deepest horror, without feeling a chill come over you and your blood almost coagulate in your veins. What, sin against God! Why, if the thought does not shock and agonize you, if the expectation that you shall sin does not seem even more terrible to you than death, where is your conscience, in what state of mind are you? Have you any sympathy with heaven? No, indeed. And perhaps I might and ought to say that if you can think of sinning without the most excruciating agony, you are even more callous than they are in hell.

How the Conscience Becomes Seared

The conscience becomes seared by the will resisting the affirmations of reason. The conscience is now generally supposed to be a function of the reason. Whether it is regarded in this light or not, certainly it becomes seared when the will opposes and continues opposed to the decisions of the reason.

The conscience becomes especially seared when the will persists in courses directly denounced or condemned by the conscience. In such cases the conscience soon becomes indignantly silent and leaves the soul stupefied to pursue its course of disobedience. It is often seared by a person's resorting to sophistry to justify any course of disobedience.

The conscience becomes seared by breaking resolutions. When you allow yourself to break or violate a resolution to do your duty, you have done much to sear and stifle your conscience. When you violate your promise on any subject, you have done much to sear your conscience. If you persist in this violation, your conscience will become seared with a hot iron.

Conscience becomes seared by diverting the attention of the mind from the moral character of your own actions. If you permit yourself to pass along without attending to the moral quality of your actions, your conscience will soon become seared with a hot iron.

Indulgence in known sin of any kind will greatly and rapidly sear your conscience. Especially indulgence in presumptuous sins or those sins already put under the condemning sentence of your conscience. Whenever conscience has called your attention to the sinfulness of any act or course of action and you still persist in it, this is a presumptuous sin. Such a course will soon cause your conscience to become seared with a hot iron.

If you indulge in anything when you doubt the lawfulness of it, you can sear your conscience. In speaking on the subject of meats offered to idols, the apostle Paul says, "he that doubteth is damned (or condemned) if he eat" (Rom. 14:23). He obviously recognized the principle that whatever is of doubtful lawfulness is to be omitted on pain of condemnation; if persisted in, the conscience will soon become seared. Many indulge in things after they have first doubted their lawfulness; but directly, their conscience becomes so seared that they no longer think with any degree of uneasiness whether it is doubtful or not, and they come to have no doubts about it simply because their conscience has become seared with a hot iron.

By making hypocritical professions the conscience becomes seared, by insincere professions of friendship, or by any insincerity whatever the conscience will soon become so seared that insincerity can be practiced without remorse.

Holding on to a hope of salvation that is pronounced hypocritical by the conscience will sear the conscience, while the hope of salvation, perhaps, will grow firmer and firmer. As the conscience becomes seared, less and less doubt will be entertained of its genuineness.

By indulging the appetites and passions, conscience becomes seared. When people allow themselves to eat too much at improper times and eat improper kinds of food merely to gratify their appetites, their conscience will soon become so seared that they can indulge in such things without reservation. They can then go on and break down their health and even destroy their lives by these indulgences, and then stupidly and madly ascribe their broken down health and premature death to a mysterious providence.

By indulging ill tempers, pride, vanity, envy, jealousy, ambition, prejudice, hatred, whatever unholy temper is indulged, you will soon so sear the conscience as to leave the mind in a state of great apathy with regard to its real moral character.

By indulging evil habits of any kind, such as using tobacco in any form or intoxicating drinks, by indulging in solitary sins or secret wickedness of any kind, the conscience becomes seared in an awful and alarming manner. How often do we find people who can indulge themselves in the filthy use of tobacco (and sometimes even ministers of the Gospel), without remorse.

Conscience is seared by evil speaking. When you allow yourself to speak unnecessarily of a brother's faults, or even uncharitably to speak of the wickedest man on earth, you do much to sear your conscience and blunt your moral sensibilities.

By making self-justifying excuses, the conscience becomes seared. Whenever you resort to any form of excuse for sin, you not only harden your heart but sear your conscience, until by and by you may come into such a state as to be in a great measure satisfied with your own excuses and fatally deceive your own soul with respect to your salvation.

You sear your conscience by procrastinating the performance of duty. Whenever you defer the performance of present duty or decline or neglect to attend to that which ought to be done at the present time, you sear your own conscience.

By attempting to defend error, the conscience becomes seared. Very often people have attempted to defend that which they knew to be error, and they have ended in believing their own lie to the destruction of their souls. It is a fearful thing to attempt to defend error on any subject, and very few courses are more certain to result in a seared conscience, a hard heart and a ruined soul.

By watching for the halting of others, the conscience becomes seared. By giving their attention to the sins of others, many people have overlooked their own sins until their conscience has become seared with a hot iron. In this state of mind, they can see enough to blame in others, but very little to blame in themselves. They can become censorious and denunciatory, and wonder at the long-suffering of God in sparing others in the midst of their awful iniquity. They can be almost insensible to the fact that they themselves are among the greatest sinners outside of hell.

By neglecting to administer reproof to those whose sins are known to us, the conscience soon becomes so seared that we can indulge in the same things ourselves with very little compunction.

By resenting or resisting reproof when admonished by others, by calling it censoriousness and denunciation, by objecting to the manner and spirit of reproof instead of exclaiming with David when reproved by Nathan: "I have sinned against the Lord," your conscience becomes seared. This is one of the ways in which I have observed that ministers are exceedingly apt to sear their own conscience. You may have observed that some are particularly apt to resist and resent reproof and sear their own conscience in a most alarming manner. And they are not ashamed to manifest a spirit under reproof which they would not hesitate severely to rebuke in anyone else.

By mocking God in prayer and in other devotional duties, you sear your conscience. This also is one of the ways in which church officers, and especially ministers of the Gospel, are exceedingly in danger of searing their conscience. If they allow their religious exercises to become professional rather than strictly devotional, if they allow themselves to pray and preach and exhort because it is their business, when their hearts are not deeply imbued with the spirit of devotion, then conscience soon becomes so seared that they are ripe for ecclesiastical denunciation, excision, and opposition to revivals and reform. How often and how distressingly has this been manifest! And what is worse than all, the conscience becomes so seared that for these things they will not allow reproof if faithfully administered and with the utmost kindness, without manifesting great indignation and perhaps a spirit of revenge. Oh, with what pain do I say this of some of the ministers of the everlasting Gospel.

By grieving and resisting the Holy Spirit, many sear their conscience. Many stifle and quench conviction until they have only a little more moral sensibility than a beast. Others neglect and refuse to act on light as fast as it is received or they neglect to reach after light on every question of duty.

The conscience is seared by neglecting universal reformation. If reformation is not universal, it cannot truly go forward at all. "Whosoever shall keep the whole law, and yet offend in one point, he is guilty of all" (James 2:10). The indulgence of any form of sin renders all obedience for the time being impossible. It is a state of mind directly opposite that of holiness. If in anything you neglect to reform, if you do not extend reformation universally over the whole field of moral obligation, your conscience will soon become seared with a hot iron.

By transacting business on worldly principles, you sear your conscience. No one can adopt the common business maxims of the world and act upon them with a clear conscience. The law of God requires you to love your neighbor as yourself. Therefore, who can adopt the principle of making the best bargain possible and of consulting only self-interest without deeply and rapidly searing his conscience?

By engaging in party politics, you will sear your conscience. By this I do not say that all attention to politics will sear the conscience. For as human governments are necessary, politics are to be a part of everyone's religion. But mark what I say. No one can go with a party as a party and vote for the candidates and support the measures of a party without a proper regard to the moral character of the candidates and measures, without rapidly and deeply searing his conscience. How many young converts have rapidly and ruinously backslidden by engaging in party politics and by transacting business upon worldly principles. As certain as your soul lives, if you do these things your conscience will become seared with a hot iron.

By exaggerating or putting a false coloring upon facts related by you, or by hypocritically covering up the real truth where truth ought to be known, conscience becomes seared. By dishonesty in small matters, by taking trifling advantage in weights and measures, by a little negligence in the transaction of business for others, by going late to work, by squandering scraps of time, by standing still or giving other inattention to business when in the employment of others, and by thousands of nameless little dishonesties, the conscience becomes deeply and ruinously seared.

By speaking evil of others, by receiving much good at the hand of others without any endeavoring to repay them or do them good, you will sear your conscience. I might pursue this part of the subject to any length, but must break off here.

The Consequences of a Seared Conscience

One consequence of a seared conscience is a certain delusion with regard to your character and what you deserve. If your conscience becomes so seared as not to call particular attention to the moral quality of your actions, you are already under a deep and damning delusion with regard to your real character before God.

You will develop a false security arising out of a delusion in respect to what you really deserve. A false hope of salvation may be and probably will be another result of a seared conscience. If your conscience is seared, you will almost naturally mistake a mere antinomian religion for true Christianity, and hold on to a hope that is as thin as a spider's web.

A seared conscience will give you a false peace, or lead you to mistake apathy on moral subjects for that peace which those have who love the law of God.

A seared conscience will lead to abandonment by the Spirit of God. Indeed, the very fact that your conscience is seared is an evidence that the Holy Spirit has forsaken you. And when your conscience becomes seared, it may prevent His return forever.

You may be given up to the buffeting of Satan, until he may bewilder, harass, and deceive you; till he has led you to destroy your own life. You may be given up to believe a lie about damnation. You might be given false anticipations in regard to your future usefulness. If your conscience has become seared, you may rest assured you will do little or no good in the world. And as a general truth, you will be useless in proportion as your conscience is seared.

Another consequence may be a broken down constitution. If you have—and will have—no conscience in regard to your physiological and dietetic habits; if you will neglect or resist the light, and even sneer at reforms, you may expect, sooner or later, to experience at least the penalty of violated physical law in a broken down constitution and a premature grave.

Another consequence may be worse than a useless life. Persist in your dietetic errors, trample down the laws of your being, and madly presume upon the strength of your constitution, until you become a dyspeptic or until some form of chronic disease has seized upon you, and ten to one your life will be worse than useless in the world. In such circumstances, you may be so hardened and your conscience so seared as not to be ashamed to complain of your ill-health and think yourself abused if you do not have the sympathy and assiduous attention of all around you. But mark what I say. In such cases, God deeply abhors the diseased state of your body that you have caused as much as if you had those forms of disease that are universally known to be a consequence of vile indulgences. If you had one of those diseases, you would expect contempt rather than pity and sympathy. And how is it that your conscience is so seared with a hot iron that you can have any other form of disease which is the result of a reckless violation of physical law without shame and deep remorse? For myself, I cannot be sick, unless I have been placed in such circumstances as necessarily to overwork my organs, without feeling the deepest shame and remorse. Sickness is the result of violated physical law; and when that violation can be avoided, it is a deep sin and shame which produces sickness. But all this you may overlook, and will overlook, if your conscience becomes seared. And you may go down to your grave and to hell under the deep abhorrence of God for your reckless violations of the laws of your being; pitying yourself, and ascribing both your disease and death to a mysterious providence.

If you sear your conscience, your influence will be pernicious upon all who come within its reach. If they have confidence in you, they will be emboldened to practice what they see you practice, to say, do and neglect what they behold in you. And thus you may become a pest and a curse to the community in which you live.

You may become a great annoyance to those who are around you. I would as soon have a pestilential disease in my family as a person with a seared conscience, who can violate the Sabbath by improper conversation, improper reading, a trifling and gossiping spirit, who has no conscience in respect to attending to those things that are expected of him, and who can say, do, and omit many things that are inconsistent with the law of love, and yet have no conscience about it. Such a person is an insufferable annoyance and a nuisance in any family.

If your conscience is seared, you may in all probability ruin your posterity, if you have any. Your reckless violations of the law of love will inculcate lessons upon them that will probably ruin their souls.

If your conscience is seared, you will entail ruin upon the country in which you dwell in proportion to the amount of your influence. Are you a minister, a deacon, an elder, a man or woman of leading influence? How dreadful must be your recklessness when your conscience has become seared with a hot iron! Perhaps you can use or sell intoxicating drinks; perhaps you can use or sell tobacco; perhaps you can encourage the church and community in the use of tea and coffee and other worse than useless articles of luxury and have no conscience about it; perhaps you can listen to the appeals and wails of six hundred million heathen and complain of hard times, and yet have no conscience on the subject. Perhaps in a great measure through your example, the church and the community of which you are a member are expending vastly more than necessary, merely to gratify their appetites and indulge their lusts rather than to save a world from eternal hell, and you have no conscience about it. "Oh shame, where is thy blush?" Oh man, where is your conscience?

If your conscience becomes seared, you will certainly do much to depress the standard of holiness, to resist the principles of reform, and to hinder the conversion of the world. You will block reform and be a real and terrible curse to the world while imagining that you are in a good degree useful.

If your conscience becomes seared, you may, as Achan did, bring the curse of God upon the community to which you belong.

If you are an impenitent sinner, if your conscience becomes seared, it will effectually prevent your conversion.

If you have ever been converted and your conscience becomes seared, it will effectually prevent your sanctification.

If it becomes seared, it may lead you into a deep delusion in respect to the degree in which you are sanctified, and you may vainly imagine that you live without sin while you are in the gall of bitterness and bond of iniquity.

If your conscience becomes seared, you will feel very little horror at the idea of sinning against God. With a seared conscience, you can expect to sin, more or less, as a thing of course from day to day without feeling such abhorrence of sin as to make you avoid it as you would avoid the gates of hell. Nay, if your conscience becomes seared, you may plead for sin and defend it as something unavoidable, which nobody is expected to live without. You may wallow in your iniquities with little more remorse than a swine.

From this subject we can see why many have no conscience on a great variety of moral questions. Few things are more common than to find even those who profess to be Christians, when expostulated with about certain habits and practices which are manifestly sinful when viewed in the light of God's law, have no conscientious scruples and indeed have no conscience upon the subject. They can practice many forms of intemperance, trifle with their health, squander their time and money, neglect to save, do much to injure the world in many ways, and yet have no conscience about it.

Their having no conscience on such questions is no proof that they are not guilty in the sight of God, and that their practices are not contrary to the law of God. Their consciences are seared and for the time being maintain an indignant silence. But does this prove that what they are doing is not displeasing to God?

A silent or a seared conscience is conclusive evidence that you are wrong. Conscience is never silent with respect to what is right and will always smile its approbation and fill the mind with peace when you do right. When, therefore, you have no conscience at all upon a subject; when you are not impressed with a sense of doing either morally right or wrong; when you are neither filled with peace nor stung with remorse, you may rest assured that you are wrong, and that conscience is maintaining an indignant silence.

A person who professes to be a Christian and who also has a seared conscience is more injurious to the cause of Christ than many infidels. Who professes to look to an infidel as an example on moral subjects? But let a professing Christian have a seared conscience and make no scruple to practice any form of intemperance, trifle with the Sabbath, become excited in party politics, transact business upon selfish principles, engage in novel-reading, squander his money upon his lusts, throw away his time, speak evil of his neighbors, or indulge in any form of sin, and his example is a thrust at the very vitals of the Christian faith. Why? Because he professes to be a Christian! People take it for granted that almost anything he may do is right, or that to say the least it is not inconsistent with salvation. And thus multitudes are emboldened in sin.

Many mistake a seared conscience for an approving one. They profess to be conscientious in what they are doing, evidently meaning by this that they feel no compunction in doing as they do, while it is evident that they have not the peace of God and the deep approbation of conscience in the course they are pursuing. Now, the absence of the approving smiles of conscience should teach them that they are laboring under a delusion in supposing themselves to act in accordance with the dictates of conscience.

You see from this subject how many professors of religion manage to retain their hope of salvation, even though they are as much in selfishness and sin as they are in the world. The fact is, their conscience has become seared with a hot iron. Having very little sense of moral obligation, they pass along securely with a lie in their right hand. To them the words of the prophet Isaiah apply with great emphasis: "A deceived heart hath turned him aside, that he cannot deliver his soul, nor say, Is there not a lie in my right hand?" (Isa. 44:20).

There are many whose consciences are seared on almost all moral subjects and seem to have been so for a long time. They seldom or never appear to be impressed with the deep conviction that they deserve the damnation of hell. Others seem to have a conscience measurably awake on some subjects, but profoundly asleep upon other subjects, where they have for a long time resisted truth and indulged in sin.

It is easy to see why some become universalists and reject the idea that sin deserves eternal punishment. Since the world began, I doubt whether there was ever a case in which a person became a universalist before his conscience became seared. I do not believe that it is naturally possible for a person with a thoroughly developed and active conscience to doubt the justice of eternal punishment.

You see the importance of cultivating, especially in children, a quick, sound and thorough conscience. The ability to reason should be developed as early as possible, so as to give conscience at the earliest possible hour an influence over their will before their habits of indulging the flesh have become too much confirmed to render it hardly possible for them to be converted.

Do you see why there is so much indulging the flesh without remorse among those professing faith, even though they are expressly commanded to "put on the Lord Jesus Christ, and make not provision for the flesh, to fulfill the lusts thereof" (Rom. 13:14)? In general, they are just as eager in their inquiries and efforts to obtain those things that will gratify their appetites as most of the ungodly are. They are as great epicures. They seem to take as much pain and are at as much expense to gratify their tastes and seem to lay as much stress upon mere gustatory enjoyment, as if to gratify their appetites is the purpose for which they live. Many of them will manifest as much uneasiness, and even disgust and loathing, at a plain, simple, wholesome diet as ungodly sinners do. And yet, they appear to have no conscience on the subject. Further, they not only gratify their appetite for food or drink, but their hearts seem set upon gratifying all their animal appetites and passions; and instead of keeping their bodies under subjection, they seem to have given up the rein to appetite. The apostle Paul might say of them, "Whose god is their belly, and whose glory is in their shame, who mind earthly things" (Phil. 3:19).

Do you see why so many can allow themselves to be ignorant on so many important practical questions without remorse? They never have examined many of the questions of great importance that have been pressed upon their attention, and when the means of knowledge are within their reach, they have no conscience about them.

When the conscience becomes seared upon one subject, it will in all probability become seared upon other subjects. By a natural process it will ultimately become generally seared and prepare the way for embracing universalism and infidelity. I might easily explain the philosophy of this, but have already said so much in this discourse that I must defer the explanation.

Do you see the infinite importance of a quick and searching conscience? It is wholly indispensable to growth in grace. There can be no such thing as a healthy piety without it. But a quick and searching conscience is especially important to a Gospel minister. If his conscience is seared, many sins will be practiced by him and allowed to exist among his people without his reproving or even seeing them. This subject shows why so many forms of sin are allowed to exist in some churches; so much selfishness, worldly-mindedness, pride, vanity, luxury, speculation, novel-reading, party-going, evil-speaking,and many forms of sin are allowed to exist from year to year without rebuke and without appearing to be perceived by the minister. Now, who does not see that such a minister is "a blind leader of the blind?" His conscience is so seared that he has very little moral sensibility. If his conscience were awake, such a state of things would wring his heart with insupportable anguish. He could not hold his peace. He would cry out in his pangs. His soul would be in travail day and night. He would lift up his voice like a trumpet and rebuke those iniquities.

Do you see the grand secret of the barrenness of many ministers? Having a seared conscience they know not how to bring the church under conviction for their sins. They do not know how to develop the conscience either of saints or sinners. They know not how to enter into the secret workings of the human heart and ferret out the various forms of iniquity that are lurking there. They do not know how to carry the light of the law of God into every department of human action, and to so develop conscience as to send a pang of agony along every fibre of the moral nature while indulging in any form of sin. The fact is, if a man would get at the conscience of others, he must have a conscience himself. And again, I say, a minister with a seared conscience is "a blind leader of the blind."

Let this subject be a warning to young men who are in a course of preparation for the gospel ministry. My dear brothers, I beseech you to remember that your consciences need to be cultivated as much as your intellect. And do remember that a thorough preparation for the ministry implies the education of the whole man. Unless your moral powers are developed and your conscience quickened and kept in a state of intense sensibility, however great your intellectual progress may be, you can never be a useful minister.

We see from this subject why so few young men do, as a matter of fact, make thorough, efficient and successful ministers. Why, in how many forms of sin do they habitually indulge while in college, and indeed through all their course of education? While they are disciplining their intellect and acquiring a knowledge of the sciences, they are benumbing and searing their consciences. They are, as it were, putting out the eyes of their minds on moral subjects. In short, they are doing just what will effectively disqualify them and render it impossible that they should ever make successful ministers. My dear young brothers, if in your education you indulge any form of sin; if you do not as assiduously cultivate a tender conscience as you pursue any branch of education whatsoever, you not only entirely overlook what constitutes a thorough course of preparation, but, on the contrary, you are taking a course that is a mere mockery upon the idea of a thorough preparation for the ministry.

We see that it is utterly in vain to talk so boastingly about a thorough course of training for the ministry, while so much sin is allowed among the young men in the course of training and so little pains are taken to develop and quicken their consciences and sanctify their hearts. As a matter of fact, the present courses of education for the ministry are to a great extent a failure. It is in vain to deny this. It is worse than in vain. It is errant wickedness to deny it. "Facts are stubborn things." And the average rate of ministerial usefulness throughout the whole of Christendom affords a demonstration of this truth that ought to alarm and agonize the church and cause those of us who are engaged in educating ministers to tremble and inquire upon our knees before the blessed God what it is that makes so great a majority of the young men who are trained under those influences so nearly useless in the church of God. Will this be called censoriousness? It is the solemn truth. I say it with pain and agony; but say it I must, and say it I would, if I knew it would cost me my life. Beloved brethren, unless there is more conscience in the Christian ministry, a broader, deeper, more efficient and practical knowledge of the claims of the law of God, a deeper, quicker, more agonizing insight into the depths of iniquity of the human heart, a greater abhorrence of every form of sin, a more insupportable agony in view of its existence in every form and in every degree, the world and the church too will sink down to hell under our administration.

I appeal to you, my brothers, who are already in the ministry; I appeal to your churches; I appeal to the onlookers, and inquire: How many forms of sin are allowed to exist in you and in your churches without anything like that pointed rebuke which the nature of the case demands? My brothers, do not many of you satisfy yourselves simply with preaching against sin, while you are afraid to so much as name the different forms of sin that exist among those to whom you are preaching? Do you not preach against sin in the abstract, with very little or no descending to particulars? Do you arraign selfishness in all the various forms that it exists among your people? Do you rebuke their pride, self-indulgence, vanity, luxury, speculations, party spirit; and indeed, my brothers, do you name and bring the law and Gospel of God fully to bear upon the various forms of iniquity in the details that exist among your people? Or are the consciences of some of you so seared as to render you almost blind to anything like the details of the sins that exist around you?

Not long ago a discerning man said that his minister preaches against sin, but he does not tell what sin is. He preaches against sin in general, but never against any particular sin. He denounces it in the aggregate, but never meddles with it in detail as it exists among his people. I do not give the words but the substance of his remarks. Now, my beloved brethren, of how many of us could such a testimony as this be borne with truth? How many such ministers would it require to convert the world? Of what use is it to preach against sin or in favor of holiness in the abstract, without entering into the details so as to give our people a true idea of what sin and holiness are?

Do you see the importance of praying continually for a quick and tender and powerful conscience? Do you see the importance of great watchfulness lest we should abuse and seduce our conscience by indulgence in sin? Do you see the great importance of faithful dealings with the consciences all around you, so as to keep your own and their consciences fully awake and as quick and sensitive as the apple of the eye? Do you see the importance of self-examination in regard to the real state of our consciences, whether they are fully awake to the whole circle of moral duties and obligations, or whether they are asleep and seared on a great many questions that come within the cognizance of the law of God? One grand design of preaching the Gospel is to develop and quicken conscience until it gains the ascendancy in the mind and exercises that influence over the will that belongs to it.

Do you see why converts backslide so soon after a revival? It is because so little pains are taken to quicken, develop, and keep their consciences awake on every subject. If they are allowed to practice any iniquity; if they are not urged up continually to a full and complete renunciation of every form of sin; if they are not urged to aim at holiness and expect to get away from all sin, they will assuredly indulge in various forms of sin. Their consciences will become more and more seared, until they can shamelessly backslide and disgrace the cause of Christ.

From this study, you can see what infinite evil has resulted to the church, and is still resulting, from the denial that people are expected to live without sin in this life. Why, this denial is to my mind one of the most death-dealing errors that can be held up before the eyes of sinners. Are people to be generally taught that they are not to expect, and even that it is a dangerous heresy to expect to live, even for a single day, without going into rebellion against Almighty God? Are they thus to be taught to expect to sin? Who does not see that this must result in their indulging in sin with very little remorse or self-abhorrence?

The doctrine of sanctification in this life appears differently to one who has a quick and sensitive conscience. Let a person's conscience become so thoroughly awake that the thought of sinning is to him as terrible as death, so that conscience will roll a wave of unutterable pain across his mind and weigh him down with agony at every step he takes in sin; let his conscience be in such a state as to agonize his soul to a degree that will cause the perspiration to pour out from his body almost in streams, and then present to that soul the offer of a full salvation. Tell him, if he will confess his sins, Christ "is faithful and just to forgive us our sins, and to cleanse us from all unrighteousness" (1 John 1:9). Announce to him the fact that the Gospel has provided a salvation from sin in this life, and he will perhaps answer you at first, "This is too good to be true! Oh, that it were true!" But turn the subject over and present the scripture promises and see with what eagerness he will grasp at them. "Oh," he will cry out, "this is indeed a Gospel suited to the circumstances and character of people! This is a salvation worthy to be from the Son of God."

How can this doctrine be doubted by the church without absolute horror? Why, beloved, suppose a person's conscience were thoroughly awake, until sin should appear to him in a great measure as it does to the inhabitants of heaven. Then announce to that soul that he must expect to live in sin as long as life lasts, that he must expect to sin against God every day till he dies. Why, I think, he would shriek and scream and faint and die with agony. "How horrible!" he would exclaim. "With such a conscience as this inflicting on me the pangs of the second death every time I sin, must I continue to sin as long as I live? Is there no hope that I shall escape? Has the Gospel made no provision for my entire sanctification in this life? Then woe is me! I am undone. And if it is heresy to believe I shall escape from my sin before I die, oh, that death would come upon me this moment." This has been the actual feeling of many whose consciences have become thoroughly awake, and who were taught that there was no such provision in the Gospel that they might reasonably expect a present deliverance from all sin. Indeed, the denial of the attainability of a state of entire sanctification in this life to an individual whose conscience is thoroughly quickened and full of power would agonize him like the thrusting of a poisoned dagger into his heart. It seems to me that within the last two or three years, I have sometimes felt as if I could not live if I did not believe the doctrine of a full salvation from sin existed in this life.

How sad is the spiritual state of those who manifest an *unwillingness* to have this doctrine true! There are those who manifest the greatest lack of candor in weighing the evidences in its favor and seem disposed to resort to any excuse to disprove it. From their writings and their sayings they have every mark of an utter loathing to have this doctrine true. Now I ask, what must their spiritual state be? What is the state of their conscience? How much do they sympathize with the inhabitants of heaven in regard to the exceeding sinfulness of sin? Do they feel horror-stricken at the idea of sinning against God? Do they know what it is to have the perspiration flow like rain when they fall into the slightest sin? Are they crying out in their prayers for a deliverance? No, but they are denouncing as heretics and fanatics those that do, and yet still reaching after and expecting a full salvation!

You see, until the conscience of the church is quickened, little can be done for the salvation of the world. Look at the tobacco-chewing minister, see that whiskey- or beer-drinking deacon. Why, how many forms of luxury and self-indulgence are allowed into the church without any conscience while the world is going down to hell? Even agents of tract societies, missionary societies, and others working for the spread of the Gospel will go through the country smoking and chewing tobacco, drinking tea and coffee, and thus by their example encouraging the church in the use of these pernicious articles. They are spending more—perhaps ten times as much—every year for these deleterious luxuries as they give for the spread of the blessed Gospel.

It is amazing that tobacco-chewing ministers can (as they have in some instances, as I have been informed) find fault with others for letting down the claims of the law. They seem, in the same breath, to find fault with others for insisting upon physiological and dietetic reform, and indeed, for pressing the subject of reform so extensively as they do, and yet complain that their teaching is letting down the claims of the law of God. A few months ago, one of the eastern papers, in reviewing one of my sermons, protested in the most earnest manner against my extending the claims of the law too far. The writer said the law of God was itself strict enough, and that he must protest against it being extended beyond its real meaning. My beloved brethren, what consistency is there in maintaining at the same time two such opposite sentiments as are often maintained upon this subject? But let me say again that until the conscience of the ministry and of the church of God is thoroughly quickened upon the subject of universal reformation, the world can never be converted.

How is it possible that ministers can waste God's money, set such an example to the church, and abuse their own bodies and souls by the habitual use of tobacco (one of the most hurtful and disgusting practices that ever disgraced mankind) without compunction of conscience, and yet complain of anyone letting down the claims of the law of God, and even go so far as to write pastoral letters against the heresy of letting down the law of God, while they have no conscience on the subject of such practices? How can people be so engaged to defend the purity, the strictness, and the honor of the law of God while in the very face of their churches and in the face of heaven they can indulge in such things as these. I would say this with the utmost kindness and yet faithfulness to them and to God, to the church, and to my own soul. I must say it though with unutterable grief.

Strangely, many churches who are living in the habitual indulgence of many forms of sin can manifest alarm at the idea of letting down the claims of the law of God. They hardly seem to have thought of practicing any self-denial, of keeping their bodies under, of crucifying and mortifying the flesh. Almost innumerable forms of sin are allowed to exist among them without their blushing or being at all ashamed of them. And yet, they manifest a great degree of alarm lest the claims of the law should be let down and some forms of sin allowed to escape detection and pass without rebuke.

There are many things in the present day that strongly remind us of the conduct of the Scribes and Pharisees, whose fears were greatly excited on the subject of our Lord Jesus Christ's letting down the law of God. They accused him of violating the Sabbath, having a wicked spirit, and even being possessed by the devil. They seemed to be horrified with His loose notions of the claims of the law of God. They were exceedingly zealous and cried out with great vehemence and bitterness against His lack of principle and firm adherence to the law of God. I would not on any account make any such allusions as this or say one word unnecessarily to wound the feelings of anyone. But it seems to be important at the present time to call the attention of the church to the great inconsistency of exclaiming against this letting down the law of God, while they are indulging with so little remorse in great multitudes of most obvious and even flagrant violations of the law. And while we contend for universal reformation and obedience to the law of God, they are opposed to us on the one hand for our strictness and on the other for our looseness. Nor can they contend that our strictness extends only to some subjects of minor importance, for we do insist upon universal obedience to the law of God in *heart and life*.

It is impossible for me to understand how some could really be in love with the law of God, earnestly and honestly engaged in supporting it in all the length and breadth of its claims, and yet indulge in so many forms of violating it with so little compunction or misgiving. Is there not, my beloved brethren, some delusion in this? Can anyone be deeply and thoroughly honest in defending the purity and strictness of the law that says: "Thou shalt love thy neighbor as thyself," while he holds slaves, uses or sells alcohol as an article of common use, and encourages the church in using tobacco and other worse than useless narcotics and filthy things to the great injury of their health and to the robbing of the treasury of the Lord?

Can you see the mistake of supposing that conscience will always admonish us when we do wrong? When it has become seared on any point we may continue in that form of iniquity without experiencing the rebuke of conscience. If you take it for granted that you are not sinning because you are not rebuked by your conscience, you will probably sleep on until you are in the depths of hell. Can you see the danger of this belief? There is no safety in stopping short of universal reformation in heart and life.

A generally seared conscience is fearful evidence of a state of hopeless reprobation. A mind with a seared conscience is like a tub without a bottom: Truth flows right through it, and there is no such thing as influencing that person by the truth. You may as well expect to influence a mere brute by moral considerations as a person whose conscience is asleep or seared. Perhaps you can now understand why so many can ridicule important branches of reform and even scoff at them. Many cry out upon these reforms as legal, self-righteousness or something which overlooks the Gospel. Here it is of the utmost importance to remember that to do anything from a mere constrained compliance with the demands of conscience without a love to what is right for its own sake, is by no means obedience to the law of God. Conscience enforces moral obligation and love complies with it. Conscience decrees *oughtness*, or that you *ought* to do thus and thus. Benevolence walks up, joyfully and instantly, to meet the imposed responsibility. Never forget that love is the substance of all obedience to the law of God, and that whenever the dictates of conscience are outwardly complied with for other than disinterestedly benevolent reasons, this is in reality regarding neither the demand of conscience nor of God; for conscience demands that right shall be done, and done from love for God and love for right. Whatever is not of love is not obedience to God.

Love or benevolence without a most strict regard to the injunctions of conscience is also a downright absurdity. Benevolence without universal obedience is inane. If there is love, there will be a most punctilious wakefulness to every affirmation of conscience. And I do not hesitate to say that he who can call this a legal instead of a Gospel righteousness is an antinomian. He is guilty of a fundamental and soul-destroying error.

Conscience will not always remain silent. A man may in this life pervert and silence his conscience, and even destroy his moral agency by making himself a lunatic. But understand, the time is coming when God will secure the fixed attention of the mind to those great moral truths that will arouse and arm the conscience with a thousand scorpions. When it awakes in eternity, its rebukes will be terrible beyond all description and imagination. How often it awakes even here toward the close of life, and inflicts the sharpest and most unutterable pangs upon subjects where it has long been silent.

Cases have occurred under my own observation in which conscience has been so quickened upon some subjects of which it had been nearly entirely silent, as to pierce the soul with such agonies as were almost entirely insupportable. Instances have occurred where people have fallen like dead men under the rebukes of conscience. In some cases people who have been the most hardened, whose consciences have been for years seared with a hot iron, have been made to wail out, even in this life, like a soul in the prison of despair. Oh, sinner, oh, professor of faith, do not suppose that you can always through time and eternity stupefy and benumb your conscience and drown the clamors of your outraged moral nature. It will, by and by, speak out with terror and in a voice of thunder. It will sit and gnaw upon your soul, and prove itself to be the "worm [that] dieth not" (Mark 9:44). It will transfix your soul as with the arrow of eternal death.

6

CONDITIONS OF BEING KEPT*

"Wherefore, let them that suffer according to the will of God commit the keeping of their souls to Him in well-doing, as unto a faithful Creator" (1 Peter 4:19).

We must learn in what sense the trials, temptations and sufferings of Christians are according to the will of God. We must learn what it means to commit the soul to God and to well-doing. If your soul is committed to God, it will inevitably be kept, but there are several mistakes we must avoid in considering this subject.

The trials, temptations and sufferings of the saints in this life are according to the will of God, but not in the sense that God has any pleasure in these afflictions for their own sake. God does not regard pain or suffering of any kind as a good in itself. He never takes pleasure in the sufferings of any being because of their sufferings.

The trials and sufferings of the saints are not to be regarded as according to the will of God in such a sense that He does not sympathize with the saints in their sufferings; for He really does sympathize with all the kindness of parental feeling.

We should not consider our sufferings as according to the will of God in the sense that He does not regard them as evils in themelves. On the contrary, trials, temptations and sufferings *are* looked upon by God as serious evils.

God feels afflicted with the sufferings of the saints, as perfectly good parents would feel in view of the afflictions of their children if all the results of these afflictions were present with them as they are with God.

The trials, temptations and sufferings of Christians are according

---

The Oberlin Evangelist, lecture 33, May 26, 1841. For twenty-one additional sermons on faith see *Principles of Faith*.

to the will of God, but not in the sense that He in all cases approves the means by which they are afflicted; for He often feels utterly opposed to the means by which His people are afflicted. Nor are these sufferings according to His will in such a sense that He would not prevent them, if He *wisely* could.

Sufferings and trials are according to His will in the sense that upon the whole, under all the circumstances of the case, He prefers they should take place. That is, He prefers it as the lesser of two evils, and considers it a lesser evil than for Him to intervene by His omnipotence and prevent it.

They are according to His will in the sense that He often sees them to be indispensable to the highest good of the saints themselves. The moral tendency of these afflictions is such that they will often teach His people lessons which they will learn in no other way. Sufferings are often an indispensable condition of sanctification and salvation. Therefore, they are regarded by Him as for His glory and the highest good of the universe. No thanks to those who are the guilty instruments of afflicting the saints; for they do not mean to glorify God. They are earthly, wicked, and selfish in their intentions; but God often overrules and calls in the wrath of man to praise Him, and the remainder of wrath He will restrain.

When He views these afflictions, temptations, trials and sufferings He rejoices in the *results*, but not in the *means*. He only rejoices because these are the necessary means of effecting His benevolent ends.

Commit Your Soul to God

We must know what is intended by committing the soul to God. In this text, the word *commit* is a form of the same word that is often rendered *faith* in the New Testament; and in this connection it conveys a very correct idea of the real meaning of the term *faith*, or of the true nature of faith. Faith means to trust and confide. Faith is not a mere emotion of the mind, but is an act of the will; a yielding up or giving over of the soul to God for safe keeping. It is like committing a treasure to someone to be kept for us. It is like a bride committing herself to her husband, giving herself away, committing her honor and her all into his hands, and thus uniting her destiny with his. It is a *state* or an *abiding* trust or confidence in contrast to a single act of will. Such a state keeps the soul at rest or in peace.

What is intended by committing the soul to God in well-doing? This means to deliver up your whole being to doing and suffering the whole will of God, joyfully and calmly; while leaving the results with Him. Observe, the will controls the actions of body and mind. *Committing* the soul to Him in well-doing is that act of the will by which all the powers of body and mind, so far as they are under the control of the will, are delivered up or consecrated to the *service* of God. All our powers are delivered up to Him to do His *whole will*, calmly and unhesitatingly leaving the results entirely with Him.

To illustrate what is intended, take the case of Abraham when he was commanded by God to forsake his country and his kindred for a land that God would show him. Without stopping to be informed respecting the land, how far off, where it was, or what sort of a country it should be, he instantly obeyed and went forth at the bidding of God. He went off not knowing whither he went. He took it for granted, as something settled beyond all question, that God would guide him rightly. He obeyed implicitly, and thus committed his soul to God in well-doing; that is, in implicit obedience.

Consider the case of God commanding Abraham to offer up Isaac, his son of promise, "his only son Isaac, whom he loved." What an amazing trial of his faith! This son, of whom it had been said he should be the father of many nations, was to be slain by his own father's hand. Abraham was placed under circumstances immensely interesting and trying. But behold his confidence! Notice how he *committed* everything to God in implicit obedience. He went forth prepared to render unqualified obedience to God—trusting that if he was slain God was able to raise him again from the dead; from whence also he virtually received him; or as God expresses it, "received him in a figure" (Heb. 11:19).

Faith is confidence reposed in God upon *God's own conditions*. God has informed us that people may trust in Him for safe-keeping upon conditions of implicit obedience and not otherwise. He does not allow people to repose confidence in Him, that He will keep and save them, if they disobey Him. "And why call ye me Lord, Lord, and do not the things which I say?" (Luke 6:46). Therefore, it is upon God's own conditions that the soul is to be committed to Him; this is the thing the apostle requires in the text.

When you commit your soul to well-doing, you give yourself up to the promotion of God's glory and the good of the universe with the steadfast confidence that your soul and interests are safe in His hands. It is giving yourself up in implicit obedience to God with the fullest assurance that you need not concern yourself about the results. It is thus giving yourself up with the entire willingness that the results shall be in all respects according to the will of God. It is actually going forward in the discharge of every duty in such confidence in God, in respect to the results, as to feel no anxiety or worry respecting the disposition God will make of your soul.

Your Soul Will Be Kept

If your soul is committed to God in the sense of our text, it will inevitably be kept. It will be kept, because God is a steadfast God. He is described in the text as a *faithful* Creator. There is no reason to distrust Him. He will not and cannot abuse your confidence. He is not only faithful, but infinitely faithful, and will heartily and certainly fulfill all His pledges and keep that which you commit to Him in well-doing.

He is *able* to keep your soul. He is described in the text as the Creator of the soul. If He was able to make it, He is certainly able to keep it. He is infinitely willing to keep it, or He would not have given His Son to die to redeem it. He would not have taken such pains to get possession of your soul if He was not willing to keep it. He would not use so many means with such long-suffering, and exercise such great self-denial as to give the life of His beloved Son to redeem your soul from the hands of public justice, and to persuade you to commit your soul to Him, unless He was willing with all His heart to keep it when you commit it to Him upon His own conditions.

His honor demands that He should keep the soul when thus committed to Him in well-doing. From the very constitution of their nature, moral beings regard a breach of sacred confidence or trust as a most dishonorable and hateful offense, as deserving the severest reprobation. What an infinite dishonor it would be to God to allow a soul to be lost which was committed to Him upon His own conditions for safekeeping.

He regards every soul thus committed to Him as He does the apple of His eye. He says that he who touches you touches the apple of His eye (see Zech. 2:8).

God regards the soul as worth keeping. He has given an intimation of the light in which He regards the value of the soul in the Atonement of Christ. Oh, who should know the value of the soul more than the God who made it? Who knows what eternity is more than God? Who can form an idea of what an immortal soul can suffer or enjoy more than God? Whose eye has beheld, whose heart has pondered, and whose mind has compassed the capabilities of the soul to endure or to enjoy except God? Shall not God keep a soul, a deathless soul, a soul made in His own image, a soul for whom His Son has died? Shall He not keep it when committed to Him upon His own conditions? Shall He carelessly throw it away? Shall He neglect it and allow any to pluck it out of His hands? Oh, tell it not, for it cannot be.

If you commit your soul to Him, God will keep your soul, because He knows you will not keep it yourself. If your soul were left with you, it would be lost forever. More than this, He sees that you have lost it already; that you have sold it into perpetual slavery; that it is already bound over and sentenced to eternal death; that unless it is committed to Him it must inevitably lie down in everlasting sorrow. How infinitely important, then, that the soul should be instantly committed to Him in well-doing.

Some Mistakes to Avoid

Some are mistaken with regard to this subject. Some have an antinomian faith. They trust that God will keep and save their souls, yet they have not complied and do not comply with the only conditions upon which they are at liberty to trust in God. Instead of committing their souls to Him *in well-doing*, and instead of implicitly obeying God, they think that Christ's righteousness will answer for them in such a way that they shall be saved on account of Christ's obedience whether they render a personal obedience or not. This is a horrible delusion. An imputed righteousness in this sense is one of the grossest blunders and most shocking errors people ever make.

Others are not expecting to be saved without good works. However, they are taking a passive attitude and waiting for God in some mysterious way to move upon them and influence them to obey Him. Thus, instead of actually going forward to the exercise of their own agency, they are, as they suppose, trusting in God while professedly waiting for divine influence. Is this committing the keeping of their souls to Him in well-doing?

Others engage in what they call well-doing from mere considerations of duty. They do not have any of the faith that works by love. They have in reality no faith in Christ. They do not commit the keeping of their souls to Him in affectionate confidence, but go about with what they call the discharge of duty, impelled by other considerations than those of faith and love. They have no rest and no deep peace of mind in what they call their well-doing. Now, this shows that they are mere legalists and know not what faith is as expressed in this text.

Many mistake *emotions of assurance* for *faith*. An emotion of assurance is wholly an involuntary state of mind. It is by no means to be mistaken for faith. Faith is an act of the will, and because it is an act of the will it is connected with its outward manifestations by a natural necessity. It is impossible for real faith not to produce corresponding outward conduct, as impossible as it is that our bodies should not be influenced by our wills. There may often be highly wrought emotions of assurance without any real faith, and yet nothing is more common than for people to mistake these two states of mind. But they are entirely different. Faith, as I have already said, is an act or choice of the will, a committing or giving up the soul to God in implicit obedience. Therefore, everything which is called faith that does not manifest itself in obedience to God is not the faith of the Gospel. It is a mere antinomian faith. It is an emotion and not at all an act of the will.

Others mistake a single act of faith for that *state* of faith which habitually trusts or commits the keeping of the soul to Him in well-doing all the time. Now there is certainly a difference between a first or single act of faith and a state of confidence. Let the case of a wife illustrate what I mean. Suppose a woman, under circumstances of excitement and being pressed hard by the persuasion of her friends, consents to become a wife and by one act commits herself to the honor, protection and guidance of her husband. But, suppose that she should soon fall back and lose her confidence in him, become distrustful insomuch that she could not trust him out of her sight without fearing he was in company with some other woman or engaged in what he ought not to be, keeping herself in continual worry lest he should be guilty of some act of infidelity to her or be unable or unwilling to support her, and thus she should become full of anxiety night and day. But suppose, on the other hand, that she had so fully committed herself so that she could honestly say from that time forward that never for one moment had she distrusted her husband in any respect or in the least degree whether at home or away. In whatever company and in whatever circumstances, she had always maintained the most implicit and unshaken confidence in him, insomuch that her soul had been as entirely at rest in respect to him as if she had known it was naturally impossible for him to do wrong or betray her confidence. Now, committing your soul to God in well-doing must not merely be a single act. It must be a continuous act or state of the will. Unless it is this, a persistent state that holds out to the end, God has not promised to keep the soul.

Others are attempting to get faith by works. Instead of confiding at once in God by a simple act of committing all to Him, they strain to achieve faith. By laborious efforts they try to force themselves into the exercise of those emotions of assurance which they suppose to constitute faith.

Others speculate about the philosophy of faith to the neglect of the objects of faith. They turn their attention to dissecting their mental exercises and settling certain philosophical questions instead of pouring their intense energies upon those truths that are to be believed. Instead of looking at Jesus Christ and attentively considering the truths of His precious Gospel, they turn their attention to within themselves and look into the darkness of their own minds to shed light upon the subject of faith. This is about as wise as if a man seeking for light should shut his eyes at high noon and turn in to examine the anatomy and physiology of his eye with the philosophy of vision.

Still others are trying to live by faith without works. They forget that a faith without works is dead, or that it is a mere emotion and not an act of the will, and therefore has no virtue in it. "Show me thy faith," wrote James, "without thy works, and I will show thee my faith by my works . . . wilt thou know, O vain man, that faith without works is dead?" (James 2:18–20).

True Faith

Always remember that faith works. Faith is an active principle. Faith is itself an action, an effort of the will, and will automatically exhibit itself in works. Some, indeed, are endeavoring to live by faith without works, and others by works without faith. And oh, how rare a thing it is to find those who have the faith that works by love!

All the Christian graces, so properly called, are acts of the will and are connected with their outward manifestations in a corresponding course of action by natural necessity. Therefore, faith is also an act of the will and is connected with corresponding works and works of love by natural necessity. No other faith than that which works—and works by love—is evangelical or saving faith. Evangelical faith is a trusting or committing of the soul to Christ in well-doing. It is infinitely important that this is borne in mind.

What numerous blunders have been made by theological writers on the subject of faith. Some hold it to be a passive state of mind, thus confusing it with the perception of truth. Others have confused it with emotion, or a full assurance that the Gospel or the promises are true. Others still have made it only indirectly voluntary and have supposed it to have moral character only because it is indirectly produced by an act of the will in directing the attention to the examination of the evidence.

Evangelical faith seems to have been quite extensively understood to be synonymous with conviction or the persuasion of the mind that something is true. These and similar blunders upon this subject have led many Antinomians and heartless professors of religion to settle down upon the supposition that they are Christians. They assume that they can have true faith, true love and true repentance, while these graces do not manifest themselves in benevolent outward conduct. How infinitely important it is, therefore, to understand that repentance, faith and love are all acts of the will, or choices; and must of necessity manifest themselves in corresponding outward conduct.

The love that constitutes true Christian faith is good-willing, or benevolent, and not complacent in God or any other being. We are as entirely involuntary in the exercise of complacent love toward God as we are in the exercise of complacency toward any other object that is to us naturally beautiful and lovely. So, repentance is an act of the will, and does not consist at all in those emotions of sorrow that are often supposed to be repentance. Repentance, when properly considered and resolved into its proper elements, is precisely synonymous with regeneration or a change from selfishness to benevolence. Sorrow for sin is a mere consequence connected with repentance by a natural necessity, just as complacency in God is connected with benevolence and faith. Therefore, do not overlook in your own experience, or in your account or estimation of your character, the fact that all the Christian graces, or all that in which there is true virtue, consist in acts of will which must of necessity manifest themselves in corresponding outward acts, otherwise you will totally deceive yourself.

Since it is true that no faith is evangelical except that which works by love, so it is also true that only works of faith are acceptable. Works not connected with and originating in faith are only works of law, by which no flesh can be justified.

The text is a beautiful description of true religion. It is admirably guarded and beautifully expressed. It sums up the whole of religion in the short sentence: "Commit the soul to Him in well-doing." This is the very direction (amplified, explained and illustrated) that answers the important question, "What shall I do to be saved?" This text says nothing about waiting for a mere feeling or emotion. It requires at once an act of will which is directly within our power. If there is anything in the universe over which man has control, it is over his own volitions. It is absurd and contradictory to say he cannot will. The thing then to be done, the thing required in the text, is at once to put forth the act of committing the soul to God in well-doing.

All faith and trust in God that does not work, and work by love, is tempting God. It is trusting Him without complying with His express conditions. It is presumptuous and a blasphemous abuse of God. It is the greatest dishonor to God, and that which He supremely resents and abhors, for anyone to claim or pretend to trust in Him without habitually obeying Him. So all works without faith are tempting God; for they are setting aside His conditions and are a wicked attempt to be justified directly or indirectly by works of the law, which He has declared to be impossible.

The Good From Affliction for the Saints

The afflictions, temptations and trials of the saints are designed and calculated to strengthen their faith. When they have passed through those scenes and have had much experience of the faithfulness of God, they can speak from experience. The faithfulness of God with them is not a matter of theory but of certain knowledge. The sharper the trial, the greater the triumphs and the deeper the rest of the soul when it is over. This is the natural result of learning by experience the great faithfulness of God. As the apostle wrote, "Now no chastening for the present seemeth to be joyous, but grievous: nevertheless, afterward it yieldeth the peaceable fruit of righteousness unto them which are exercised thereby" (Heb. 12:11).

God sometimes allows people to fall into sin because they are presumptuous in running into temptation. They pray, "Lead us not into temptation," and then rush right into it. Because they do not watch, God allows them to fall. Unless they will watch, He cannot by any possibility prevent their falling.

It is impossible for a faith that does not work—and work by love—to be a saving faith. In other words, it is impossible for God to save the soul, through the medium of faith, that is not holy or does not consist in an act of will and connect with a corresponding course of life by a natural necessity. If the Christian graces were mere emotions instead of choices, they might exist forever without any virtue or holiness in the mind. If faith were a mere antinomian perception of the truths of the Gospel, a mere emotion or felt assurance of being kept or saved which Antinomians have, there would be no tendency to salvation in it, nor would there be any possibility that salvation should be connected with it. All virtue consists of intentions or acts of the will. And a faith that is not an act of will is a dead faith, a faith connected with damnation and not with salvation.

Always remember that whenever you are living in the neglect of any known duty or in any form of known disobedience, your faith is vain: It is not faith, it is a mere emotion and not an act of will; for if it were an act of will it would be connected with a discharge of all known duty by an act of necessity.

One grand reason for keeping the saints for a time in this world is to develop and strengthen their graces, to confirm them in holiness. Holiness is always pure in kind. It is always obedience to God. In the interim it may acquire permanence by the teaching and discipline that confirms and perpetuates faith and all those states of mind and acts of will of which faith is the condition.

In this state of existence, the saints are educated for future usefulness. It may be and probably is true that the saints will hereafter be employed in works of love under circumstances that will require just that degree of knowledge and strength of virtue which they acquire in passing through the scenes of tumult with which they are surrounded in this life. Here they are made familiar with temptation and with the faithfulness of God. Doubtless, they will henceforth need this experience in order to act well in the labors to which God shall call them. We may rest assured that our discipline here is not in vain, and that God would not allow His children to pass through such scenes if it could be wisely avoided.

It is a great evil and a great sin to cast away your confidence in God in an hour of trial. You have heard of the patience and confidence of Job. Satan accused him before the sons of God of having a selfish religion:

> Doth Job fear God for nought? Hast thou not made an hedge about him, and about his house, and about all that he hath on every side? Thou hast blessed the work of his hands, and his substance is increased in the land. But put forth thine hand now, and touch all that he hath, and he will curse thee to thy face. And the Lord said unto Satan, Behold, all that he hath is in thy power; only upon himself put not forth thine hand. So Satan went forth from the presence of the Lord.
>
> And there was a day when his sons and his daughters were eating and drinking wine in their eldest brother's house: And there came a messenger unto Job, and said, The oxen were plowing, and the asses feeding beside them: And the Sabeans fell upon them, and took them away; yea, they have slain the servants with the edge of the sword; and I only am escaped alone to tell thee. While he was yet speaking, there came also another, and said, The fire of God is fallen from heaven, and hath burned up the sheep, and the servants, and hath consumed them; and I only am escaped alone to tell thee. While he was yet speaking, there came also another, and said, The Chaldeans made out three bands, and fell upon the camels, and have carried them away, yea, and slain the servants with the edge of the sword; and I only am escaped alone to tell thee. While he was yet speaking, there came also another, and said, Thy sons and thy daughters were eating and drinking wine in their eldest brother's house: And, behold, there came a great wind from the wilderness, and smote the four corners of the house, and it fell upon the young men, and they are dead; and I only am escaped alone to tell thee. Then Job arose, and rent his mantle, and shaved his head, and fell down upon the ground, and worshipped, and said, Naked came I out of my mother's womb, and naked shall I return thither: the Lord gave, and the Lord hath taken away; blessed be the name of the Lord. In all this Job sinned not, nor charged God foolishly. (Job 1:9–22)

Now see the great confidence of this man of God? In an hour of trial and temptation he did not (like many professors of religion now) cast away his shield. But his trial is not yet ended:

> Again there was a day when the sons of God came to present themselves before the Lord, and Satan came also among them to present himself before the Lord. And the Lord said unto Satan, From whence comest thou? And Satan answered the Lord, and said, From going to and fro in the earth, and from walking up and down in it. And the Lord said unto Satan, Hast thou considered my servant Job,

that there is none like him in the earth, a perfect and an upright man, one that feareth God, and escheweth evil? And still he holdeth fast his integrity, although thou movedst me against him, to destroy him without cause. And Satan answered the Lord, and said, Skin for skin, yea, all that a man hath will he give for his life. But put forth thine hand now, and touch his bone and his flesh, and he will curse thee to thy face. And the Lord said unto Satan, Behold, he is in thine hand; but save his life.

So went Satan forth from the presence of the Lord, and smote Job with sore boils from the sole of his foot unto his crown. And he took him a potsherd to scrape himself withal; and he sat down among the ashes.

Then said his wife unto him, Dost thou still retain thine integrity? curse God, and die. But he said unto her, Thou speakest as one of the foolish women speaketh. What? Shall we receive good at the hand of God, and shall we not receive evil? In all this did not Job sin with his lips. (Job 2:1–10)

How affecting and remarkable it is that Job's confidence should have been so unwavering under such trials as these. One messenger comes upon the heels of another; and while one is yet speaking another comes, and another, and another, and another bringing messages still more afflicting and overwhelming. He was very rich, but one thing goes after another till he is left a beggar. Still his children are left to him; but while the news of the destruction of the remains of his fortune still rings in his ears, a messenger comes to inform him of the instantaneous death of all his children. He then stands naked before the Lord, and cries out, "Naked came I out of my mother's womb, and naked shall I return thither: the Lord gave, and the Lord hath taken away; blessed be the name of the Lord" (Job 1:21).

But still his wife is left—his dearest earthly friend, his richest earthly treasure. She is not only alive, but she has not forsaken him. Her countenance, her support and her counsel are still with him. But ah! When Satan but touches his person, then she forsakes him. His three friends come to taunt him. He is accused of being a hypocrite, and his wife, confident of his sincerity, and thinking him abused, advises him to curse God and die. But hear the man of God: "Thou speakest as one of the foolish women speaketh. What? Shall we receive good at the hand of God and shall we not receive evil? Though he slay me, yet will I trust in Him . . ." (Job 2:10, 13:15).

How infinitely different was this conduct of Job from many who profess to be Christians in the present day. Often professors seem to be like soldiers who carry their shield when there is no danger; but as soon as they come into danger, where they have occasion to use it, they cast it away and flee. They give up their confidence in God "which hath great recompense of reward," and turn their backs upon God and shamefully apostatize.

Suppose a man were going to sea and God should inform him that he would encounter great storms and go through much tribulation; nevertheless, he should ride them all out in safety, and "not a hair of any man's head should perish." With this promise in his hand, he embarks and sets his feet upon the deck of the ship and feels that he is as safe as if upon eternal rock. But he is scarcely out of sight of land before a tempest arises. The heavens gather blackness, the blazing lightning flashes around him and now he is lifted upon the mountain wave, and the ocean yawns as if it would lay bare its very bottom to receive the plunging and struggling ship. The tempest roars so loud that the voice of the thunder cannot be heard. The captain with his trumpet is obliged to shout at the top of his voice in every man's ear to be heard and understood. The elements are conspired against him. The rattling hail, the forked lightning, the deafening roar of the tempest, the mighty wrestlings of the waves, all exhibit around him an indescribable scene of terror and consternation. But God rides upon the storm and amid the mighty rollings of the ship, when the daring seamen from the highest yards are rolled and pitched as if to be thrown a great distance by the mighty sweepings of the sea. Why, if his faith is firm in God, the man can stand upon the deck and in every rolling and lurching of the ship cry out, "Hold on, for God has spoken, and not a hair of any man's head shall perish. I believe in God. Let the winds blow on, and let the elements conspire against this trembling ship; though every joint shall groan, and every butt should seem about to spring—though wave after wave should make an entire breach over us from stem to stern; yet, as God is true, the hair of no man's head shall perish." Why, with the promise of God in his hand, he could ride the world around in the midst of the most terrific hurricane and be as calm as if sitting by his fire at home.

But suppose that with such a promise as this in his hand, and with the express intimation that he must pass through great storms and tribulations to enter the haven of rest, the man had so little confidence in God that unless it was fair weather all the time he was in a state of continual distrust. Every appearance of a storm would make him tremble. He would cast away his confidence and before the whole ship's crew he would dishonor God and give up all for lost. The shipmen and the passengers would say, "What sort of a Christian is this, and what must he think of his God to have no confidence in the stability of His promise? He is in a state of continual distress until he sees with his eyes that there is no danger." Oh, the miserable unbelief, the God-dishonoring distrust and casting away of confidence with which the church of God is cursed. How greatly this grieves the Spirit of the Lord and how greatly it offends against the generation of God's children. What a stumbling block to the saints, and what ruin it brings upon the world.

Beloved, when you are called to pass through trials and deep waters of affliction, these are your golden opportunities to honor the blessed God and exhibit the value and power of your Christian faith. These are the bright spots in your history, in which you have an opportunity to make the deepest impression upon the world. Have you never known that the blood of the martyrs was the seed of the church? Their confidence in God in the midst of the fires of martyrdom was to the bystanders the overwhelming demonstration of the truth and value of their Christian faith. What, then, do you mean by casting away your confidence in an hour of trial? Why do you not hold on? Why do you not, when you have the opportunity, show yourself a good soldier of Jesus Christ?

> Am I a soldier of the cross,
> A foll'wer of the Lamb;
> And shall I fear to own his cause
> Or blush to speak his name?
>
> Shall I be carried to the skies,
> On flow'ry beds of ease,
> While others fought to win the prize,
> And sail'd through bloody seas?
>
> Are there no foes for me to face,
> Must I not stem the flood;
> Is this vain world a friend to grace,
> To help me on to God?
>
> Sure I must fight, if I would reign;
> Increase my courage, Lord,
> To bear the cross, endure the shame,
> Supported by thy word.
>
> The saints, in all this glorious war,
> Shall conquer, tho' they die;
> They see the triumph from afar,
> With faith's discerning eye.
>
> —Isaac Watts

7

THE NECESSITY OF HUMAN GOVERNMENT*

"Cry aloud, spare not, lift up thy voice like a trumpet, and show my people their transgression, and the house of Jacob their sins. Yet they seek me daily, and delight to know my ways, as a nation that did righteousness, and forsook not the ordinance of their God: they ask of me the ordinances of justice; they take delight in approaching to God.

Wherefore have we fasted, say they, and thou seest not? Wherefore have we afflicted our soul, and thou takest no knowledge? Behold, in the day of your fast ye find pleasure, and exact all your labours. Behold, ye fast for strife and debate, and to smite with the fist of wickedness: ye shall not fast as ye do this day, to make your voice to be heard on high. Is it such a fast that I have chosen? A day for a man to afflict his soul? Is it to bow down his head as a bulrush, and to spread sackcloth and ashes under him? Wilt thou call this a fast, and an acceptable day to the Lord? Is not this the fast that I have chosen? To loose the bands of wickedness, to undo the heavy burdens, and to let the oppressed go free, and that ye break every yoke? Is it not to deal thy bread to the hungry, and that thou bring the poor that are cast out to thy house? When thou seest the naked, that thou cover him; and that thou hide not thyself from thine own flesh?

Then shall thy light break forth as the morning, and thine health shall spring forth speedily: and thy righteousness shall go before thee; the glory of the Lord shall be thy rear ward. Then shalt thou call, and the Lord shall answer; thou shalt cry, and he shall say, Here I am. If thou take away from the midst of thee the yoke, the putting forth of the finger, and speaking vanity; and if thou draw out thy soul to the hungry, and satisfy the afflicted soul; then shall thy light rise in obscurity, and

---

*The Oberlin Evangelist, lecture 34, June 9, 1841. Preached on the day of the National Fast on May 14, 1841.

thy darkness be as the noon day: and the Lord shall guide thee contin-
ually, and satisfy thy soul in drought, and make fat thy bones: and thou
shalt be like a watered garden, and like a spring of water, whose waters
fail not." (Isaiah 58:1–11).

On this day of the national fast, I will discuss what is implied in an acceptable fast and the importance of abstaining from food on such occasions. I will show the principle upon which God deals with nations as such, and notice the design, propriety and use of national fasts. I will also point out the duty of citizens and especially Christian citizens in respect to fasting, and notice some of the national sins which call this nation to fasting, humiliation and prayer.

First, I will discuss what is implied in an acceptable fast. It implies repentance. Fasting without repentance must be an abomination. It implies such a degree of sorrow and concern as to destroy, for the time being, the appetite for food.

Everyone is familiar with the fact that when the mind is strongly exercised and a high degree of emotion exists, it temporarily destroys the appetite. Children arising in the morning to go on a journey are much too excited to eat. Just so, when people lose their friends, or anything else occurs that produces a strong excitement of mind, they naturally reject their food. This fact is easily accounted for on physiological principles. When the mind is strongly exercised, there is a powerful determination of blood to the head. Also, when the appetite for food is excited, there is a determination of blood to the stomach. Therefore, when the mind is strongly exercised, there is naturally a lack of appetite for food.

Hence, acceptable fasting implies abstinence from food for the time being. It implies confession of sin to God and to those who have been injured. It implies restitution, so far as restitution is in your power. It implies reformation.

Abstinence from food is important. If a requisite state of mind exists, health demands abstinence from food. When the brain is strongly exercised by the mind, if food is taken into the stomach, it will not, ordinarily, be digested; for the reason that there is so much blood flowing to the brain as to deprive the stomach of the amount of blood required for the purposes of digestion. In such cases food should not be taken since it will seriously impair the health.

In such cases as above, food cannot be taken without serious detriment to the required state of mind. If the blood is diverted from the head to the stomach, the strong exercise of the mind must necessarily, in a great measure, cease. But if the blood is not diverted from the head sufficient for digestion, the fermentation of food in the stomach—although it may not actually annihilate those exercises of the mind—

must necessarily greatly impede them.

In such cases, abstinence greatly favors the healthy action of the mind, and leaves it free to pursue its investigations and to exercise its affections without being under the necessity of competing with the stomach in its efforts to retain a sufficiency of blood for the brain. Who does not know that when he has taken a full meal, he is disqualified, for a time, for close and vigorous thought? This is a physiological result. The stomach must have the excitement of a considerable determination of blood to that organ, or the process of digestion cannot go forward. And if, soon after eating a full meal, your mind is by any means lashed into a state of powerful excitement, you are nearly or quite sick in consequence.

Judicious fasting greatly aids the mind in gaining an ascendance over the bodily appetites and passions. This, also, is a physiological fact easily explained. But into this I cannot here enter.

Human Governments Are a Divine Institution

I remark upon the divine authority of governments in this place, because of the manifest propriety of recognizing them upon a celebration of a national fast. You will indulge me in speaking more at length upon this topic, since their divine authority has recently been questioned. And I will quote from my recently published *Skeletons on Theology*[1], and then consider the sins of our nation:

FIRST: Human governments are a necessity of human nature.

1. There is a material universe.
2. The bodies of men are material.
3. Any action wastes these material bodies, and consequently they need continual sustenance.
4. Hence, we have many bodily wants.
5. Hence, the necessity of worldly goods and possessions.
6. There must be real estate.
7. It must belong to somebody.
8. There must, therefore, be all the forms of conveyancing, registry, and in short, all the forms of legal government, to settle and manage the real estate affairs of men.
9. Men have minds residing in a material body, and depend upon

---

[1]Finney's *Skeletons on Theology* has been reprinted by Bethany House Publishers as *The Heart of Truth*. Since Finney never completed the first volume of his two-volume systematic theology, *The Heart of Truth* contains in a brief form what Finney probably would have included in the first volume of his systematic theology. Half of what Finney intended to publish in his two volumes can be found in *Finney's Systematic Theology*, also published by Bethany House Publishers.

the organization and perfection of this body for mental development.

10. The mind receives its ideas of external objects, and the elements of all its knowledge through the bodily senses. It therefore needs books and other means of knowledge.
11. Hence, for this reason men also need property.
12. Moral beings will not agree in opinion on any subject without similar degrees of knowledge.
13. Hence, no human community exists, or ever will exist, that on all subjects will agree in opinion.
14. This creates a necessity for human legislation and adjudication, to apply the great principle of moral law to all human affairs.
15. There are multitudes of human needs and necessities that cannot properly be met, except through the instrumentality of human governments.

SECOND: This necessity will continue as long as human beings exist in this world.

1. This is as certain as that the human body will always need sustenance, clothing and other things.
2. It is as certain as that the human soul will always need instruction, and that the means of instruction will not grow spontaneously without expense or labor.
3. It is as certain as that people of all ages and circumstances will never possess equal degrees of information on all subjects.
4. If all people were perfectly holy and disposed to do right, the necessity of human governments would not be set aside, because this necessity is founded in the ignorance of mankind.
5. The decisions of legislators and judges must be authoritative, so as to settle questions of disagreement in opinion, and secure and protect all parties.
6. The Bible represents human governments not only as existing, but as giving their authority and power to the support of the church in its most prosperous state or in the Millennium. It proves that human government will not be dispensed with when the world is holy. Read Isaiah 49:22, 23: "Thus saith the Lord God, Behold, I will lift up mine hand to the Gentiles, and set up my standard to the people: and they shall bring thy sons in their arms, and thy daughters shall be carried upon their shoulders. And kings shall be thy nursing fathers, and their queens thy nursing mothers: they shall bow down to thee with their face toward the earth, and lick up the dust of thy feet; and thou shalt know that I am the Lord: for they shall not be ashamed that wait for me."

THIRD: Human governments are plainly recognized in the Bible as a part of the moral government of God. Study the following texts:

124

1. He changeth the times and the seasons: he removeth kings, and setteth up kings: he giveth wisdom unto the wise, and knowledge to them that know understanding. (Dan. 2:21)

   This matter is by the decree of the watchers, and the demand by the word of the holy ones: to the intent that the living may know that the Most High ruleth in the kingdom of men, and giveth it to whomsoever he will, and setteth up over it the basest of men. That they shall drive thee from men, and thy dwelling shall be with the beasts of the field, and they shall make thee to eat grass as oxen, and they shall wet thee with the dew of heaven, and seven times shall pass over thee, till thou know that the Most High ruleth in the kingdom of men, and giveth it to whomsoever he will. (Dan. 4:17, 25)

   Let every soul be subject unto the higher powers. For there is no power but of God: the powers that be are ordained of God. Whosoever therefore resisteth the power, resisteth the ordinance of God: and they that resist shall receive to themselves damnation. For rulers are not a terror to good works, but to the evil. Wilt thou then not be afraid of the power? Do that which is good, and thou shalt have praise of the same: for he is the minister of God to thee for good. But if thou do that which is evil, be afraid; for he beareth not the sword in vain: for he is the minister of God, a revenger to execute wrath upon him that doeth evil. Wherefore ye must needs be subject, not only for wrath, but also for conscience' sake. For, for this cause pay ye tribute also: for they are God's ministers, attending continually upon this very thing. Render therefore to all their dues: tribute to whom tribute is due; custom to whom custom; fear to whom fear; honor to whom honor. (Rom. 13:1–7)

   Put them in mind to be subject to principalities and powers, to obey magistrates, to be ready to every good work. (Tit. 3:1)

   Submit yourselves to every ordinance of man for the Lord's sake: whether it be to the king, as supreme; or unto governors, as unto them that are sent by him for the punishment of evildoers, and for the praise of them that do well. (1 Pet. 2:13–14)

   These passages prove conclusively that God establishes human governments as a part of His moral government.
2. It is a matter of fact that God does exert moral influences through the instrumentality of human governments.
3. It is a matter of fact that He often executes His law, punishes vice and rewards virtue through the instrumentality of human governments.
4. Under the Jewish Theocracy, *where God was King*, it was found indispensable to have the forms of the executive department of government.

FOURTH: Whose right and duty it is to govern.

1. I have said that government is a necessity. Human beings are, under God, dependent on human government to promote their highest well-being.
2. It is his right and duty to govern who is both able and willing in the highest and most effectual manner to secure and promote individual and public virtue and happiness.
3. Upon him all eyes are or ought to be turned, as one whose right and whose duty it is to sustain to them the relation of ruler.

FIFTH: In what cases human legislation imposes moral obligation.

1. Not when it requires what is inconsistent with moral law.
2. Not when it is arbitrary or not founded in right reason.
3. But it always imposes moral obligation when it is in accordance with moral law or the law of nature.

SIXTH: It is the duty of all men to aid in the establishment and support of human governments.

1. Because human governments are founded in the necessities of human beings.
2. As all men are in some way dependent upon them, it is the duty of every man to aid in their establishment and support.
3. As the great law of benevolence or universal good-willing demands the existence of human governments, all people are under a perpetual and unalterable moral obligation to aid in their establishment and support.
4. In popular or elective governments, with every man having a right to vote, every human being who has moral influence is bound to exert that influence in the promotion of virtue and happiness. And as human governments are plainly indispensable to the highest good of man, he is bound to exert his influence to secure a legislation that is in accordance with the law of God.
5. The obligation of human beings to support and obey human governments while they legislate upon the principles of the moral law is as undeniable as the moral law itself.

SEVENTH: It is a ridiculous and absurd dream to suppose that human governments can ever be dispensed with in the present world.

1. Because such a supposition is entirely inconsistent with the nature of human beings.
2. It is equally inconsistent with their relations and circumstances.
3. Because it assumes that the necessity of government is founded alone in human depravity; whereas the foundation of this necessity is human ignorance, and human depravity is only an additional reason for the existence of human governments. The primary idea of law is to teach; hence, law has a *precept*. It is authoritative, and therefore has a *penalty*.
4. Because it assumes that men would always agree in judgment,

if their hearts were right, irrespective of their degrees of information.

5. Because it sets aside one of the plainest and most unequivocal doctrines of revelation.

It is important to consider several objections to these ideas:

Objection: The Kingdom of God is represented in the Bible as subverting all other kingdoms.

Answer: This is true, and all that can be meant by this is that the time will come when God shall be regarded as the supreme and universal sovereign of the universe; when His law shall be regarded as universally obligatory; when all kings, legislators, and judges shall act as His servants, declaring, applying and administering the great principle of His law to all the affairs of human beings. Thus God will be the Supreme Sovereign, and earthly rulers will be presidents, governors, kings, and judges, under Him, and acting by His authority as revealed in the Bible.

Objection: God only providentially establishes human governments, and does not approve of their selfish and wicked administration. He only uses them providentially, as He does Satan, for the promotion of His own designs.

Answer:

1. God nowhere commands mankind to obey Satan; but He does command them to obey magistrates and rulers. Study the following texts:

   Let every soul be subject unto the higher powers: for there is no power but of God: the powers that be are ordained of God. (Rom. 13:1)

   Submit yourselves to every ordinance of man for the Lord's sake: whether it be to the king, as supreme; or unto governors, as unto them that are sent by him for the punishment of evildoers, and for the praise of them that do well. (1 Pet. 2:13–14)

2. He nowhere recognizes Satan as His servant, sent and set by Him to administer justice and execute wrath upon the wicked; but He does this in respect to human governments. Study the following text:

   Whosoever therefore resisteth the power, resisteth the ordinance of God: and they that resist shall receive to themselves damnation. For rulers are not a terror to good works, but to the evil. Wilt thou then not be afraid of the power? Do that which is good, and thou shalt have praise of the same: for he is the minister of God to thee for good. But if thou do that which is evil, be afraid; for he beareth not the sword in vain: for he is the minister of God, a revenger to execute wrath upon him that doeth evil. Wherefore ye must needs be subject, not only for wrath, but also for conscience' sake. For, for this cause pay ye tribute also: for they are God's ministers, attending continually upon this very thing. (Rom. 13:2–6)

3. It is true indeed, that God approves of nothing that is ungodly and selfish in human governments. Neither did He approve of what was ungodly and selfish in the Scribes and Pharisees; and yet Christ said to His disciples, "The Scribes and Pharisees sit in Moses' seat: all therefore whatsoever they bid you observe, that observe and do; but do not ye after their works: for they say, and do not" (Matt. 23:2–3). Here the common sense principle is recognized, that we are to obey when the requirement is not inconsistent with the moral law, whatever may be the character or the motive of the ruler. We are always to heartily obey as unto the Lord, and not unto men, and render obedience to magistrates for the honor and glory of God, and as doing service to Him.

Objection: Christians should leave human governments to the management of the ungodly, and not be diverted from the work of saving souls to intermeddle with human governments.

Answer:

1. This is not being diverted from the work of saving souls. The promotion of public and private order and happiness is one of the indispensable means of saving souls.
2. It is nonsense to admit that Christians are under an obligation to obey human government and still have nothing to do with the choice of those who shall govern.

Objection: We are commanded not to avenge ourselves, that "Vengeance is mine, and I will repay, saith the Lord." It is said that if I may not avenge or redress my own wrongs in my own person, I may not do it through the instrumentality of human government.

Answer:

1. It does not follow that because you may not take it upon yourself to redress your own wrongs by a summary and personal infliction of punishment upon the transgressor that human governments may not punish them.
2. Because all *private* wrongs are a *public* injury; and, irrespective of any particular regard to your personal interest, magistrates are bound to punish crime for the public good.
3. It does not follow because while God has expressly forbidden you to redress your own wrongs by administering personal and private chastisement, He has expressly recognized the right and made it the duty of the public magistrate to punish crimes.

Objection: Love is so much better than law; since where love reigns in the heart, law can be universally dispensed with.

Answer:

1. This supposes that if there is only love there need be no rule of duty.
2. This objection overlooks the fact that law is in all worlds the

rule of duty, and that legal sanctions make up an indispensable part of that circle of motives that are suited to the nature, relations and government of moral beings.

3. The law requires love; and nothing is law, either human or divine, that is inconsistent with universal benevolence. To suppose that love is better than law is to suppose that obedience to law sets aside the necessity of law.

Objection: Christians have something else to do besides meddle with politics.

Answer:

1. In a popular government, politics are an indispensable part of religion. No one can possibly be benevolent or religious without concerning himself to a greater or lesser extent with the affairs of human government.

2. It is true that Christians have something else to do than to go with a party to do evil, or to meddle with politics in a selfish or ungodly manner. But they are bound to meddle with politics in popular governments for the same reason that they are bound to seek the universal good of all people.

Objection: Human governments are nowhere expressly authorized in the Bible.

Answer: This is a mistake.

1. Both their existence and lawfulness are as expressly recognized in the above quoted scriptures as they can be.

2. If God did not expressly authorize them, it would still be both the right and the duty of mankind to institute human governments; because they are plainly demanded by the necessities of human nature. It is a first truth of reason that whatever is essential to the highest good of moral beings in any world, they have a right to and are bound to do. So far, therefore, are men from needing any express authority to establish human governments, that no possible prohibition could render their establishment unlawful. It has been shown in my lectures on moral government[2], that moral law is a unit, that it is a rule of action which is in accordance with and demanded by the nature, relations, and circumstances of moral beings, and therefore is an obligatory requirement of them. It is moral law, and no power in the universe can set it aside. Therefore, were the Scriptures entirely silent on the subject of human governments, and on the subject of family government, as it actually is on a great many important subjects, this would be no objection to the lawfulness, expediency, necessity and duty of establishing human governments.

---

[2]See *The Heart of Truth* and *Finney's Systematic Theology*.

Objection: Human governments are founded in and sustained by force, and this is inconsistent with the spirit of the Gospel.

Answer:

1. There cannot be a difference between the *spirit* of the Old and New Testaments, or between the *spirit* of the law and the Gospel, unless God has changed, and unless Christ has undertaken to make void the law, through faith, which cannot be. "Do we make void the law through faith? God forbid: yea, we establish the law" (Rom. 3:31).

2. Just human governments, and only such governments are contended for, will not exercise force unless it is demanded to promote the highest public good. If it is necessary to this end, it can never be wrong. Nay, it must be the duty of human governments to inflict penalties, when their infliction is demanded by the public interest.

Objection: There should be no laws with penalties.

Answer: This is the same as to say, there should be no law at all; for that is no law which has no penalty, but only advice.

Objection: Church government is sufficient to meet the necessities of the world without secular or state governments.

Answer: What! Church governments regulate commerce, make internal improvements and undertake to manage all the business affairs of the world! Church government was never established for any such end; but simply to regulate the spiritual, in distinction from the secular, concerns of people; to try offenders and inflict spiritual chastisement, and never to perplex and embarrass itself with managing the business and commercial operations of the world.

Objection: Were all the world holy, legal penalties would not be needed.

Answer: Were all people perfectly holy, the *execution* of penalties would not be needed; but still, if there were law, there would be penalties, and it would be both the right and the duty of magistrates to inflict them, should their execution be called for.

Objection: It is asserted, that family government is the only form of government approved of God.

Answer: This is a ridiculous assertion:

1. Because God as expressly commands obedience to magistrates as to parents.

2. He makes it as absolutely the duty of magistrates to punish crime as of parents to punish their own disobedient children.

3. The right of family government is not founded in the arbitrary will of God, but in the necessities of human beings; so that family government would be both allowable and obligatory,

even if God had said nothing about it.

4. So, the right of human government has not its foundation in the arbitrary will of God, but in the necessities of human beings. The larger the community, the more absolute the necessity of government. If, in the small circle of the family, laws and penalties are needed, how much more in the larger communities of states and nations? Now, neither the ruler of a family, nor of any other form of human government, has a right to legislate arbitrarily, or enact, or enforce any other laws, than those that are in accordance with the nature, relations and circumstances of human beings. Nothing can be law in heaven; nothing can be law on earth; nothing can be obligatory on moral beings, but that which is founded in the nature, relations, and circumstances of moral beings. But human beings are bound to establish family governments, state governments, national governments, and, in short, whatever government may be requisite for the universal instruction, jurisdiction, virtue and happiness of the world.

5. Therefore, all the reasons for family government hold equally in favor of state and national governments.

6. There are vastly higher and weightier reasons for governments over states and nations than in the small communities of families.

7. Therefore, neither family nor state governments need the express sanction of God to render them obligatory; for both the right and duty of establishing and maintaining these governments would remain, even if the Bible had been entirely silent on the subject. But on this, as on many other subjects, God has spoken and declared what is the common and universal law, plainly recognizing both the right and duty of family and human governments.

8. Christians, therefore, have something else to do other than confound the right of government with the abuse of this right by the ungodly. Instead of destroying human governments, Christians are bound to reform them.

9. To attempt to destroy, instead of reforming human governments, is the same in principle as is often pleaded by those who are attempting to destroy rather than reform the church. There are those, who, disgusted with the abuses of Christianity practiced in the church, seem bent on destroying the church altogether, as the means of saving the world. But what mad policy is this!

10. Some argue that selfish people need and must have the restraints of law; but Christians should not have any part in restraining them by law. But suppose the wicked should agree among themselves to have no law, and therefore should not attempt to restrain themselves nor each other by law; would it

be neither the right nor the duty of Christians to attempt their restraint through the influence of wholesome government?

11. It is strange that selfish men should need the restraints of law, and yet that Christians have no right to meet this necessity by supporting governments that will restrain them. What is this but admitting that the world really needs the restraints of governments, that the highest good of the universe demands their existence; and yet, that it is wicked for Christians to seek the highest good of the world by meeting this necessity in the establishment and support of human governments! It is right and best that there should be law. It is necessary that there should be. Therefore, universal benevolence demands it; but it is wicked for Christians to have anything to do with it! This is peculiar logic.

EIGHTH: God has made no form of church or state government universally obligatory.

1. As a matter of fact, nowhere in the Bible has God given directions in regard to any particular form of church or secular government.

2. It is also certain that God did not consider the existing forms, either of church or state government, as of perpetual obligation. He did not give directions in regard to particular forms of government, either church or state, for the following reasons:

a. No such directions could be given without producing great revolutions and governmental opposition to Christianity. The governments of the world are, and always have been, exceedingly various in form. Therefore, to attempt to insist upon any particular form as being universally obligatory would be calling out great national opposition to religion.

b. No particular form of church or state government either is now, or ever has been, suited to all degrees of intelligence and states of society.

c. The forms of both church and state governments need to be changed with any great elevations or depressions of society in regard to their intelligence and virtue.

NINTH: The particular forms of church and state governments must and will depend upon the virtue and intelligence of the people.

1. Democracy is self-government and can be safe or useful only as far as there is sufficient intelligence and virtue in the community to impose by mutual consent salutary self-restraints, and to enforce by the power of public sentiment and by the fear and love of God the practice of those virtues which are indispensable to the highest good of any community.

2. Republics are another and less perfect form of self-government.

3. When there is not sufficient intelligence and virtue among the

people to legislate in accordance with the highest good of the state or nation, then both democracies and republics are improper and impracticable as forms of government.

4. When there is too little intelligence and virtue in the mass of the people to legislate on correct principles, monarchies are better calculated to restrain vice and promote virtue.

5. In the worst states of society, despotisms, either civil or military, are the only proper and efficient forms of government.

6. When virtue and intelligence are nearly universal, democratic forms of government are well suited to promote the public good.

7. In such a state of society, democracy is greatly conducive to the diffusion of knowledge on governmental subjects.

8. Although in some respects less convenient and more expensive, in a suitable state of society a democracy is in many respects the most desirable form either of church or state government, for the following reasons:

    a. It is conducive to general intelligence.

    b. Under a democracy, the people are more generally acquainted with the laws.

    c. They are more interested in them.

    d. This form of government creates a more general feeling of individual responsibility.

    e. Governmental questions are more apt to be thoroughly discussed and understood before they are adopted.

    f. As the diffusion of knowledge is favorable to individual and public virtue, democracy is highly conducive to virtue and happiness.

9. God has always providentially given to mankind those forms of government that were suited to the degrees of virtue and intelligence among them.

10. If they have been extremely ignorant and vicious, He has restrained them by the iron rod of human despotism.

11. If more intelligent and virtuous, He has given them the milder forms of limited monarchies.

12. If still more intelligent and virtuous, He has given them still more liberty and providentially established republics for their government.

13. Whenever the general state of intelligence has permitted it, He has put them to the test of self-government and self-restraint by establishing democracies.

14. If the world ever becomes perfectly virtuous, both church and state governments will be proportionally modified and employed in expounding and applying the great principles of moral law to the spiritual and secular concerns of men.

15. The above principles are equally applicable to church and state governments. Episcopacy is well suited to a state of general

ignorance among the people. Presbyterianism, or Church Republicanism, is better suited to a more advanced state of intelligence and the prevalence of Christian principle. While Congregationalism, or Spiritual Democracy, is best suited and only suited to the state of general intelligence and the prevalence of Christian principle.

16. God's providence has always modified both church and state governments so as to suit the intelligence and virtue of the people. As churches and nations rise and fall on the scale of virtue and intelligence, these various forms of government naturally and necessarily give place to each other. So ecclesiastical and state despotism, or liberty, depends naturally, providentially, and necessarily upon the virtue and intelligence of the people. That form of government is obligatory when it is best suited to meet the necessities of the people for the following reasons:

a. This follows as a self-evident truth from the consideration that it is necessity alone that creates the right of human government. To meet these necessities is the object of government; and that government is obligatory and best which is demanded by the circumstances, intelligence, and morals of the people.

b. Consequently, in certain states of society it would be a Christian's duty to pray for and sustain even a military despotism. In a certain other state of society, to pray for and sustain a republic. In a still more advanced stage of virtue and intelligence, to pray for and sustain a democracy; if indeed a democracy is the most wholesome form of self-government, which may be doubtful.

TENTH: The true basis on which the right of human legislation rests.

Under this heading, I need only to repeat the substance of what has already been said, that the right of human legislation is founded in the necessities of mankind; that the nature and ignorance of mankind lie at the foundation of this necessity; and, that their wickedness and the multiplicity and variety of their needs are additional reasons demanding the existence of human governments. Understand, then, that the foundation of the right of human governments lies not in the arbitrary will of God; but in the nature, relations, and circumstances of human beings.

ELEVENTH: Revolutions become necessary and obligatory when the virtue and intelligence or the vice and ignorance of the people demand them.

1. Naturally, when one form of government no longer meets the necessities of the people, it is the duty of the people to revolutionize.

2. In such cases, it is in vain to oppose revolution; for in some way the benevolence of God will bring it about. Upon this principle alone can what is generally termed the American Revolution be justified. The intelligence and virtue of our Puritan forefathers rendered a monarchy an unnecessary burden, and a republican form of government both appropriate and necessary. And God always allows His children as much liberty as they are prepared to enjoy.

3. The stability of our republican institutions must depend upon the progress of general intelligence and virtue. If in these respects the nation falls short, if general intelligence and public and private virtue sink to that point below which self-control becomes impossible, we must fall back into monarchy, limited or absolute; or into a civil or military despotism, all in accordance with the national standard of intelligence and virtue. This is just as certain as that God governs the world, or that causes produce their effects.

4. Therefore, it is the maddest conceivable policy for Christians to uproot human governments while they ought to be engaged in sustaining them upon the great principles of the moral law. It is certainly stark nonsense, if not abominable wickedness, to overlook either in theory or practice these plain, common sense and universal truths.

TWELFTH: Human legislation is valid.

1. Human legislation is valid when called for by the necessities; that is, by the nature, relations, and circumstances of the people.

2. The kind and degree of human legislation which is demanded by the necessities of the people is obligatory.

3. Human legislation is utterly null and void in all other cases whatever; and I may add that divine legislation would be equally null and void unless demanded by the nature, relations, and necessities of human beings. Consequently, human beings can never legislate in opposition to the moral law. Whatever is inconsistent with supreme love for God and equal love for our neighbor can by no possibility be obligatory.

4. We may yield obedience when the thing required does not involve a violation of moral obligation.

5. We are bound to yield obedience when legislation is in accordance with the law of nature.

6. We are bound to obey when the thing required has no moral character in itself; upon the principle that obedience in this case is a lesser evil than revolution or misrule.

7. We are bound in all cases to disobey when human legislation contravenes moral law, or invades the rights of conscience.

National Fasts

We must now consider the principles upon which God deals with nations. Each nation is regarded by God as a unit. Nations are regarded as public persons; as amenable to Him for their conduct; as bound by the principle of moral law. Nations are bound to legislate and adjudicate in accordance with the law of nature or that rule of conduct which requires every moral being to love God with all his heart and his neighbor as himself.

God's dealings with nations are only providential and necessarily confined to this world. Nations, as such, do not exist in a future world. As nations, He treats them according to their outward conduct. Nations have no private character. Their character is public. They are regarded as public persons and treated according to the manner in which they outwardly demean themselves towards God and His government. Upon this tenure the Jews manifestly held their worldly possessions. In every age, God's treatment of nations as such has demonstrated the truth that nations are providentially treated according to their public acts. Indeed, as nations they have no other than public acts. For what individuals do is not regarded as a national act, unless these individuals are heads of government and acting in a governmental capacity.

As the righteous and the wicked are mingled together in human governments, they are providentially treated alike. It is improper and impossible, when dealing with a nation as such, to make a distinction between the righteous and the wicked. In eternity, God will treat rulers and rule according to their private characters, as they shall appear in the light of the moral law.

We must now consider carefully the design, propriety and use of national fasts. It is not part of the design, either of private or public fasting, to make amends for past wrongs by doing penance. National fasts are designed as a public recognition of national responsibility to God. They are designed as a public confession of national sins; as a public profession of national repentance and renunciation of them.

This is eminently proper in respect to national sins. For, as national sins are always public sins, they should always be publicly confessed and renounced. This should be done by the executive magistrate of the nation. Indeed, there seems to be no other way to put away national sins, so as to dispense with the necessity of national judgments, but by the appointment of national fasts, national confessions and national repentance. Since national sins are not private sins, private repentance will not meet the demands of the divine government. If God does not punish nations for their sins, there must be some public reason for withholding His judgments. And as this is with nations a state of reward or retribution, God's relation to the universe demands that He should visit national sins with national judgments, unless they are nationally renounced; that is, renounced by a national public appointment of a fast, which is the most emphatic form of making a national confession.

National fasts are useful since they often avert the judgments of God. The case of Nineveh is an illustrious example of this.

National fasts are a public and national rebuke of infidelity, and a public acknowledgment of the existence, government and goodness of God. They tend to arouse and quicken the public conscience. They give ministers an opportunity to expose and rebuke national vices.

We must recognize the duty of citizens, and especially of Christian citizens, in respect to fasts. It is their duty to abstain from the ordinary business of life. Public fasts are to be publicly celebrated. Both magistrates and people are bound to lay aside their ordinary business and attend to the solemn and public confession of their sins.

It is their duty to attend public worship and unite in public confessions. And were it possible for this whole nation to assemble at Washington, and there, with the President at their head, unite in the public confession and renunciation of their sins, it would undoubtedly be their duty. On such occasions, it would no doubt be eminently proper for the governors and heads of departments in the several states and for the houses of congress to be assembled (and thus the representatives of the whole people) to appear before the Lord to make public confession of the sins of the nation.

It is the duty of all citizens to use whatever appropriate means are within their power to bring about a complete national reformation.

The Sins of the Nation

Today, we need to consider some of the national sins which call this nation to fasting, humiliation and prayer.

We must consider the outrageous injustice with which this nation has treated the Indians of this country. The shameless wickedness of this nation in respect to the manner in which the Indians have been deceived when making treaties with them. The shocking and disgraceful manner in which these treaties have been violated by this government is almost too bad to name. Who can mention or think of these things without grief and indignation? How these helpless Indians have been trampled down and in multitudes of ways oppressed and injured until their cry has come up into the ears of Jehovah!

I notice the hypocrisy of this nation in shedding British blood in defense of principles which, when applied to this nation's own wrongs, this nation has always denied. As the very basis of the Revolution, it was publicly declared that "*All* men were born free and equal, and endowed by their Creator with certain inalienable rights; among which are life, *liberty*, and the pursuit of happiness." Now, at the very time at which this declaration was made, the very men who made it and the nation that proclaimed these truths as an excuse for revolution and war stood with their unsanctified feet upon the necks of the prostrate slaves! From that day to this, this nation as such has continued, publicly and practically, when these wrongs were held up to view, to deny the principles upon which the Revolution was based. This nation both maintains and denies these great truths: When she is oppressed, she maintains them and fights in defense of them; when she is accused of oppression, she denies them, and is ready to fight in support of the opposite doctrine.

I notice the national treatment of the question of the abolition of slavery as another of those heinous sins for which this nation ought to blush. Is it not astonishing that in this government the friends of the oppressed are not even allowed to petition? Our government will not so much as allow itself to be asked to "undo the heavy burdens." Concerning oppression they speak loftily. And could we this day meet with the public assemblies in the city of Washington, we might perhaps hear the conduct of Abolitionists in seeking the abolition of slavery pointed out as one of the great sins of the people, in endeavoring, as they would express it, "to dissolve the Union."

We must notice the great wickedness in forming and in attempting to support a Union upon such principles. It is "a league of iniquity." The nation never had a right, in their constitution or in any other way, to recognize the lawfulness of slavery, and guarantee the protection of states in holding their fellow human beings in bondage. The compact was an utter abomination. The Union was a league against God. And now our public men make this excuse for supporting slavery: That by the stipulations of the constitution they are bound to do so. Now, admitting that the constitution does ever so expressly contain such stipulations, are they, can they be binding? What! Can it be obligatory on the nation, or any set of people, to violate the great law of love because they have promised to do so? Suppose the different states had entered into a stipulation to carry on the slave trade forever, could such a promise as this be binding on any of them? Suppose each state had promised to fit out and keep upon the high seas a certain number of pirate ships to rob all the nations of the earth, to supply the public treasury with funds; could such an abominable compact be binding? Would any state have a right to abide by such a stipulation as this? No, no more than a contract to keep up a perpetual war with heaven could be binding. The fact is, neither individuals nor nations can ever bind themselves by any promise to do wrong, to violate the law of love. Can a man render it lawful for him to murder, by promising to murder? If this be so, any sin may cease to be sin, and become obligatory and consequently a virtue simply by promising to do it. It is lamentable and shameful that this nation should try to preserve the Union based upon such principles as these. If the Union cannot be preserved, except by abiding by a stipulation to sustain slavery, or not to interfere with it, let it be given up. It is in the highest degree rebellion against God to attempt to support it upon such principles.

I call your attention to the national desecration of the Sabbath, especially by the Post Office Department. In this department of our government, our nation has literally "framed iniquity by a law," and absolutely legislated in direct opposition to the law of God. It is by no means unusual that this department is so often crippled in its movements; that its accounts are so often embarrassed. The curse of God is upon it. This is just what might be expected, for it is managed by a host of Sabbath-breakers. If this department of government be not yet sorely rebuked than it has been, and if the government should in general continue in its present form, if the Post Office Department continues its shameless violation of the Sabbath, I shall be disappointed if God does not mark it yet more signally with His curse.

Again, I notice the national love of money, which is the root and foundation of this public desecration of the Sabbath. This nation has seemed to be ready to go to almost any length in obtaining wealth, and to set aside the law of God whenever it has interfered with its grasping after worldly goods.

I notice the notorious licentiousness and intemperance of many of our rulers. It is commonly reported, and I suppose truly, that during the sessions of Congress the city of Washington exhibits a scene of most disgusting licentiousness and intemperance on the part of many of those who are entrusted with and voluntarily put into places of power and made the conservators of the public morals.

I notice duel-fighting and murderous deeds that are practiced almost every year in Congress. Is it too much to say that no nation is so wicked as this? Where can a nation be found so enlightened on religious subjects as this nation, yet so recklessly, perversely, and even wantonly trampling down the government of God?

I notice the wickedness of political contests, and especially the great sins that were committed during the election of the late President. We are assembled to celebrate a fast appointed in view of the recent death of that President. Now who can wonder that he was taken away by a stroke of Divine Providence in the very beginning of his official career? Who ever witnessed such disgraceful and wanton scenes that disgusted the eyes and grieved the hearts of the friends of virtue during that political struggle? What low, vulgar, indecent, and in many instances, profane measures were resorted to? They are too bad to name. Who does not know that "Tippecanoe" and "Hard Cider," and almost every other abomination were the watch-words and the measures for carrying that election? My soul mourns when I say it. God forbid that I should say it to bring a railing accusation against my country. Were they not already public I would never make them so. I call your attention to them that they may be confessed among the guilt and God-dishonoring sins of this nation.[3]

There are numerous other sins of this nation to be confessed and put away. But I have not time to call your attention to any more at present.

The Sins of the Church

As Christians, we ought to confess and lament the sectarianism and divisions of the church. These lie at the foundation of and give countenance to the strivings, slang and slander of party politics. Who can look into the religious periodicals without agony at seeing that there is almost as much party spirit, division, censoriousness and slander in the church as among party politicians. Indeed the difficulty is that the politics existing in the church are continually keeping in countenance those political contests that are working the destruction of this nation. I say this with humiliation and trembling, because it has become so common to accuse those who would deal faithfully with the sins of the church as being slanderers.

As Christians, we ought to confess the wickedness of the church in view of its bearing toward and treatment of those national sins of which I have spoken. What is the conduct of the church as a body, and what is her attitude in respect to the dreadful sin of slavery? Oh, tell not the shameful story in Gath, nor let the sound reach Askelon, that the American Church is to such a shameful extent an apologist for slavery. And what has the church, as such, ever done to reprove and rebuke this nation for its treatment of the Indians? Why has not her voice been heard? Why has not the church as a body respectfully remonstrated? Why has she not at least lifted up her voice and wept in view of these abominations? And what is the conduct of the church in respect to party politics? Why, there have always been professed Christians enough in this country to hold the balance of power. It has always been in the power of Christians to elect or defeat the election of any candidate for President who has ever been proposed. If only the church would be in earnest in maintaining correct principles, if they be agreed to let the world know that they would vote for no man who did not fear God, then no party in that case would think of proposing a can-

---

[3]Editor's Note: The President was William Henry Harrison, who defeated the Indians in the Battle of Tippecanoe in 1811. He ran against the incumbent President, Martin Van Buren. The Whigs proudly presented Harrison as "the log cabin, hard cider" candidate.

didate of loose or even doubtful character. If they would be united in going always for the man of the highest moral standing, such candidates, and such only, would be proposed by the respective parties. But as it is, they have adopted the miserably wicked policy of choosing between two moral evils. Instead of choosing the best of two good men, they consent to vote for the least immoral of two bad men, thus rendering themselves responsible for the sins of this nation. It is completely within the power of the church to rebuke effectively and put away all the sins that disgrace the nation. And how long shall the skirts of the church be defiled with these abominations?

The righteous may well be expected to share largely in national judgments. They really deserve it. How absurd it is to say that Christians have nothing to do with human governments. They should immediately set about the moral reformation of government. But here the question arises, "How can such a reformation be brought about?" I answer:

1. It never can be brought about by a kind of party movement, such party men and party measures as have brought this nation to such a pass of wickedness. Such party measures can never work a reformation of public morals. They are of themselves a vile and loathsome offense to public morals.

2. The needed reformation can never be brought about by contending for truth in a wrong spirit. There is something very remarkable in the providence of God in this respect. Facts in the history of the world demonstrate that God would rather even truth should suffer a temporary defeat than triumph when maintained in a bad spirit. Besides, there is something in the spirit which in such instances contradicts the truth and prevents it from being received as truth. Whenever any set of men, however much truth they may have on their side, get into a wrong spirit in the proclamation and defense of it, they may expect that God will give them up to defeat. Men who hold the truth are very apt to be presumptuous, to take it for granted, and to boast that they shall prevail because they have the truth. But mark me, and mark the fact when you will, that in this they will be disappointed. The truth will indeed eventually prevail, but not in their hands. God will give them over as individuals and as a party to ultimate defeat. And in His own time, through other instruments, He will cause His truth to prevail.

3. This reformation must be brought about and may be brought about by promoting union among Christians, and by extending correct views on the subject of Christian responsibility in regard to their relation to government. Anything that will unite the Church and consolidate her efforts, and direct them wisely on this point, will correct the national morals. Nothing else can.

The private views, character, or motives of the rulers in appointing a fast have nothing to do with the obligation of citizens in respect to its observance. If the ruler were an infidel, or whatever his private views or designs might be in appointing a public fast, it is the business and duty of the people to celebrate the fast and confess and lament the real sins of the nation. If the present chief magistrate of the United States had been consulted in respect to the sins he would have the people confess, it is very probable that among them he would have mentioned the efforts of abolitionists to effect the overthrow of slavery, or as he would more probably have expressed it, the heinous crime of northern interference with the domestic institutions of the South and an unrighteous attempt to divide the Union. Now with his private opinion on such questions the nation has nothing to do. Our business is to confess, among other enormities, the disgraceful and God-provoking sin of slavery, together with the wicked opposition of this nation to the efforts of abolitionists to bring about its overthrow.

Before I close this discourse, I must add a few words on the necessity of abstinence from food, since in many cases abstinence is entirely indispensable to a right state of religious feeling. If the alimentary organs be continually taxed to the amount of their capability, the mind can be exercised to but a limited extent. Especially is it next to impossible that much emotion should exist while the digestive organs are laboriously employed in the process of alimentation. As I have before remarked, so great a determination of blood to these organs is imperiously demanded during the process of digestion, that the mind, whose organ is the brain, must be comparatively, and in many instances to a great degree, sluggish in its operations. Who has not learned by his own experience that if he is about to make a great mental effort, he must not indulge himself in a full meal immediately preceding it? Many people, either because they are so much under the dominion of their appetite or because they have imbibed a false notion, say that to skip a meal now and then will seriously impair their health. They continually and regularly load their alimentary organs to such an extent as to render it impossible for their minds to be strongly exercised on any subject. Fasting is often useful, and sometimes indispensable, as a means of giving the mind a thorough opportunity to exercise itself without being impeded in its action by a determination of the blood to the alimentary organs.

In fasting, people should always guard against a self-righteous state of mind. Self-righteous fasting is worse than no fasting at all.

Public or private fasting without reformation is a great abomination to God. It is to be hoped that our President did not intend to substitute national fasting for national reformation. But we shall see what course they will take in regard to slavery, the treatment of the Indians, the sanctification of the Sabbath, licentiousness, dueling, intemperance and other evils at the next session of Congress. Our rulers may expect, of course, that the people will have their eye upon them, and anxiously wait to see whether they expect to escape the judgment of God by fasting without reformation. Oh, it would be dreadful, if, notwithstanding their fastings, they should persist in their sins! If they should forget that the fast was a national fast, and merely expect the reformation of individuals without national reformation, it would be but the more offensive to God. And our fasting would but hasten our destruction.

Let Christians everywhere continue to pray that God may reform the nation, and that our rulers may not be guilty of so gross a hypocrisy as to appoint a national fast and then persevere in our national abominations. If they do this, it will not be surprising if the nation should soon be called to mourn the death of another President, or that some judgment infinitely more deplorable than this should soon desolate our country.

All of us, and certainly those of us who are and from principle always have been opposed to those sins are to be especially on our guard in contemplating the sins of this nation, lest we imbibe a censorious, angry spirit, instead of feeling a deep and real sorrow for those sins. It is of no use to scold about our national sins. Our business is to lament them, to warn, entreat, respectfully expostulate, petition Congress and petition God that they may be put away.

Let no man say that ministers are out of their place in exposing and reproving the sins of this nation. The fact is, ministers and all other men not only have a right but are bound to expose and rebuke the national sins. We are all on board the same ship. As a nation, our very existence depends upon the correct moral conduct of our rulers. And shall they deafen their ears to our petitions, expostulations, and entreaties? Shall ministers be told, shall any man be told, that he is meddling with other men's matters, when he reproves and rebukes the abominations of slavery? As well might a man be accused of meddling with that which does not belong to him, who is on board a ship in the midst of the Atlantic Ocean, because he should expostulate with and rebuke a man who should attempt to scuttle the ship.

8

MEDIATORSHIP OF CHRIST*

"For there is one God, and one mediator between God and men, the man Christ Jesus" (1 Timothy 2:5).

In discussing this subject, I shall show what a mediator is and what is implied in the existence of that office. I will indicate some essential qualifications for the office of mediator and on what conditions the purpose of the mediatorial office can be accomplished. Finally, I will apply these principles to Christ as mediator between God and men.

A mediator is one who undertakes to bring about a reconciliation between contending parties. If there is no controversy, there is no room for a mediator, and no reason for the existence of such an office. A mediator is not an arbitrator. An arbitrator is one to whose judgment both the law and the facts are submitted for adjudication in a case of right. A mediator is one who interposes on behalf of the offending party and undertakes to bring the parties into a state of reconciliation. In this case, the fact or question of right is already decided, and the thing to be accomplished is to remove difficulties, fulfill conditions and effect a reconciliation upon the acknowledged principles of right or public justice.

One of the things implied in the existence of that office is the presence of two or more parties with a controversy between them. There must be some hindrance in the way of their adjusting their own difficulties properly. This hindrance may arise out of an indisposition in one or all the parties to adjust their differences; or, it may arise out of the inability of the offending party to make the satisfaction which is rendered indispensable by the relations and circumstances of the offending party.

---

*The Oberlin Evangelist, lecture 35, June 23, 1841. See also, "Christ Our Advocate" and "Christ Our Mediator" in *Principles of Faith*, pp. 159–181.

Let us now consider the essential qualifications for the office of mediator. A mediator must be in a position to understand the whole controversy in all its bearings and tendencies. He must possess the confidence of all the parties. If he has not their confidence, they will not voluntarily submit the question in dispute to his mediatorial adjustment. Therefore the confidence of the parties is indispensable to his success. He must sustain such relations to the parties as to be the suitable person to discharge the functions of that office. He must be both able and willing to fulfill all the indispensable conditions of the reconciliation.

Certain conditions must be fulfilled for the purpose of the mediatorial office to be accomplished. The mediator must be consecrated to the office by the consent of all parties. The mediator must consent to undertake and accomplish the work of bringing about a reconciliation. The parties involved must accept the conditions proposed by the mediator, and they must actually fulfill these conditions.

Christ as Mediator

Now, we must apply these principles to Christ as mediator between God and men. The office implies the existence of two parties. Both parties are mentioned in the text: on the one hand, Jehovah; on the other, man as a race. These are the parties between whom Christ is appointed to act as mediator.

The existence of a mediator implies that a controversy exists between the parties. That there is a controversy between God and men is one of the most notorious facts in the universe. It is impossible that God should approve the conduct of mankind. It cannot be that He does not disapprove, and that He is not highly displeased with the course of conduct pursued by our race. He cannot but know what the conduct of mankind is. He cannot but disapprove of their conduct. For Him to approve their conduct would be to become as bad as they are. He cannot possibly be a virtuous being, unless He highly and infinitely abhors the selfishness of mankind.

Nor can it be possible that selfish men, remaining selfish, love God. They are hostile to God, because He is so holy as to require of them entire benevolence on pain of eternal death. This He ought to require. Nothing less than this can He require and be virtuous. But, because of this very requirement people hate Him; and because they hate Him for His goodness, He must certainly, and, if He is a good being, must necessarily abhor them.

The actual state of things in the world shows that the world is full of blasphemous opposition to the government of God on the one hand, and that, on the other hand, God is sweeping the nations from time to time with the broom of destruction. It is manifestly open, outrageous war between God and men. God is exercising as much forbearance all along as the nature of the case admits; while men, encouraged by His forbearance, are pushing their desperate opposition in the most fool-hardy and blasphemous manner. To maintain that there is no contro-versy between God and men is to deny one of the most universally evident facts that exists in the universe.

I said that the existence of a mediator implies a difficulty in the way of the parties coming together and adjusting their own matters of difference, and that this difficulty might arise out of an indisposition in one or both the parties to have the matter adjusted, or out of the relation of the parties to each other. Hence, I observe the necessity of a mediator between God and men did not arise out of any unmerciful disposition on the part of God, or any disinclination on His part to pardon sin, if it could be safely done in consistency with the stability of His government. God is love; so He is of course infinitely disposed to do good whenever He wisely can. It is absurd to say that an infinitely benevolent Being should not be merciful in His disposition, and that He should not actually exercise mercy in the pardon of crime, when-ever it can be done consistently with the public interest.

On the part of man there actually is and always has been a most pertinacious indisposition to have this matter adjusted, and to become reconciled to God. Therefore, if people ever are to be reconciled, some-one must undertake the mediatorial office who is able to bring about the requisite change in the temper of their minds toward God.

A difficulty arose out of the relation of the parties to each other, or rather, out of God's relation to the universe. Since God is the lawgiver, public justice demanded either that He should execute the law when it was violated, or provide a substitute that would as effectively sustain the government as the execution would. Hence, from the relation of God to the universe, it is plain that He must exact a condition as indispensable to effecting a reconciliation between Him and men. This condition mankind could not fulfill. The necessity, then, of a mediator, was two-fold:

1. To meet the demands of public justice and provide a substitute for the execution of law upon mankind.

2. To subdue the selfish and turbulent spirit of the offending party, to humble mankind and make them willing to confess, repent and be reconciled to God.

As I said, a mediator must possess a nature and be in a position to understand the whole controversy in all its bearings and tendencies. Christ has the omniscience of God, together with the experience of a man, and is, therefore, the only being in the universe who in the same sense could understand the precise attitude of affairs between God and men. As God, He knew and had always known the precise adaptedness of the law to the nature and circumstances of mankind. He had seen sin at its first entrance into the world; and beginning with the first human pair, He had seen it like a fountain opened in a mountain, running and spreading itself as it advanced, first a rill, then a brook, next a river, and finally an ocean, extending through all the ranks of mankind and filling the earth, and finally pouring the immense stream of human population over the vast cataract of death to be swallowed up in the dreadful vortex of damnation.

As a man, He had the experience of a man and knew all the difficulties in the way of rendering perfect obedience to the moral law under circumstances of the severest temptation. If any allowance should be made under the government of God for sin in the circumstances in which mankind was placed, the man Christ Jesus had the opportunity to know and must of necessity have tested the question in His own personal experience.

A mediator must sustain such relations to the parties as to be the person to whom the office naturally belongs. Christ sustained to the universe the relation of an Executive Magistrate. It was, therefore, His duty to execute the law or to provide a substitute for its execution. That He sustains this relation to the universe is evident from His own assertions. It is said of Him, "The government is upon his shoulder . . . He is head over all things to the Church . . . All power in heaven and earth is in his hands . . . The Father judgeth no man, but hath committed all judgment to the Son." He will judge the world, and distribute the rewards of eternity. He commissions ambassadors, which none can do but the Supreme Executive Magistrate. These, with many other considerations that might be adduced, render it certain that Christ sustains to the universe the relation of the Supreme Executive. It therefore belonged to Him either to execute the law, or to provide such a substitute for its execution as fully to meet the demands of public justice. As God, He was infinitely concerned to secure the stability of His government and the virtue of the universe. Being also man, and sustaining the same relation to men that He did to God, rendered it peculiarly proper that He should interpose His influence with His Father, who in this respect sustained the relation of the lawgiver, on behalf of His fellow men.

A mediator must possess the confidence of both parties. That Christ actually possesses the confidence of the Father, we have the fullest assurance in the Father's own assertions: "Thou art my beloved Son, in whom I am well pleased." That He deserves the confidence of men will be questioned by none but infidels. And I may say further that He actually possesses the confidence of everyone who is benefitted by His mediatorial interposition. Everyone knows that faith or confidence in

Christ is insisted on everywhere in the Bible as wholly indispensable to being interested in His salvation. So that, as a matter of fact, the mediator must and does possess the confidence of all the parties who are to be or can be benefitted by His interposition.

I said a mediator must be able and willing to fulfill the indispensable conditions of reconciliation. Christ being God and sustaining to the universe the relation of the Executive Magistrate, He could, by offering His own person, more than satisfy the demands of public justice; that is, His death, as their substitute, would be a higher evidence of His regard to the law and determination not to relinquish its claims than would be the infliction of its penalty on all mankind. Public justice demands that the law should be sustained for the protection of public and private interests.

Law is public property, and every subject of any government is interested in the execution of any law when its penalty is incurred. The very establishment of government is a pledge on the part of the lawgiver that he will protect the public interests and do all that the nature of the case admits to secure public virtue and happiness. In other words, to secure universal respect and obedience to the laws. The execution of the penalty is designed and calculated to prevent future breaches of the law, to secure respect and obedience to the law by demonstrating both the intention and the ability of the lawgiver to redeem his pledge and protect the public interests.

Now who cannot see that if the lawgiver himself will consent to suffer as the substitute of his guilty subjects, it will do much more to sustain his government, to create confidence, love and energetic attachment to him, than merely to execute the law upon the offenders? Mercy must not, and in a perfect government cannot be exercised and the penalty of law set aside, without such a satisfaction made to public justice as will be equivalent to the execution of the law.

Let me illustrate this by supposing a mighty earthly sovereign at the head of an immense army marching to effect some important object. Discipline in his army is altogether indispensable. Therefore, his orders must be most rigorously enforced or insubordination will defeat the enterprise. But on one occasion he issues an order against which a whole regiment rebels. Now what shall be done? It is a valuable regiment. The sovereign pities them and yet abhors their disobedience. Either his authority must cease, that regiment must be put to the sword, or some governmental expedient must be devised that will as effectually secure future obedience as the execution of the law would do. An order is issued for the whole army to form a hollow square. In the center of this a vast scaffold is erected over which an immense velvet pall is thrown. The implements of punishment are prepared. The whole army with trailed arms and standards dragged in dust, muffled drums, and solemn death marches, are gathered, as they suppose, to witness the execution of the rebellious regiment. They wait in breathless expectation for the order for the regiment to be put to death. In the mean time, this regiment is drawn out and paraded by itself alone around the scaffold. Everything is gloomy. Sorrow fills every countenance. Every heart is heaving. Deep sighs are heard on every side and the whole mass of minds is heaving with excitement, and agonized with the dismal prospect. At this moment, the sovereign, attended by his guards, is seen to ride within the square. He dismounts, lays aside his royal robes, uncovers his head, and arrays himself in the humble attire of a servant. Every eye is upon him. Unutterable astonishment and wonder fill every mind. No one can imagine what is now to be done. Leaving his attendants behind him, he meekly ascends the scaffold, unattended, unarmed, and thus addresses the rebellious regiment: "You have disobeyed my orders. You deserve to die! But my compassion bleeds over you. To wholly set aside the penalty which you deserve, simply upon your bare repentance and return to duty—I cannot, dare not, and must not do. I cannot offer you forgiveness on any such conditions. My authority must be sustained. Discipline in my army is wholly indispensable. So much do I regard public justice that sooner should heaven and earth pass away than I would set aside the execution of law in a manner that would weaken my authority. But on the other hand, so much do I have compassion in your case, so much do I love and pity you, that for the sake of being able to offer you a pardon upon conditions that will not destroy the discipline of my army I am willing and about to suffer in your stead."

So saying, he uncovers his shoulders and receives upon his naked back one hundred stripes until the blood flows down and stains the pall beneath his feet. Indeed he suffers, until a universal wail is heard and the army refuses to look on. They cover their faces, and cry out in agony, until he bids the executioner stay his hand. He resumes his garments, bows to the army, and retires to his quarters. Now what do you think would be the effect of a transaction like this upon the discipline of his army? Who would dare thereafter to rebel, and which of that rebellious regiment, or who, of his whole army, would not instantly die to protect their sovereign rather than disobey him?

Now the design of Christ was to satisfy the demands of public justice and at once to demonstrate the infinite compassion of God for His rebellious subjects, and at the same time His unalterable determination to sustain His government and enforce obedience to His law, to protect and bless the innocent, to punish and destroy the guilty. And His relation to the universe was such that His death, I may say, was an infinitely higher expression of His compassion, on the one hand, and of His justice on the other, than could have been given in His execution of the law upon sinners.

The Atonement*

I said the mediator must be able and willing to make any sacrifice necessary in order to remove the obstacles out of the way of such reconciliation. The Atonement has been looked upon by many as an incredible doctrine, and aside from right apprehensions of the moral character of God it is altogether the most incredible thing in the universe. That God should consent to suffer for man would beggar all credibility except for the fact that His whole moral character is love or benevolence. When you consider this, and it is a truth taught by all the works and all the ways of God, the doctrine of Atonement is altogether the most reasonable and credible doctrine that can be conceived. Since God is benevolent, He certainly must be disposed to exercise mercy. But since He is benevolent, He certainly would exercise mercy with a due regard to public justice and upon such conditions that would not endanger His authority. Since God is love and infinitely wise, He devised a plan whereby the ends of public justice might be consistent with the offer of pardon. And He adopted the plan, although it called Him to great self-denial. If His own suffering in their place could be of a lesser amount than must necessarily be inflicted upon them, then it would render it proper to offer them mercy. If His suffering would prevail to bring them to repentance and make them virtuous, His love would render it certain that such would be the course of conduct He would pursue. Christ, then, was not only able but willing to offer His human nature as a sacrifice to public justice. His human nature, being taken into union with His divine nature, became a part of himself. His blood was, therefore, the blood of God. His Atonement was the Atonement of God in offering up His human nature unto death that He might give to man eternal life.

The parties must consent that He should sustain to them this relation. He should be consecrated to this office by consent of the parties. The Father, who is the offended party, has nominated and sent forth His own Son, and proposed that He should act as Mediator between God and men. He has consented to accept what He has done as satisfactory on the part of the government of God, as wholly removing out of the way every objection to a universal offer of pardon on the part of the divine government to all who will repent and return to their duty. And now the question is submitted to you, to every sinner, whether you will consent on your part to receive Christ as your Mediator. This you must do by faith. Are you willing to do it?

I said that another condition upon which the accomplishment of the great object of Christ depends is the actual fulfillment of the conditions decreed by Him as indispensable to the effecting of this rec-

---

*See also, "On the Atonement," *Principles of Victory*, p. 38.

onciliation. These conditions on the part of the sinner are as follows:

1. Repentance, or an unqualified turning of yourself both in heart and life from all iniquity, and making a consecration of your whole being to God and to His service forever.

2. Faith in Christ's Atonement as the foundation of your pardon and acceptance with God.

3. Your perseverance in holiness or true obedience to the end of life.

Your Decision

This is a summary statement of the indispensable conditions, upon the fulfillment of which depends your eternal salvation. And now what do you say? It is in vain for you to pretend to consent to the mediatorial office and character of Christ, unless you consent to and fulfill the conditions imposed by Him upon you as indispensable to your being justified through Him. This, I say, is a question for you to decide. No one can decide it for you. God, on His part, has consented. Christ, as Mediator, has thrown the door wide open before you and stands as a doorman between you and the throne of God. He, as it were, lays His hand on both the parties. The Father has committed to Him the adjustment of this difficulty on the part of the divine government. Now will you commit to Him the keeping of your soul? Will you submit yourself to His government and control? Will you give your case into His hands, to be advocated, managed and adjusted by Him? Will you consecrate your whole being to God, and from this time on know and prove by your own conduct that the controversy between you and God is at an end? Now, therefore, "as an ambassador for Christ, I pray you, in Christ's stead, be ye reconciled to God."

In the light of this subject do you see the disinterested love of Christ? Oh how infinitely wonderful that He should consent to undertake such an office as this, fully knowing as He did the immense sacrifice to which it would call Him, the immense amount of shame, persecution, agony and death; and for what? For himself? To promote some selfish interests? No! But from disinterested love for you and me. What an exhibition of self-denial! His whole life being only an accumulation of sufferings, reproach, ridicule and opposition. How great His mental agonies must have been. To live in the midst of a world created by Him, and yet ruining themselves with their blasphemous opposition to Him!

From this subject do you see for what we are to trust Christ as Mediator? We are to look to Him for sanctification, or for that measure of grace that will thoroughly cleanse us from all our sins. We are to look to Him for justification; that is, for pardon and acceptance in respect to all our past sins. We are to look to Him for preserving grace to quicken and sustain us to the end.

Do you see from this subject what it is to be a Christian? It is to heartily consent to the mediatorial work of Christ and to comply with the conditions upon which He offers to save.

Do you see the security of the saints? The controversy between them and God is at an end. Being justified by faith, they have peace with God through our Lord Jesus Christ. And now what shall be able to separate them from the love of Christ? "What shall we then say to these things? If God be for us, who can be against us? He that spared not his own Son, but delivered him up for us all, how shall he not with him also freely give us all things? Who shall lay any thing to the charge of God's elect? It is God that justifieth. Who is he that condemneth? It is Christ that died, yea rather, that is risen again, who is even at the right hand of God, who also maketh intercession for us. Who shall separate us from the love of Christ? Shall tribulation, or distress, or persecution, or famine, or nakedness, or peril, or sword? As it is written, For thy sake we are killed all the day long; we are accounted as sheep for the slaughter. Nay, in all these things we are more than conquerors, through Him that loved us. For I am persuaded, that neither death, nor life, nor angels, nor principalities, nor powers, nor things present, nor things to come, nor height, nor depth, nor any other creature, shall be able to separate us from the love of God, which is in Christ Jesus our Lord" (Rom. 8:31–39).

From this subject also we see the certainty of the final damnation of all unbelievers. Why, sinner, by your rejection of Christ the controversy between you and God, so far from being ended, is only made worse. Your guilt and final damnation are severely aggravated by your rejection of the mediatorial interference of Christ.

How infinitely foolish and mad are the expectations of some who claim that if Christ has made an Atonement sufficient for all, that all will be saved as a matter of course. Why, sinner, it would be just as reasonable as if you were starving and invited to a feast, to which you obstinately refused to go, for you to affirm that the provision was ample, had actually been made enough for all, so that no one need to famish with hunger; that therefore it mattered not whether you went to the feast or not. Why, sinner! Are you crazy? Can it be possible that the mediatorial work of Christ will save you without your own consent? Surely it cannot be. It is virtually and forever impossible.

From this subject do you see the wickedness and danger of delay? Sinner, God urges now upon you the obligation and necessity of instantly deciding whether you will consent to this plan of salvation or not. This may be the last opportunity you will ever have to make your salvation sure. Now what do you say? Do you call heaven and earth to witness and to record on your soul that you now, in the presence of God, of angels and of men, from the inmost recesses of your being, consent to the mediatorial work of Christ, and accept the conditions of salvation? Do you so decide? And is the response of your heart, "So help me God!"?

From this subject we can see the meaning of the context which has been in some instances much perverted: "I exhort therefore, that, first of all, supplications, prayers, intercessions, and giving of thanks, be made for all men; for kings, and for all that are in authority; that we may live a quiet and peaceable life in all godliness and honesty. For this is good and acceptable in the sight of God our Savior; who will have all men to be saved, and to come unto the knowledge of the truth. For there is one God, and one mediator between God and men, the man Christ Jesus; who gave himself a ransom for all, to be testified in due time" (1 Tim. 2:1-6). Some have inferred that all men will inevitably be saved. But the plain meaning of this passage, when taken together, is that God *desires* the salvation of all men. The word *will* may with equal propriety be rendered *desire*, as it often is. God really desires the salvation of all men as a thing desirable in itself; and has therefore sent forth His Son to be a mediator between himself and mankind in general, "who gave himself a ransom for all, to be testified (or, as in the original, a testimony or witness,) in due time" (1 Tim. 2:6). He has given himself as a witness or testimony of the righteousness and infinite love of God to dying men, "That [God] might be just, and the justifier of him which believeth in Jesus" (Rom. 3:26).

Now, sinner, you have before you as condensed and simple an exhibition of the gospel as I can give you in one discourse. Will you accept it, or do you reject it? "I call heaven and earth to record this day against you, that I have set before you life and death, blessing and cursing" (Deut. 30:19). Therefore choose today, and oh, choose life, that you may live!

And Christian, do you see your privilege? Do you see your obligation to Christ? Do you see your dependence upon Him? Do you understand your security in Him? Why you are to ask in His name? Why you are to approach God through Him? Do you understand the Gospel? Then cleave to the Mediator that the river of live may flow continually through your soul!*

---

*Here Finney breaks from publishing his sermons, but continues his series of *Letters on Sanctification*. These letters have been published in *Principles of Discipleship*, by Bethany House Publishers. Finney returned to printing his sermons once again with the following sermon in the July 20, 1842 issue of *The Oberlin Evangelist*.

9

THY WILL BE DONE*

"Thy will be done in earth, as it is in heaven" (Matthew 6:10b).

Every theological system and every theological opinion takes for granted and assumes the truth of some system of philosophy or psychology. No matter how much someone may condemn metaphysics, he too has his own system of metaphysics by which he interprets the Bible. Furthermore, he frames his theological opinions so they will be consistent with his own metaphysical system.

When any attempt is made to overthrow any theological error or to establish any theological truth by an appeal to our own consciousness and to the Bible as interpreted in view of the laws of mind, some cry out vehemently against metaphysics. They assume that they have made a conclusive objection when they declare of their opponents ideas, "It is metaphysical." But everyone should know that the objector himself, when he attempts to establish an opposing theory, assumes as true an opposite system of philosophy or psychology and is no less metaphysical than his opponent. He himself is metaphysical in his violent zeal against metaphysics!

The fundamental point of difference between the old and new schools of theology is in respect to the freedom of the will. From this point they diverge. When consistently carried out, the two schemes or schools differ fundamentally on most of the important questions in theology. It is in vain to attempt to cover up this fact; for anyone who has not seen it to be true is still ignorant of the great principles and legitimate bearing of the points at issue. However, few of either school are consistent throughout. Nothing is more common than to find old

---

The Oberlin Evangelist, July 20, 1842. There are no lecture numbers on any of the following sermons in this book.

school men zealously contending for doctrines that properly belong only to the scheme of the new school theologians. Perhaps it is just as common to find new school men, as they call themselves, zealously defending dogmas that properly belong to the scheme of the old school. With any consistency, new school men cannot accept, defend and embrace as true these old school doctrines. Therefore, a strange confusion and inconsistency prevails among theologians of both schools. How remarkable and even incredible that there should be so little consistency in the theological views of so great a majority of theologians of all schools.

I have stated that the point of divergence between the old and new schools is the freedom or necessity of the will. Upon this point, the old school maintains that the will always is as the greatest apparent good is; or, in other words, that the mind always chooses that which appears to be upon the whole the most agreeable and that the choice is always determined by the objective motive, or that which is presented to the mind as a reason for choice. Many of them will not say that choice is necessitated by motive, while at the same time they maintain that motive is the cause of choice as absolutely as a physical cause produces its effect. And that the difference between the determination of choice by motive and the production of an effect by a physical cause does not lie in the nature of the connection but in the nature of the terms connected—that the certainty is just as absolute in the one case as in the other. And when they explain themselves, it is obvious and self-evident that the necessity is just as great in the one case as in the other.

Those who are truly consistent with the old school maintain, and have since the days of Augustine, that men are wholly and naturally unable to do anything good; that their will is necessarily determined to do evil by what they call original sin or native depravity. They maintain that moral obligation implies no power whatsoever to act right or to do the will of God. With them, sin is a necessity of human nature since the fall of Adam. And free agency amounts only to the power of committing sin.

If, according to their view, the will is necessitated by motives, then it follows that all action is *necessary* as opposed to *free*, and the doctrine of universal fatalism is true. But if the will is free, as is maintained by the new school theologians, and all moral depravity belongs to moral action, then truly there is a system of theology directly opposite of the old school in nearly every important point.

That I may give this subject as fundamental a discussion as my time and the nature of the case admits, I will, the Lord willing, discuss the following propositions[1]:

1. How we know anything.
2. What the primary faculties of the mind are.
3. Wherein human liberty consists.
4. To what acts and states of mind moral responsibility extends.
5. What constitutes sin.
6. What constitutes holiness.
7. What constitutes the will of God.
8. How God's will is done in heaven.
9. What is implied in the sincere offering of this petition to God as found in the text?
10. Nothing short of a state of mind that can sincerely offer this petition can be true Christianity.

1. How we know anything.

Consciousness is the condition of all knowledge. I will therefore begin by giving what I suppose to be a correct definition of consciousness. Consciousness may be regarded as a power, or faculty, or as an act or state of the mind. As a power or faculty, it is the capacity or ability which the mind has to recognize or know its own existence, acts and states. As an act, or state of mind, it is the actual notice or knowledge of its own existence and state. Consciousness gives us the knowledge of our own existence. By it we certainly know that we exist. It gives us the phenomena of our mental states and acts, as well as the knowledge of the liberty or necessity of our acts or states. In short, everything that we do know is given by consciousness.

Whatever we know by consciousness we know with certainty. Consciousness gives me the fact of my existence. Consciousness is the highest evidence of the fact of my existence. It also gives me the fact of certain sensations, volitions, mental states and acts, and it gives me these with certainty. Whether or not there be in reality anything without corresponding with the sensations and mental states within, the mental states themselves as given by consciousness are matters of fact of which I have absolute knowledge by my own consciousness. When a person thinks or reasons, whether he thinks or reasons according to the truth or not may be doubted. It cannot be doubted whether he thinks or reasons, since he is conscious of thinking and reasoning. My thoughts and reasonings are matters of fact given me by my own con-

---

[1]Note: In this sermon I have maintained the subject heading numbers to help you refer quickly to the subjects in question, and to help you see at a glance the logical outline of the numerous topics presented here.

sciousness, of which I am therefore absolutely certain. In short, every mental phenomenon is given by consciousness. Every act and state of mind is a reality, just as it is given by consciousness. And whatever else is true or false, the phenomena of mind given by consciousness must be facts, must be incontrovertible verities, because they are perceived by the mind to be facts.

2. What the primary faculties of the mind are.

Consciousness does not directly give us the faculties themselves, but the mind infers them from phenomena perceived by consciousness. Every phenomenon, act or state of mind implies a corresponding faculty; that is, the mind possesses the power to perform that act. In other words, it is able to act in that manner. When, therefore, consciousness gives us certain classes of actions, we affirm with intuitive certainly that the mind possesses corresponding faculties.

There are three primary or fundamental classes of actions: Acts or states of the intellect, acts or states of the sensibility, and acts or states of the will.

By this language I mean that men certainly possess a faculty by which they think, reason, judge and affirm certain truths. The faculty which does these things I call intellect, and suppose it to include understanding, reason and conscience. By the sensibility I mean the faculty of feeling. This comprehends emotions, desires, affections, and, in short, whatever we mean by feeling. By the will I mean the power of choice, or ability to choose or refuse whatever is an object of choice. Please understand, then, the primary faculties, as implied in the phenomena given by consciousness, are intellect (or intelligence), sensibility, and will.

3. Wherein human liberty consists.

This is a fundamental point for discussion. And to this problem two different answers are given by the different schools in theology. The old school gives this answer: Liberty consists in the power of doing as you will; that is, in carrying out and accomplishing the object of your volitions. With them, human liberty does not consist in an ability to choose in any direction in view of an object of choice; but simply in acting according to your choice without restriction—because they maintain that choice itself is invariably and necessarily determined by motive. But to this definition of free agency or human liberty it is justly objected that it is not liberty at all. Action is necessitated by volition or choice; and a man cannot but do as he wills or chooses. If I will to move, my muscles move of necessity, and there is no liberty between the volition and the action. The will moves the muscles, and a man cannot act against his will; for his will is the cause of his actions. This every man knows by his own consciousness with absolute certainty. Human liberty, then, does not and cannot consist in doing as you will, irrespective of the question of how it comes to pass that we *will* as we do.

Human liberty does not consist in a self-determining power in the will. For the will is not an agent, but only a capacity or power of an agent. It is not the will, therefore, that determines its own choices, but it is the agent himself that wills or chooses.

It does not consist in the power to decline all choice in view of motives or objects of choice. The mind is under a necessity of choosing in some way in view of an object of choice, and a refusal to choose, could this be, would be itself a choosing not to choose.

Human liberty does not consist in the power to choose without a motive or object of choice. The mind must necessarily have some object of choice, or it cannot choose. Choice implies that something is chosen; therefore, to choose without a motive or object of choice is absurd.

It does not lie in the necessity of choosing what, in the judgment of the mind, is most worthy of choice. For this we have the testimony of our own consciousness, since we certainly know that very often we do not choose that which in the judgment of our mind is most worthy of choice.

Nor does it lie in the necessity of choosing that which appears the most agreeable to the mind. For, as a matter of fact, we certainly know that we often do choose that which, in no proper sense, can be called agreeable to us.

Positively speaking, human liberty does consist in the sovereign power of choosing in any direction in view of any motive or object of choice. In proof of this, I observe:

First, nothing else than this can be liberty. For we are conscious that action is compelled or necessitated by choice.

Second, to force or necessitate volition (were this possible) is as inconsistent with liberty as to force action against choice. If I should seize your hand and put a dagger in it, and compel you to stab a man, this action is not yours, but mine. But suppose I had power to force your will to act on your muscles, and should compel you to will to stab a man, and the muscular action and stabbing should follow of necessity from your volitions, this action would no more properly be your own than if I forced your muscles contrary to your will.

Third, we just as certainly know that we are free in this sense as we know that we exist or that we choose at all. Consciousness gives us not only our existence as a fact, our mental states and acts as facts, but it gives us absolutely the freedom or necessity of our acts. Hence, of some acts and states of mind, we say with certainty, "I could not help it," because we are conscious of being in the most proper sense involuntary in those states of mind. Consciousness always gives us not only our acts and mental states, but also the fact of their freedom or their necessity. And everyone knows when he has chosen in any direction in view of an object of choice, that, all the circumstances being the same, he was able to choose or might have chosen the opposite.

Fourth, that this is true is manifest from the universal affirmation of praise and blameworthiness in respect to our moral actions. No one can, by any possibility, blame or praise himself or anyone else except upon the assumption that under the circumstances he might have chosen differently. No one can really doubt the liberty of the will in this sense, and still affirm the praise or blameworthiness of any act.

We have seen, then, that liberty cannot consist in outward action because consciousness affirms that this is directly necessitated by choice.

Liberty cannot consist in feeling or emotion, because consciousness testifies that our feelings are involuntary states of mind. Feelings are not acts or states of the will, but of the sensibility. We cannot exercise feelings and emotions directly as we do volitions or choices. If we desire to feel upon any subject, we direct our attention to a consideration of that subject, and corresponding feelings exist in the mind of course, just as naturally as we experience the sensation of vision when we direct our eyes to an object of sight. But we can never directly will emotions or feelings into existence. Nor can we suppress them when they do exist, except by diverting our attention and thoughts from the objects that produce them. Feelings then are always indirectly necessitated or promoted by choice. Human liberty, then, cannot consist in the feelings.

Since human liberty cannot consist in acts or states of the *intelligence*, or in acts or states of the *sensibility*, it must consist in the sovereign power of willing or choosing in any direction in view of an object of choice.

4. To what acts and states of mind moral responsibility extends.

The law of God is the rule of moral action, and the measure of its claims is the measure of moral responsibility.

The law of God levels its claims to the present ability of every subject of God's moral government. Its language is "Thou shalt love the Lord thy God with all thy heart, and thy neighbor as thyself." The true meaning of this law is that every moral being shall consecrate all his powers, whatever they are at the present moment, to the service of God. Our consciousness informs us that by willing we control the acts and states of the intellect: that we think, reason, judge and affirm by voluntarily controlling the attention of our mind. Consciousness also testifies that we feel by directing our attention to objects calculated to excite feeling, and that we act by willing to act. Thus by legislating over the voluntary power of the mind, the lawgiver proposes to secure the entire consecration of the whole being to the great ends of benevolence.

But the thought which I wish to impress here is: The law levels its claims to present ability. The law does not say, "Love the Lord thy God with the strength you possessed when you were a child, and serve Him only with the powers you had then." The law says we are to love God with all the powers we have at present. If your capacity to serve God and to promote the great ends of benevolence has been increased, either by the grace of God or by their diligent use and development in the exercise of your own agency, the law does not satisfy itself with claiming the measure of obedience you might have rendered before this increase of ability. The law requires that all your present strength and power shall be completely and unreservedly consecrated to God.

So, on the other hand, if your ability has been in any way diminished, either by your own act or in any other way, the law requires nothing more except that whatever power you have left be consecrated unreservedly and perfectly to God. If your ability has been abridged by your own fault, you are guilty for thus abridging it, and for this you may be punished. But you cannot be held responsible for not doing what you are no longer able to do. For example, suppose it were my duty last week to visit and warn a certain sinner to flee from the wrath to come, but the man is now dead and beyond my reach. For not warning him when I had opportunity I am guilty. But I am now under no obligation to warn him, for the simple reason that I am naturally unable to do so. I may justly be punished for my former neglect, but I cannot be held responsible for not warning him at the present time. If I cut off a hand, I can no longer be required to use it, though I may be guilty for cutting it off and held responsible for that act. In such cases, God requires repentance for the act that abridged our capacity, but in no case requires that which has become naturally impossible.

When a person loses the ability to pay his debts, and that too by his own fault, he is no longer under a moral obligation to pay them any faster than he has power to do so. He may be punished for rendering himself unable, but he can no more be under a moral obligation to pay them while unable, than to warn a man who is dead to flee from the wrath to come. The reason why he is no more under moral obligation in the one case than in the other is precisely the same, namely, that he has no power to do so.

So if a man becomes deranged by his own fault, he is not a moral agent while deranged, but his great sin lies in having made himself deranged.

The spirit of the legal maxim that a man shall not take advantage of his own wrong, is that the guilt of the act which incapacitates a man for duty is equal to the guilt of all the default of which it is the cause.

Some maintain that the law of God does not limit its claims to present ability, but that it requires the same degree of service now, the same amount of love and zeal and consequent usefulness in us, that the law might have required had we never curtailed our ability by sinning, but on the contrary had fully developed our powers by perfect and perpetual obedience. To this I answer:

First, that it must be, and so far as I know is admitted by those who hold this doctrine, that to render this degree of service is naturally impossible in this state of existence.

Second, that the law might just as reasonably require that we should undo all that we have done, or make up for our default by future works of supererogation, both of which are equally impossible. If the law may require the one, notwithstanding it is naturally impossible, it may with equal propriety and justice require the other.

Third, if the same degree of service could be required now that might have been rendered had we never sinned, obedience to the law of God is naturally impossible in this state. But there is no reason from the Bible or philosophy to believe that that obedience, in the case of those who have lived in sin any portion of their lives, will ever be possible. Everyone understands that people know much less of God, and are therefore naturally able to love Him much less and to render Him a much less effectual service than they might have done had they always employed their powers of moral agency rightly. If anyone affirms that the saint in heaven will not be correspondingly unable to render the same amount of service that he might have done had he never sinned, the burden of proof is wholly upon him who makes the affirmation.

Fourth, that the Gospel or anything else can so change our powers as to make us able to perform in any world all that we might have done had we never sinned is a sheer assumption.

So of our ignorance: We cannot be under obligation to do that of which we are entirely ignorant, although our ignorance is our fault. Read James 4:17: "Therefore to him that knoweth to do good, and doeth it not, to him it is sin." Here it is as fully implied as possible that if a person does not know to do good he is not under obligation to do it. Our obligation is first to know what duty is and then to do it. To do that of which we are entirely ignorant is naturally impossible and can no more be morally binding upon us than it is to warn a dead man. Nor does it alter the case if our ignorance is our own fault. If our ignorance is our own fault, then the sin lies in being ignorant, and not in omitting to do that of which we have no knowledge. Therefore the spirit of the legal maxim, *Ignorantia legis non excusat*, (Ignorance of the law is no excuse) is that the guilt of willful ignorance is equal to all the default of which it is the cause, and not that a man can be under moral obligation to perform impossibilities.

If the law requires the same amount of love and service that we might have rendered had we acquired all the knowledge possible, I see not how any saint in heaven can ever perfectly obey, for it will always remain true that he might have known numerous truths and relations more than at any given time he will know, had he not sinned in neglecting to know the truth. So that if the law requires at present, and will forever require, all of every moral being that might have been required had he never sinned, it must remain true forever, not only that every saint on earth, but for all that appears, every saint in heaven will forever continue to fall short of rendering the obedience the law requires, and therefore live eternally in sin.

It is not a little curious and amazing that the same person, as is often the case, should maintain the doctrine of a natural ability in man to do all his duty, and also that it is the duty of every individual to render the same service to God in kind and in degree that might have been rendered had he never sinned, and still further admit that this degree of service in this state is naturally impossible. I not infrequently meet with people who call themselves new school theologians, who strongly contend for the doctrine of natural ability to do all God requires, and who will insist on people being entirely holy, and urge and command the church to forsake all sin, and yet inconsistently and absurdly maintain that to forsake all sin, and to entirely obey the law would imply the rendering of the same degree of service that they might have rendered had they never sinned, which they themselves admit to be impossible. I had in substance the following conversation with a brother:

"Do you believe in the doctrine of natural ability: That men are able to do all that God requires of them?"

"Yes," he replied, "and I insist as much as you do upon their doing all their duty and being entirely holy."

I asked: "Do you believe that doing their whole duty and being entirely holy implies entire obedience to the law of God?"

"Yes, be sure I do."

"And you believe that men are naturally able to do this?"

"Yes," was his reply, "and I insist upon it as much as you do."

I then asked, "Do you believe that the law of God levels its claims to the present ability of men, so that men are entirely able perfectly to obey?"

"No," he replied, "and I think there is your error. You so explain the law as to bring it down to the present ability of man."

"How else," I asked, "should I do? If I insist upon man's natural ability to perfectly obey it, am I not bound so to expound it as to level its claims to their natural ability? But what do you do? Do you believe that the law of God requires of a man the same degree of love and service and efficiency that he might have rendered had he never sinned?"

"Yes," said he, "and this is the very point where we differ. I exalt the law and maintain that God requires that every moral agent, however long he has sinned, however ignorant he may be, and however much he may have curtailed his natural ability by sin, should render the same degree of service he would have done had he never sinned; while you," he continued, still addressing me, "so expound the law as to level its claims to the creature's present natural ability."

"And, my brother," I asked, "which is most consistent? I so expound the law as to level its claims to the present natural ability of the subject, and then consistently urge him up to immediate and perfect obedience. You maintain that he is able perfectly to obey, but yet that the law requires that which you confess to be naturally impossible, and then absurdly call upon him to perform that which is by your own showing naturally impossible. Now what consistency or candor is there in your professing to believe in his natural ability to do all his duty, and then maintaining that the law requires natural impossibilities, and all at the same breath denounce him for not keeping the whole law; maintaining that he is able to keep it, and yet inconsistently contending that it requires that which you confess to be naturally impossible? You are bound, as an honest man, to give up the doctrine of natural ability; to publish to the world that people are entirely unable to obey the law of God; and no longer insult their intelligence and outrage their sense of justice by requiring them to perfectly obey it; or else to so interpret it as to bring obedience within the limit of their natural ability, and cease to denounce those as heretics who consistently and conscientiously do this. I say that you are obligated to do this."

Now here let me ask: Is it not a shame and a sin for persons to hold and teach the doctrine of natural ability and to perfectly obey the law while holding that the law requires natural impossibilities? Is it not a shame and a sin to call upon people to universally and perfectly obey the law on pain of eternal death, and then accuse those of being heretics and far gone in error, who are consistent enough, while they maintain the doctrine of natural ability, to maintain also that the law levels its claims to the present ability of people, and for this reason call upon all people, everywhere, unreservedly and perfectly to obey it?

The very language and spirit of the law manifestly levels its claims to present human ability. The question therefore is what are people naturally able to do or avoid? Observe, the point of inquiry before us now is: To what acts and states of mind does moral responsibility extend? Since I have shown that the law is the standard and that it levels its claims to present ability, the true inquiry is what acts and states of mind are possible to people, or what acts and states of mind can be avoided by them?

We have already seen that consciousness gives us the phenomena of our own minds, and that whatever we know with certainty we know through the medium of our own consciousness. It teaches us that the will is the controlling faculty of the mind, that volition necessitates outward action. Volition also necessitates thought, feeling or emotion by directing the attention of the mind to subjects of thought and to objects calculated to excite emotion. Consciousness then teaches us that whatever is possible to man he can do by willing, and anything that does not follow the act of his will is naturally impossible to him. *If he cannot do it by willing and endeavor, and by sincerely intending and aiming to do it, it is naturally impossible to him. Consequently man cannot be responsible for anything which he cannot do or avoid, by willing and endeavoring to do or avoid it.*

For example: If I will to move and my muscles do not obey volition, muscular action is impossible to me. If I will to think and thought does not follow, if I will to feel and direct my attention to corresponding objects and emotion does not follow, thought and emotion at the time are impossible to me. In short, whatever does not follow volition directly or indirectly as the natural and necessary result of volition is impossible to me. So if I will to avoid anything whatever, and the thing follows in spite of my volition, it is unavoidable by me. If by will and endeavor I cannot avoid it, the thing is necessary in such a sense that I am not responsible for its occurrence. Man therefore is not responsible:

For his nature being what it is;

Nor for the existence of his constitutional appetites and propensities;

Nor for the existence of the appetites or propensities under the appropriate circumstances of his being;

But he is responsible for their guidance, control and subjection to the law of God insofar as they are subject to the control of his will.

Look to the law and the testimony. The law of God is the rule, and by it we know to what acts and states of mind moral responsibility extends.

The law of God is in spirit a unit. Love, or benevolence, is the fulfilling of the whole law. That all the law is fulfilled in one word is repeatedly asserted in the Bible.

The love which constitutes obedience to the law of God is an act or state of the will, and consists in supreme, disinterested benevolence. This is all that the law requires; and man is responsible, and can be responsible only for this state of the will. If he is perfectly, universally and disinterestedly benevolent, he perfectly obeys the law of God. Whatever emotions, thoughts, acts or states of mind do not follow from this state of the will, as its natural and necessary sequence, are naturally impossible to him, and therefore moral obligation cannot extend to them. Whatever thoughts, emotions, acts or states of mind come to pass, notwithstanding this perfectly benevolent state of the will, he has no power to avoid. Therefore, such acts, emotions and states of mind can have no moral character. To maintain the contrary of these positions is not only to set all true philosophy aside, but is also a flat denial of the Bible itself.

It is abundantly taught, and again and again asserted in the Bible, that love, or benevolence, is the fulfilling of the law—that all the law is fulfilled in one word, *love*. And it should ever be borne in mind, and well considered by all, that the Bible takes the very same ground upon this subject as true philosophy. Benevolence is good-willing. It is willing the good of being for its own sake, and on account of its intrinsic value; consequently, it is the very nature of benevolence to will every good according to its relative value as perceived by the mind.

Every mind is to be guided by its own best judgment in respect to the relative value of different interests, except where God has revealed their relative value; in which case, this revelation is to decide for us. But in applying the great principle of the law of God to human conduct, we are obviously guided, not by the infinite views which God has, nor by the high views which the angels have, nor by the views which any other beings except ourselves have, of the relative value of different interests. We must judge for ourselves, under the best light afforded us, what is the relative value of the different interests with which we are surrounded, and how the law of God requires us to conduct ourselves in respect to them. And every being wills right, or just as the law of God requires him to will, when he regards and treats every interest according to its relative value as understood by his own mind. When he wills every good for its own sake, and the promotion of every interest according to its relative value in his own best judgment, he fully obeys the law of God.

We have seen that the will necessitates thought, action and feeling. Therefore, moral character cannot strictly belong to thought, action or feeling. If I will to stab a man, moral character does not attach to the dagger, to the hand that holds it, to the muscle that moves it, but to the mind in the exercise of willing. The same is true of thought or feeling. The mind is strictly responsible only for its voluntary acts. And the moral character of all acts and states of mind is found in that act of the will that produced them by a natural necessity.

We have seen, and know by our own consciousness, that man is free and sovereign. He is, therefore, responsible for any act or state of mind that can be produced or avoided directly or indirectly by willing and endeavor, and for nothing more or less. Hence, the law of God makes all virtue to consist in benevolence. Since the Bible is inspired by God, it teaches a correct philosophy and insists that all virtue consists in benevolence.

If the will, then, is conformed to the law of God, nothing can be morally wrong for the time being. For whatever does not follow by natural necessity from this state of the will is naturally impossible to us. So, on the other hand, if the will is wrong, nothing can be morally right; for, whatever acts or states of mind result from a wrong choice by a natural necessity have the same character, so far as they have any character at all, with the choice that produced them. This is the philosophy of total depravity. We truly say, if a man's heart is wrong everything that he does is wrong. By his heart we mean his choice, intention, purpose. If his intention or choice be selfish, nothing can be morally right; because his character is as his intention is; and it is naturally impossible that the emotions and actions which follow from a selfish intention should be morally right. If this is not true philosophy, then the doctrine of the total depravity of the unregenerate is not true.

The doctrine of total depravity as consisting in the selfish state of the will and of entire holiness as consisting in the benevolent state of the will, must stand or fall together. If anything about a person can be sinful, while his will is in a perfectly benevolent state, it must be true that when the will is in a perfectly selfish state, some things or many things in the same mind may be at the same time truly holy. And if a person can be all the while sinning, while his heart or will is in a state of disinterested benevolence, he can all the while be partly holy, while his heart or will is unregenerate and in a state of entire selfishness. If the emotions and actions of a person whose will is in a perfectly benevolent state can be sinful, then the emotions or actions of a person who is in a perfectly selfish state can be holy. So also, if the actions and emotions which follow from a selfish state of the will must of necessity be sinful, so the actions which follow from a benevolent state of the will must in the same sense be holy.

Remember, therefore, that whoever maintains that present sinfulness can be predicated of a person in a perfectly benevolent state of the will, must also admit that holiness may be predicated of one in a perfectly selfish state of the will. This is the doctrine of the Bible and of true philosophy: "True benevolence, or the willing of every good according to its relative value as perceived by the mind and for its own sake, is the whole of virtue." God's interest is to be willed as the supreme good, and every other interest according to its relative value, so far as we are capable of knowing. This is holiness, and nothing else is.

5. What constitutes sin.

We have seen that the primary faculties of the human mind are intellect, sensibility, and will. We have seen that the mind, in its voluntary actions, has respect to motives. It is not compelled to choose, but in every instance of choice it is free and sovereign. We have seen also that virtue and vice, or holiness and sin, lie in the choice or voluntary actions of the mind, and not in outward actions or involuntary states of mind.

I now observe that motives are addressed to the mind, either through the intelligence or the sensibility, and in no other way. By this I mean that by the use of the intellect, or through the medium of the feelings, the mind perceives things which it accounts an object of choice. The sensibility (or feelings) invites the will or mind to seek the gratification of the appetites or propensities as an end, or for the mere sake of the gratification. The intelligence points to God and His law, and the reason affirms that the mind ought to obey God rather than to seek the gratification of the sensibility. Through the intelligence is revealed to the mind the existence, character and claims of God. And the law of universal benevolence is seen by the intelligence to be obligatory. Now to will in accordance with the impressions of the sensibility, and to seek as the great end of life the gratification of the propensities, is what the Bible denominates the "carnal mind," or "minding of the flesh." This is the very essence of sin. It is enmity against God. Understand, then, that sin consists in the committal of the will (or in the devotion by the will of the whole being) to self-interest or self-gratification. This choice of our own gratification as the supreme end of life is the wicked heart, and all the forms of sin are only developments and necessary results of this supreme choice or intention of the mind. This is total moral depravity—enmity against God—entire consecration to self-gratification.

6. What constitues holiness.

In a word, holiness is the obedience of the will or heart to the law of God as this law lies revealed in the intelligence. I have just said that sin consists in the supreme devotion of the will, and consequently of all the powers of the mind to self-gratification. On the contrary, holiness consists in the supreme devotion of the will, and consequently of the whole being to the glory of God and the good of the universe. This entire consecration to the glory of God and the good of the universe is the whole of virtue in any being and in every world.

7. What the will of God is.

The will of God is expressed in His law. He is himself in the same state of mind in which He requires all moral beings to be; that is, in a state of universal and disinterested benevolence. Holiness is a term that expresses the moral character of this state of His will or heart. Love or benevolence is the fulfilling of the law; and conformity of will in any being to the law of universal love is holiness. We have seen that the will of God as expressed in His law is that every interest shall be willed for its own sake and according to its relative value. This is the will of God: "Moral agents should be universally and perfectly benevolent."

8. How God's will is done in heaven.

We are directed in the text to pray that the will of God may be done on earth as it is done in heaven. The will of God is done in heaven perfectly and universally, so far as it is known. Since only God is omniscient, all other beings in heaven must be of course continually learning new relations, and consequently their obligations must continually increase, corresponding to their increased knowledge. The obedience of heaven, therefore, must keep pace with increasing knowledge, and therefore its inhabitants must continually grow in holiness.

9. What is implied in a sincere offering of this petition to God as found in the text?*

What is the real state of mind in which an individual must be to sincerely offer this prayer?

It implies that the petitioner has confidence in the wisdom of God. If he did not believe that God was wise he could not innocently pray that God's will might be universally done. It implies confidence in His benevolence. If God is not benevolent, we have no right to pray that His will may be universally done. And if we do not believe Him to be

*See also, "The Lord's Prayer," "Acceptable Prayer," and "The Kingdom of God Upon Earth" in *Principles of Devotion*, pp. 84–134.

universally and perfectly benevolent, we have no right to offer such a petition.

It implies that the petitioner believes that the petition is according to the will of God. In other words, that it is the will of God that His will should be done as perfectly on earth as it is done in heaven. It implies a belief in the petitioner that it is possible that the will of God should be done on earth as it is done in heaven. For if he does not believe it possible, he cannot sincerely pray that it may be so.

It implies the belief that grace has made provision for his doing the will of God on earth as it is done in heaven. If he does not believe that such a thing is possible or that grace has made provision for the attainment of any such state, he mocks God in making such a request. And if he does not believe it to be according to the will of God that persons are to attain to such a state on earth, it is downright rebellion in him to ask it.

It implies a willingness that God should require of all people just what He does require, for surely if the petitioner does not heartily consent to the requirements of God, he cannot sincerely pray that He may be universally obeyed.

It implies that the petitioner is willing that God should require of him in all respects just what He does require. For how can he sincerely say "Thy will be done on earth as it is done in heaven," unless he is willing that God should require of him just what He does require.

As we have seen that willing and doing are connected by a natural necessity, and that a person naturally and necessarily acts as he wills, the sincere offering of this petition implies that the petitioner really does the will of God so far as he knows it, as really as they do in heaven. If the will is in sincere conformity with the true spirit of the petition, everything else that is under the control of the will must of necessity correspond with this state of the will. Consequently, whenever a soul is in such a state as to offer this petition to God sincerely, he must, for the time being, be really doing the will of God, as truly, and in his measure as perfectly as they are in heaven.

It implies that the petitioner holds himself and all that he has as fully and sacredly and practically at the disposal of God as do the inhabitants of heaven, so far as he knows the will of God. It implies that he actually does all in his power to promote this end, so far as he has knowledge, as they do in heaven. It implies a state of will or heart in perfect conformity with the will of God, so far as he knows His will.

It implies the same perfection for the time being, and according to his knowledge, that is in God and in the inhabitants of heaven. Do not be startled at this, for the whole of God's moral perfection lies in the benevolent state of His will. And whoever wills in perfect accordance with His will, so far as His will is known, whether on earth or in heaven, is in his measure, as really perfect as God is.

10. Nothing short of a state of mind that can sincerely offer this petition can be true Christianity.

Nothing short of this state of will or heart is conformity to the nature of things. Everything short of this state of the will is rebellion, and is virtually saying, "Let not the will of the Lord be universally done." Since this state of mind consists in willing every good for its own sake, and according to its relative value, nothing more or less than this state of mind can, by any possibility, be virtue.

God cannot allow anything less than this to be virtue, nor can He require anything more. Since His will is in all things perfectly right, He can require nothing less than that every moral agent should be entirely conformed to it so far as he knows it. He can never discharge any being from this obligation, nor accept that as obedience and call it virtue that is not precisely according to His will. If it is not according to His will, it must be opposed to His will, and can by no possibility be true Christianity.

Coming into this state of mind is what we mean by conversion or regeneration. It is a change in the ultimate choice or intention of the mind, in other words, a change from selfishness or the choice of self-gratification as the great end of life to disinterested benevolence. This, and nothing short of this, is regeneration or the new birth. It is and must be the beginning of true Christianity. This is holiness. This is sanctification, and the uninterrupted continuance of it is a state of sanctification. And if, as new relations are perceived, the will comes into immediate conformity to all these new relations, and remains in this state of conformity, such a mind is in entire harmony with the will of God and can sincerely say, "Thy will be done on earth as it is done in heaven."

Let me conclude by saying that this petition in the mouth of a selfish being is hypocrisy. It must be in all cases downright hypocrisy for a selfish person to offer this petition to God. This petition is hypocrisy on the lips of anyone whose will is not in entire and universal harmony with the will of God so far as His will is known. If there is anything in which the will is not entirely conformed to the known will of God, in offering this petition, the petitioner is a hypocrite, and abuses, flatters, and mocks God.

Now we can see what Christ intended by the command, "Be ye therefore perfect, even as your Father which is in heaven is perfect" (Matt. 5:48).* Many feel shocked at the idea of anyone being—even for a moment—without sin in this life. And to expect to be, in any proper sense, perfect in this life is with them wholly out of the question.

---

*See also, "Christian Perfection, I, II" for two sermons on this verse in *Principles of Holiness*, pp. 17–53.

From the manner in which they speak of the subject of perfection, it would seem Christ's command to be perfect as God is perfect is a most extravagant requirement, and something which Christ did not so much as even expect would be obeyed in this world. If they are consistent they must also suppose that in requiring us to offer this petition to God, He must have intended that we should use the language of hyperbole, and not that we should seriously expect or even suppose it possible that the will of God should be done on earth by any human being as it is done in heaven. But the truth is, Christ simply intended to require people to be truly Christian. Nothing short of that state of the will that is for the time being as perfectly conformed to the will of God as is the will of the inhabitants of heaven, can by any possibility be true Christianity. Do not rebel in anything against the will of God, but be upright, sincere or perfect—which is the same thing. Every moral being that can sincerely offer this prayer is and must be in his measure—for the time being, so far as the state of his heart is concerned—as perfect as God.

In another sense, every moral being in the universe comes infinitely short of being as perfect as God is. God's knowledge is infinite, and His will is entirely conformed to His infinite knowledge. The knowledge of every other being is finite, and conformity of will to finite knowledge must of necessity fall infinitely short of conformity of will to infinite knowledge.

Entire conformity of heart or will to all known truth is moral perfection in the only sense in which a moral being is ever perfect. If a little child had but one moral truth in his mind, entire conformity of heart to that truth would be in him moral perfection. Nothing less in him could be virtue, and nothing more could be required. Whether one, ten, ten thousand, or ten thousand million truths and relations are apprehended by the mind, nothing short of conformity to them all can by any possibility be virtue. "For whosoever shall keep the whole law, and yet offend in one point, he is guilty of all" (James 2:10). In God nothing can be virtue short of conformity to all the truth known to Him. The same is true of the highest moral agent as well as the lowest. And nothing more or less is properly intended by moral perfection than universal conformity to all known truth.

Let not the distinction between perfection as a state and perfection as an act be overlooked. The thing for which we are required to pray in the text is a *state* of perfection, or of entire conformity to the will of God, and that this may be as universal on earth as it is in heaven. A state of mind that can habitually offer this petition must be in entire conformity to all known truth; or in other words, it must be in that state intended by entire consecration to God. If you ask whether a state of entire sanctification is attainable in this life, I will answer by inquiring whether a state of mind that can sincerely and habitually offer this petition to God is attainable.

The petition for pardon in the Lord's Prayer must respect past sin, and cannot respect the state of mind in which this petition can be offered sincerely. For a man cannot be sinning while he is sincerely saying, "Thy will be done on earth as it is in heaven."

What perfect mockery it is to teach thoughtless children to say the Lord's Prayer and offer this petition. And what a dreadful influence it must have upon them to teach them to offer this prayer without instructing them with reference to its meaning, and informing them of the great wickedness of insincerity.

How this petition must sound to God, as it is used in the church service and repeated by hundreds and thousands of thoughtless sinners who neither know nor care what they say! Many offer it and mean nothing by it; and some offer the petition and leave it for others to do the will of God, considering, it would seem, that it is their part to offer the petition and leave it for others to live according to it.

The request for pardon is never lawful and acceptable to God, unless the mind is in a state in which it can sincerely make this petition. If this petition cannot be sincerely offered, and the soul cannot sincerely say "Thy will be done on earth as it is in heaven," it is in a state of present rebellion against God, and therefore it has no right to ask for forgiveness.

A great many have, I fear, fallen entirely short of conceiving rightly the nature of true Christianity. It is high time that the subject were thoroughly investigated, and that the Lord's Prayer in its true spirit and meaning were deeply pondered by the church. We must raise the question, "What is implied in the sincere offering of this prayer to God?" Unless this fundamental inquiry is stated and pressed, until the church comes to an intelligent understanding of it, false hopes will continue to be cherished and thousands of professing Christians will go down to hell.

10

DANGER OF DELUSION*

"Therefore we ought to give the more earnest heed to the things which we have heard, lest at any time we let them slip" (Hebrews 2:1).

In remarking upon this text, I shall attempt to show what constitutes true Christianity and that the true idea of Christianity is rare. Furthermore, I shall show that you must have a true idea of Christianity before you can have true faith in your soul. I will show how people are often in danger of losing the true idea of Christianity, because they are always in danger of delusion. Finally, I will show how we must retain the true idea of Christianity in order to maintain a true practice of our faith.

What Constitutes True Christianity

True Christianity does not consist in any course of outward action. Outward actions, when viewed apart from the intention of the mind, can have no moral character at all. They are always necessitated by acts of the will. Therefore Christianity cannot consist in mere outward actions.

Moral character does not consist in inward emotions or mere feelings, for these are involuntary states of mind produced by directing our attention to objects that excite these feelings by a natural necessity; therefore, mere feeling or emotion cannot in itself possess moral character.

True Christianity cannot consist in opinion, or in holding any system of doctrine. Our opinions are the necessary result of giving or refusing our attention to evidence, and therefore opinions can have no moral character in themselves.

The Oberlin Evangelist, August 17, 1842.

True Christianity does not consist in desire as distinguished from choice. People often desire what, upon the whole, they do not choose. But desire, as distinguished from choice, can have no moral character, because it is an involuntary state of mind.

True Christianity consists in obedience to the law of God, or in living in conformity with our nature and relations. Universal reason affirms, and no one can doubt that people are under a moral obligation to understand, as far as possible, their nature and relations and the necessity to conform to them.

Reason also affirms the obligation of all moral beings to exercise disinterested benevolence. Disinterested benevolence means willing the highest good of being in general for its own sake—every good is to be regarded, willed and treated according to its relative value so far as we are able to understand its value. Disinterested benevolence constitutes that which is required by the law of God, and is expressed in the term *love*. It is choice as distinguished from mere desire. It is willing, as distinguished from mere emotion or feeling. It is willing good for its own sake, as distinguished from willing the good of others for some selfish reason. It is willing the good of beings as an end, and not as a means of promoting our own good. It is willing universal good as opposed to willing partial good. It is willing every interest according to its relative value, because it is the willing of good for its own sake and on account of its intrinsic value. Disinterested benevolence regards the ultimate intention. By ultimate intention I mean the subjective motive of the mind, or the mind's choice of an ultimate end, to the promotion of which it devotes itself.

Understand then, virtue or true Christianity consists always in the supreme ultimate intention of the mind. A person's character is whatever his subjective motive or ultimate intention is. The Bible again and again affirms that all the law is fulfilled in one word, *love*. And this love, when the term is properly defined and understood, is synonymous with the ultimate intention of disinterested benevolence. We therefore judge rightly when we say that a person's character is as his motive or intention is.

You may think from what I have said that outward action and inward feeling have no necessary connection with true Christianity, and that it may exist without corresponding feelings and actions. But I remark that the actions of the will, as we know by our own consciousness, necessitate outward actions. If I intend to go to a certain place as soon as I can, that intention will beget those volitions that give motion to the muscles. Therefore, while the intention exists, corresponding outward actions must exist. So intentions necessitate corresponding feelings. The attention of the mind is governed by the will. If I intend to feel upon a certain subject, I direct my attention to it, and corresponding feelings are the necessary result. Therefore where intentions exist, corresponding feelings must exist.

Please observe, sometimes outward actions and corresponding feelings cannot be produced by efforts of the will. For example, outward actions cannot be produced when there is a paralysis of the nerves of voluntary motion. In such cases, the muscles will not obey volition. So where the excitability of the mind is exhausted, emotions will not be the necessary result of giving the attention of the mind to certain subjects which in other cases would produce them. But except in such cases, feeling and outward action are the certain and necessary results of intention.

Therefore, where true Christianity exists, it will of necessity manifest itself in corresponding outward actions and inward feelings.

The True Idea of True Christianity Is Rare.

The common notion seems to be that true Christianity consists in emotion or feeling. Consequently, when some people relate their religious experience, they almost universally give an account of their feelings or emotions and so speak of them as to show that they suppose these to constitute Christianity. And nothing is more common than to hear people, in giving an account of what they call their religious experience, pass over entirely and not so much as once allude to that which constitutes true Christianity. It is most apparent in such cases that if they indeed have any true Christianity, they do not know in what it consists. If their ultimate intention is really holy, and if they do truly intend to glorify God and promote the highest good of being, they do not look upon this intention as constituting true Christianity, but suppose their Christianity consists in that class of feelings which are produced by their intention.

Commonly and almost universally, those professing to be Christians speak of it as something to be experienced by us, rather than to be *done*, something in which we are passive rather than active. This shows that they do not consider Christianity as consisting in intention; for who would speak of experiencing an intention? Does anyone ever speak of experiencing a choice?

It has been a common and almost universal idea that sin and holiness can co-exist in the same mind. But if true Christianity or holiness consists in supreme or ultimate intention, sin can by no means co-exist with it. For certainly, a moral being cannot at the same time have a supremely benevolent intention and a selfish intention. If virtue consists in intention, so must sin. Sin consists universally in a supremely selfish intention or in aiming at the gratification of self as the supreme end of life. Selfishness and true Christianity consist in opposite ultimate intentions and cannot co-exist in the same mind. When, therefore, it is supposed that sin and holiness can co-exist in the same mind, it is obvious that the true idea of true Christianity is not before the mind.

The current phraseology shows that some suppose Christianity can really exist in the mind in a dormant state; that like a coal of fire covered up by ashes it can remain smothered and inactive and yet be true Christianity. It is common for all types of people to speak of having Christianity, but not in exercise—that their Christianity is not active. Now this phraseology shows that at the time they have not the true idea of true Christianity in their minds, for true Christianity is nothing else but action, voluntary action, choice and intention. Intention is an act of the mind, and true Christianity is a supreme ultimate intention or act of the mind. Therefore, to talk of a Christianity not in exercise, a Christianity not active, is to talk stark nonsense. And when people use such language, they demonstrate that, at the time, they have not the true idea of Christianity in their minds.

It is very common to hear people speak of Christianity as consisting in mere desire as distinguished from choice. Choice always controls the outward conduct. But mere desire, as distinguished from choice, never does. Many people speak of desiring to live and act better than they do, and they speak of those desires which do not produce corresponding action as constituting Christianity. Now, this is a sad and fatal mistake.

Only certain gross sins are generally regarded as being inconsistent with the existence of true holiness. Some seem to generally believe that habitual drunkenness, licentiousness, lying, theft, murder, and other behaviors, would demonstrate that a person had no true Christianity. But it does not seem to be at all the general opinion that one form of habitual selfishness is just as inconsistent with true Christianity as another. People may transact business on selfish principles. They may live in vanity and in various forms of self-indulgence (and these forms of selfishness may be habitual with them); yet, they may regard themselves, and be regarded by others, as being truly religious. But this cannot be. A person can no more be truly religious and transact business upon selfish principles and for selfish reasons than he could be truly religious and be drunk every day of the week. For it makes no difference whether he devotes himself to the promotion of self-gratification in the form of obtaining wealth, or in the form of gratifying appetite for strong drink, or in other sensual indulgences. It matters not whether a woman devotes herself to dress or to the gratification of licentious appetites. A vain woman can no more be religious than a licentious woman. It does not seem to be understood, or hardly so much as dreamed of by the church in general, that one form of selfishness is just as inconsistent with true Christianity as another; and that no form of selfishness whatever can coexist with true Christianity.

It often happens that nearly all the reasons urged by ministers and others to induce people to become Christians are mere appeals to their selfishness. Now this shows that very often religious teachers themselves have not the true idea of Christianity developed in their own minds. I might appeal to my readers and ask you, "Is it common for you to hear true Christianity accurately defined? Do your teachers make such discriminations as generally to develop in the minds of their congregation the true idea of what constitutes Christianity?" I hope in many instances they do. And yet I am sure that in many instances they do not. It is the very general fault of religious teachers that they do not succeed in developing in the minds of their hearers the true idea of Christianity.

What is called "revival preaching" often consists very much in appeals to the sensibility (feelings) of man, while it leaves entirely out of view the idea of what constitutes true Christianity. In such revivals people are not made disinterestedly benevolent. It is a revival of feeling and not of true Christianity. There are a great many excitements, oftentimes, and a great many professed converts, where the idea of disinterested benevolence is not developed and scarcely a vestige of true Christianity exists. Every year I live I am more and more impressed with this, and can have no confidence in the genuineness of those revivals in which the true idea of Christianity is not thoroughly developed until it carries the will and people become truly disinterestedly benevolent.

Sin is often denounced without telling what it is. It is almost always spoken of as something different from selfishness. And when selfishness is spoken of at all as sin, it is only spoken of as being one form of sin. It often happens that selfishness ceases to be regarded as sin, and very little will be said of it as constituting sin at all, whereas selfishness, under its various modifications, is the whole of sin.

If the idea of what constitutes true Christianity were not so rare, many hopes of salvation could not possibly be entertained by the great mass of professing Christians. If people generally understood that the Christian religion is nothing less than supreme benevolent intention which necessarily begets corresponding feeling and action—if they also generally understood that one form of habitual selfishness is just as inconsistent with true Christianity as another, and that the habitual existence of any form of selfishness whatever is conclusive proof of the absence of true Christianity, how impossible would it be that hopes should be entertained either by or for the scores of selfish professing Christians that fill our churches.

The common old school notion that sin and holiness consist in the constitutional tastes or appetites of the mind and lie back of voluntary intention demonstrates that they have not the true idea of Christianity. By this I do not mean that none of them can be Christians, for they have the idea of supreme benevolent intention, but they do not understand that this constitutes true Christianity. I trust that many of them know by their own consciousness what true devotedness to God is; however, in theorizing they make that to constitute virtue which does not; and hold the "taste scheme," that is, that sin and holiness instead of consisting in choice or ultimate intention lie in the involuntary appetites and propensities.

The words that represent the Christian graces are seldom understood by those that use them. For example, the term *love*, as used in the law of God, is generally spoken of as if it meant a mere emotion or feeling of the mind. *Humility* is spoken of as if it consisted in a deep sense of unworthiness, whereas it consists in no such thing. *Love*, as we have seen, as used in the law of God, means disinterested benevolence. If humility consisted in a sense of unworthiness, the devil might be humble, and doubtless is. Convicted sinners might also be humble, and doubtless are, if this is humility. I scarcely ever in my life have heard a minister speak of humility as if he had any definitely developed idea of what it is. *Humility* must consist in a willingness to be known and appreciated according to our real character. The same mistakes are made in regard to *repentance* and *faith*. Repentance is generally spoken of as if it consisted in emotions of sorrow, whereas it consists in a change of mind, choice or ultimate intention, and is precisely synonymous with a change of heart. Faith is very commonly spoken of as consisting either in mere intellectual conviction, or in a felt assurance of the truth of a proposition, whereas it consists in an act of the will or in confiding or committing the whole being to the influence of truth.

The fact that the seventh chapter of Romans has been so generally understood as descriptive of the Christian warfare is conclusive evidence that the true idea of true Christianity is rare. In that chapter, the apostle is speaking of a legal experience as contrasted with a Gospel experience, of which he proceeds to speak of in the eighth chapter. And the fact that the church has so generally stopped short, and claimed the seventh chapter as descriptive of a Christian's experience, because it was their own experience, shows to what a limited extent the real idea of true Christianity has been developed.

I might adduce a great many other reasons, showing that the true idea of true Christianity is a rare idea; but I must continue and look at the existence of true Christianity.

The True Idea of Christianity Is Indispensable to the Existence of True Christianity.

By this, as I have already intimated, I do not mean that people may not be Christians, and yet in theory make a mistake in regard to what constitutes real Christianity. But I do mean that unintelligent action has no moral character. I mean that the true knowledge of God consists in having correct ideas of Him. God cannot be truly loved, worshiped or served, any further than He is truly known. True Christianity, as we have seen, consists in the choice of a right end. This end must be distinctly apprehended by the mind; that is, the idea must be distinctly developed and kept in view. If this end is lost sight of, there can be no true Christianity; for if the end is not in view, the intention cannot be right. Since virtue consists in intention, it is self-evident that where the true idea or end to be aimed at is not kept in view, there can be no true Christianity.

The Danger of Losing the True Idea of Christianity

This is evident from the fact that the true idea of Christianity is so rare. All ages and nations have manifested a tendency to lose the true idea of God and of true Christianity. Even the Jews, who had the living oracles of God, had, before the coming of Christ, almost entirely lost the true idea of religion and supposed it to consist in outward works.

The selfishness of mankind creates in people a strong tendency to make Christianity consist in some modification of selfishness, and to overlook the fact that Christianity consists in disinterested benevolence.

The selfishness of people creates in them a strong tendency to misunderstand the Bible. Everywhere the Bible promises reward to virtue and threatens endless evil to vice. But the Bible nowhere makes virtue to consist in aiming at the reward as an end. It always represents virtue as consisting in disinterested benevolence. Now, since people are selfish, they are extremely liable to try to escape from the penalty of sin and acquire the rewards of virtue, the great and most influential reasons for their attempts to be virtuous. They set up the rewards of virtue as an end. They aim at getting to heaven, and set about the service of God for the sake of reward. But this is not virtue. It is only serving for the loaves and fishes. There is not a particle of true benevolence in it. It is amazing to see to what extent people set about what they call the service of God from purely selfish motives. They really understand the Bible as appealing to their selfishness.

Unconverted people are universally committed to the indulgence of their feelings rather than being swayed by the affirmations of their reason and decisions of their conscience. Consequently, there is a strong tendency in them to consider Christianity as consisting in strongly excited feelings rather than in conformity to the law of God as revealed in the reason.

The selfishness of people with which we are perpetually surrounded tends strongly to divert the attention from that which constitutes true Christianity.

Among the millions of aims and intentions which people have, only one of them is virtue or true Christianity. Christ said, "Enter ye in at the strait gate: for wide is the gate, and broad is the way that leadeth to destruction, and many there be which go in thereat: because strait is the gate, and narrow is the way which leadeth unto life, and few there be that find it" (Matt. 7:13–14). There is great emphasis in this truth. The wide gate and broad way includes everyone who is actuated by any other than a disinterestedly benevolent spirit. While the narrow way includes those only who have a single eye, and are living for one end: The highest good of universal being.

In the text the apostle says, "Therefore we ought to give the more earnest heed to the things which we have heard, lest at any time we let them slip." By slip, as it is rendered in the margin, is intended "to leak out, to escape." People are extremely apt to act without considering their ultimate motive or the great and fundamental reason of their conduct, and therefore to be entirely selfish without understanding that they are so.

People constantly have Christianity represented to them in a great variety of ways as consisting in feelings, in outward courses of conduct, and in almost everything else other than supreme disinterested benevolent intention.

Finally, it is difficult to maintain a true idea of Christianity because people dislike to retain the true idea of Christianity just as they dislike to retain the true idea of God.

Retaining the True Idea and Practice of True Christianity

To retain the true idea and practice of true Christianity ask yourself about the fundamental reason of your conduct. Do nothing, and commit yourself to no course of action, without asking, "What is the great fundamental reason by which I am actuated?" Do not allow yourself to go forward without the testimony of your own consciousness that you are disinterestedly benevolent in what you do.

Keep Christ's life and temperament before you as your great example, the great and powerful instrument of making you as benevolent as He was. Faith in the truths of the Gospel, unwavering confidence that those things recorded of Christ are true, gives the life and example of Christ the greatest power over you to make you as benevolent as He is.

Pray much in the Holy Spirit. Remember that unless you pray in the Spirit, you are sure to let slip the true idea and practice of true Christianity. In order to pray in the Holy Spirit, you must watch unto prayer.

Unless you watch, you will be sure to grieve the Spirit of God away.

Be sure that you do not neglect any duty. Remember that neglect is just as absolutely a violation of the law of God as any positive crime is.

Maintain a consciousness that you do everything for the glory of God. This is perfectly practicable. A worldly man is conscious of the great end he has in view in all his ways. He knows why he labors and toils, why he refuses to make this or that expenditure, and why he makes that speculation.

Neither engage nor continue in any business except for the glory of God. Unless you are conscious that it may be pursued and that you are actually pursuing it for the glory of God, you cannot be truly religious.

Aim not merely at being useful, but aim at being useful in the highest degree. If you are disinterestedly benevolent, it will naturally follow that you will prefer a greater to a lesser good, and not satisfy yourself with doing some good when it is in your power to do more. Therefore remember, unless in your own honest estimation you are living so as, upon the whole, to promote the highest good you are capable of promoting, you are not in a truly Christian state of mind. If you think you are, it is because you have let slip the true idea of what constitutes true Christianity. Such questions as these should be started and honestly answered: "Is my present employment one in which I can be most useful? If not, is there any opening in providence for me to change it for one in which I can be more useful?" And in settling these questions, be careful that you are not influenced by any selfish considerations. So on the other hand, take an enlightened view of the subject before you decide to change your employment, if it is one that is lawful in itself. If your employment is one that is inconsistent with the highest interests of mankind; no, if it is not one that is useful, you are to abandon it at all events. But if it is one that is useful to others, whether you should exchange it for one that is more useful must depend upon your qualifications and all the circumstances of the case. If in deciding all these questions your eye is single, your whole body shall be full of light; but if your eye is evil, in other words, if you are selfish, you will wander on in perpetual error. You have already lost sight of the true idea of Christianity, and fallen from all real virtue.

If you have not done so, make a public profession of Christianity. Remember that Christ expressly requires this of you. You cannot live in the neglect of this duty (when you have an opportunity to perform it) and still retain the idea and practice of true Christianity. The very neglect is itself disobedience, and is inconsistent with the existence of true Christianity.

In making a profession of Christianity, be sure that you are not selfish in joining one or another particular church or denomination. No doubt, as a matter of fact, some people are guilty of heart apostasy in the very act of making a profession of Christianity. In uniting with the visible church they actually apostatize from God. Sometimes they are influenced by political motives, sometimes by pecuniary considerations, having an eye upon how their relation to such and such a congregation will affect their business transactions. Sometimes they are influenced by fear of expense in supporting the Gospel, if connected with a particular congregation. Or, on the other hand, by the hope that in uniting with a particular denomination their church expenses will be small. Often, in making a profession of Christianity, people are influenced by a regard to the respectability of the church or denomination to which they attach themselves. And indeed, there are multitudes of selfish considerations by which you are in danger of being influenced, and by which, if you are influenced, you really apostatize from God in the very act of making a public profession of supreme attachment to Him. One of the great reasons why many professed converts immediately backslide, after making a profession of Christianity, is, that in selecting the church or denomination to which they attach themselves, they were influenced by some selfish consideration, and actually lost both the idea and practice of true Christianity in making a public profession of it. Be sure then in making a profession of Christianity that you are honest, that your eye is single to the glory of God, that you aim at doing the highest good in your power.

Avoid sectarianism. Sectarianism is as far as possible from the spirit of true Christianity. All the arguments, by which the dividing of the church into different denominations and continuing them in this state are supported, are utterly futile, as might easily be shown were this the place for the discussion.

In recommending it to you, however, to join some church, it is of course expected that you will join some of the existing denominations. The thing intended here is that you avoid a sectarian spirit, that you love all Christians as such, that you have no zeal to build up a party, but that you live for the glory of God, the universal church, and the world.

Avoid every form and also the spirit of papacy. There is an alarming tendency in the various protestant denominations to adopt and carry out the fundamental error of papacy. The grand mistake of papacy is this: It assumes that the Bible is not a sufficiently popular standard of morals for the multitude, and that there must be some authoritative exposition of its meaning. Papacy assumes that if the unlearned are allowed to form their own opinions of the meaning of the Bible, it will lead to endless divisions and heresies. Consequently, the Pope and the decisions of the Councils were set up as authoritative standards by which the Bible was to be interpreted. The next step of course was to take the Bible out of the hands of common people inasmuch as it had been assumed that they were unable to understand it, and were therefore not allowed to interpret it for themselves. Consequently with papists, anything is heresy that is not consistent with this standard. In trials for heresy, people are not allowed to appeal from those human standards to the Holy Scriptures, because by the general consent of the papists, their standards are an authoritative exposition of what the Bible means. This I say is the fundamental error of papacy. And as I said, there is a growing tendency among all protestant denominations to adopt and carry out this very error.

Take for example the Presbyterian confession of faith, which does not in itself assume to be an infallible standard, but Presbyterians treat it as such, speak of it as such, and in all their public acts they place it above the Bible. Especially is this tendency increasing since the great division of the Presbyterian Church. Formerly, at their ordination, multitudes of Presbyterian ministers professed nothing more than to receive the confession of faith as upon the whole a correct system of doctrine, while they did not hesitate to declare publicly and positively that there were several points in that confession from which they dissented. But so much has been said about the "standards" of the church, so many accusations have been made of a departure from the "standards" and so many flat denials of this have been reiterated, that it has come now to be common to treat the confession of faith as an authoritative standard from which if men depart in any particular they are regarded as heretics.

They give to the confession of faith all the authority which papists attach to decisions of the Councils and the Pope. This is plainly evident from the fact that in all the trials that have been had for heresy, the accused is arraigned for dissenting from the "standards" of the church and from the Holy Scriptures. But in no instance that has come to my knowledge have they allowed the accused to defend himself by an appeal to the Scriptures in such a way that would set aside the confession of faith. They assume, as far as I know in all cases, that the confession of faith has settled the meaning of the Scriptures. And it is considered as entirely inadmissable to attempt to set aside the confession of faith by an appeal to the Bible. Indeed to such lengths has the Presbyterian Church proceeded, to say nothing of other churches, that in trials for heresy, it is assumed both by the accused and the accuser that the ultimate appeal is to the confession of faith, and consequently the accused feels himself obliged to show that his sentiments are not inconsistent with the confession of faith.

Let the trials of Mr. Barnes and Dr. Beecher be looked at as illustrations of this fact. Were they allowed or did they even attempt to justify their sentiments by an appeal to the Bible, or did they defend themselves by attempting to show that what they held was consistent with the "standards"? Were they allowed to say that, whatever the confession of faith might say, such and such was the doctrine of the Bible? By no means.

The fact is that it is high time for the church to open her eyes upon the appalling fact that the protestant denominations are assuming the truth of the fundamental error of papacy, are talking about their "standards" and are using their spiritual guillotine wherever and whenever there is a departure from their "standards."

The next step will be to substitute their "convenient manuals of doctrine" and their human standards in the place of the Bible to such an extent that the laity may as well be deprived of the Bible.

Not long ago, I received an invitation from the session of a Presbyterian church to come and preach to them upon the condition that I would preach nothing inconsistent with the Bible as interpreted by the confession of faith. I of course treated such an invitation in the manner in which I supposed I was bound to treat it. I felt shocked that matters had come to such a state in the Presbyterian Church that they dared to demand of a minister that he should interpret the Bible by their confession of faith. What is this but exalting the confession of faith into the very place of the Pope?

Now beloved, if you intend to preserve the idea and practice of genuine Christianity, be careful that you do not either in theory or practice adopt the great error of papacy and assume that some human standard is to be regarded as an authoritative exposition of the Word of God. Read your Bible. Let the opinions of good men, whether expressed in catechisms, confessions of faith, or in any other way, orally or in writing, have with you what weight they really deserve, but call no man master in your views of theology, and let inspiration alone be authoritative with you in matters of faith and practice.

Aim at nothing short of universal consecration to God. By universal consecration, I intend the devotion of your whole being and of all over which you have control to the service and glory of God. And remember that nothing short of entire consecration is true Christianity. If you hold back anything from God, you are and must be, for the time being, in a state of rebellion against Him.

If you would attain the true idea and practice of Christianity, make everything give place to communion with God. So arrange all your business affairs as to have ample time for much secret prayer and communion with God. You will never retain the spirit of true Christianity unless you make as real and as sacred a calculation in all your movements to have time for reading your Bible, secret prayer, and communion with God, as you do for taking your daily food. People do not enter into such business transactions as to have no time to eat. They know very well that they cannot live without eating. Therefore, whatever business they engage in, whatever course of life they devote themselves to, they always make calculation to take sufficient time for their meals. Now it should be universally understood that spiritual life can no more continue without regular and frequent seasons of prayer and communion with God than natural life can continue without daily food.

Beware of conferring with flesh and blood. By this I mean, take heed that you do not give way to a spirit of self indulgence in any form; and remember that the moment the indulgence of any appetite or passion, the love of ease, reputation, or any form of self-indulgence whatever comes to be consulted by you and allowed to have a controlling influence, you have already let slip, if not the true idea, at least the practice of true Christianity.

Beware of the influence of the customs of society and of your own habits. Examine narrowly all your own voluntary habits of eating, drinking, exercise, rest, conversation, the manner in which you spend your time, hours of rising and retiring, conversation with friends, and in short the whole round of your habits, private, domestic, public, and see that everything is just right.

Beware of the influence of public sentiment. With many, public sentiment is the rule rather than the law of good. Their inquiry seems to be not what will please God but what will please men. This is as far as possible from true Christianity. Let the Bible be your companion and your counsel. Make yourself thoroughly acquainted with the mind of the Spirit so far as possible in every passage.

Seek the most spiritual instruction within your reach. If you live in the neighborhood of various preachers, hear those who are the most spiritual, and decidedly the most evangelical. Let your reading be of a very select character. Be sure that you do not devour and swallow down the mass of the periodical literature of the day. It is in general so sectarian that it will poison you to death. Select the most spiritual memoirs and writings of all kinds within your reach. Acquaint yourselves, as far as possible, with books on natural science. Examine works on anatomy, physiology, natural, mental, and moral philosophy, and such books as will make you thoroughly acquainted with the structure and laws of the universe; for all these things declare the wonderful works of God.

Do not shrink from reproach for Christ, and for truth's sake. A great many professors of Christianity seem afraid even to form an opinion, and much more, publicly to avow it, on any unpopular question. This shows that they have a supreme regard to their own reputation, that they love the praise of men more than the praise of God. It is a demonstration that they have no true Christianity.

Above all, learn to live by faith upon the Son of God. You will never practice any of the things I have recommended unless as you live by faith. And do not make a mistake and think you live by faith, when you do not know what faith is. To live by faith is not merely to hold the opinion that you are to be pardoned and saved through faith in Christ, but it is to repose continual and implicit confidence in Him, and to really expect Him to give you continual grace and help in every time of need, and enable you to walk blamelessly in all His commandments and ordinances. It must be a matter of experience with you and not of opinion and profession merely. You must know what it is to be united to Him as the branch is united to the vine, and to receive constant nourishment and spiritual life from Him, as the branch does from the vine. And when you are exhorted to do anything else, remember that you will not do it aright, only as Christ strengthens you, which strength you are to receive by faith.

Learn to walk in the Spirit. If you read the Epistles, you will find much said of walking in the Spirit. You must know what this is by your own experience, or you will not retain the true idea or practice of true Christianity.

Beware of declining on the one hand into antinomianism, and doing nothing for the conversion of sinners, and on the other, of running into legality and bustling about with a legal zeal devoid of the peace and rest of the Gospel. Keep an equal distance from a sickly quietism, on the one hand, and from bigoted pharisaism on the other.

Aim to be all, as a Christian, that you can be, to exert the highest and best influence that is possible upon all around you, and upon the world. Keep the thought before you, that to be a Christian at all, your aim, end, or supreme intention must be to devote your whole being, all that you have and are, to the glory of God and the good of the universe. By this I do not mean that you must *intend* to be holy, for this in reality is nonsense. You must be benevolent, instead of *intending* to be benevolent. You must intend good, and aim at doing good. This is holiness; and always remember that it is one thing to be holy or benevolent, and quite another to intend to be so. Almost every sinner expects and intends to be holy at some time. It will not do for you to aim to be benevolent, but you must continue to be so.

Remember that you are a witness for God, that you are a living epistle known and read of all men, that unless your life and lips bear testimony in accordance with the grace of God, you are a false witness—a perjured wretch.

True Christianity, in the lowest degree, implies living up to the best light you have. This is not to be looked upon as some high and rare attainment in Christianity, but is in fact essential to the lowest degree of true Christianity. He that does not habitually live up to the best light he enjoys, lives habitually in sin and cannot be a Christian. By living up to the best light you have, it is intended that you do everything which you acknowledge to be duty, and live up to the standard of right which you acknowledge to be your rule of duty. If you allow yourself any omission or practice which you acknowledge to be wrong (I mean where this is habitual with you in opposition to occasional), you are not and cannot be a Christian as the Bible is true.

True Christianity of course hails every branch of reform that promises glory to God and good to others. The radical principle of all false religion, whatever be its name, is selfishness. No matter whether it be Judaism, Christianity, Islam, or by whatever name you call it, the radical principle, that which constitutes the end and aim of every false religion, is some form of selfishness.

Do you see why study, business, and other ventures are often a snare to the soul? It is not because people do too much business for God, but because they do business and study for themselves.

The state of the world and of the Church is such, and the general strain of preaching is such, that even true converts are very apt soon to let slip the true idea, and consequently to fall from the practice of true Christianity. They see so little of real benevolence, they hear so little about it, and they witness such universal selfishness, that they soon get confused, backslide, and fall into the snare of the devil. How striking and appropriate, then, is the admonition of the apostle in the text, "Therefore we ought to give the more earnest heed to the things which we have heard, lest at any time we let them slip."

11

ABILITY AND INABILITY*

"And Joshua said unto the people, Ye cannot serve the Lord: for He is a holy God" (Joshua 24:19a).

In this discussion, I shall point out the distinction between the different kinds of ability and inability to obey the Law of God which have been insisted on by different classes of philosophers and theologians. Then I will show how this distinction is nonsensical and what is intended by the language of the text and similar passages of scripture. Finally, I will discuss why the Holy Spirit is employed in the production of holiness.

A distinction between the different kinds of ability and inability to obey the law of God have been insisted on by different classes of philosophers and theologians.

Natural Ability

According to them, natural ability is to do as you will, irrespective of the question of ability to will in any direction in view of motive. In their definition of natural ability, they keep entirely out of view the doctrine which they hold to be true, that the will is invariably and inevitably determined by motives. Some state that the doctrine of natural ability is the possession of the faculties of a moral being, with the power to use them whenever and as you are disposed or choose to use them, ignoring how it comes to pass that we are disposed to use them.

These statements and definitions are specious. Remember that these same philosophers also believe that choice is necessarily deter-

---

The Oberlin Evangelist, August 31, 1842.

mined by motives. They reject the term *necessity*, and use the term *certainty*, to avoid the charge of fatalism; but so explain what they mean by *certainty*, as to show that *necessity* is really intended. They, or the leaders of their school, hold that the connection between motive and choice is the same in kind and efficiency, as that between a physical cause and its effect. So, the difference does not consist in the kind of connection, but in the terms connected. Their proposition is, *the will always and invariably is as the greatest apparent good is*; whatever appears to the mind to be upon the whole most agreeable invariably determines the choice of the mind in that direction. Indeed, the leader of this school maintains that choice is nothing else than the very state of mind referred to; that is, a thing's appearing to be the most agreeable and choosing that thing are identical. This, then, is the plain sentiment of this class of theologians: *whenever a thing is presented to the mind in such relations as to appear upon the whole the most agreeable, this is choice, or the determination of the will*. And this is what they mean by the will's invariably being as the greatest apparent good.

Clearly, the very nature of the connection between a physical cause and its effect is that of necessity. And if, according to them, the connection is the same in kind between motive and choice, then choice must be determined by necessity. You may call it *necessity* or *certainty*, or what you will, but the true idea and thing intended is *necessity*.

Moral Ability

According to them, moral ability is the presence of such motives as to determine the will by this kind of misnamed certainty. The impossibility of executing our volitions or doing as we will they term *natural inability*. Observe: Natural ability, according to them, is the power to do as you will, or to execute your volitions. Natural inability is the lack of power to do as you will. If, for example, you put forth volitions to accomplish a certain object, and are unable to execute or bring about the thing at which you aim, this is natural inability.

The absence of sufficient motives to determine the will with this kind of misnamed certainty, they call *moral inability*. It is called a moral inability, not because it is not a real inability, but because it is inability of will. If there are not sufficient motives to cause the proposed object of choice to appear to the mind upon the whole the most agreeable, or to be the greatest apparent good, in this case there is a moral inability; that is, an inability to choose in that direction. Whereas, if there are sufficient motives to make the impression of the most agreeable on the mind, in this case choice is produced, and here is a moral ability.

Gracious Ability

Another class of philosophers rejects these distinctions, and denies both natural and moral ability. They maintain a *gracious ability* to conform to the claims of God. Their gracious ability consists in this: *Through the atonement of Christ, God, by His Spirit and gracious influences, has removed inability of every kind and made it possible for people, through this gracious aid, to obey the law of God.* Without this aid, they maintain that fallen or sinful beings have no kind of ability to obey God. Hence, consistency drives them to maintain that except for the atonement and gracious divine influence, people after the fall would have been under no obligation to obey God, and that those in hell, from whom the gracious influence is withdrawn, are under no such obligation. It is easy to see, also, that if consistent, they must deny that Satan has ever sinned since his fall, or can sin, unless the atonement and gracious ability extend to him.

Observe, I do not intend that all who professedly belong to either of these schools are consistent enough to hold the whole of their theory, as I have stated it. But I have stated the doctrine of natural and moral ability and inability, and of gracious ability just as held by the leading minds of these different schools, if I rightly understand them, which I have taken much pains to do.

These Distinctions Are Nonsensical.

Their so-called natural ability is really no ability at all. Observe, their definition of natural ability is the power to act or do as you will, ignoring the question whether you have power to choose in a given case or given direction or not. Now, everyone knows that the power to act depends on the power to choose. If a given course of conduct is proposed to me, it is naturally impossible for me to pursue it unless I can choose to do so. But, according to them, if such motives are not presented to my mind so as to make that course appear the most agreeable, I am unable to choose to pursue it; therefore, I am in the highest sense naturally unable to pursue that course. Now, who does not see that an ability to act or do as you will is no ability at all, unless you have ability to choose in that direction? Therefore, is not their definition of natural ability which denies the power to choose in any direction in view of motives, nonsensical? What is it but nonsense to affirm that I am naturally able to do that which I am naturally unable to will to do? Is it not nonsense to affirm that natural ability to do a thing consists in the power to do it, if you will, while the power to will in any direction in view of motives is denied?

Their so-called natural inability, so far as morality or virtue is concerned, is no inability at all. In morals, the will is the deed. The virtue or vice of any action does not lie in any outward act, but in the choice or intention of the mind. So, if the choice or intention exists, but we are really unable to execute our intention, we are as virtuous or as vicious as if we had executed it. And this is the doctrine of the Bible; "If there be first a willing mind, it is accepted according to that a man hath, and not according to that he hath not" (2 Cor. 8:12). It should always be understood that obedience and disobedience in the eye of God consist in acts of will. If a man wills or really intends, in accordance with the will of God, although he may be unable to do as he wills or to accomplish the thing he intends, yet the will is taken for the deed, and he is as virtuous as if he did accomplish it.

If people act at all, they cannot but act as they will. Will, choice, or volition necessitates action. If I will to move my muscles, they move of necessity, if they move at all. If there is a paralysis of the nerves of voluntary motion, volition will fail to produce muscular action. So there may be an opposing force which shall overpower my volition and prevent its execution. But if I act at all, I act always and necessarily according to my will, and cannot by any possibility act against it.

Their so-called moral ability is no ability at all. For observe, according to them moral ability consists in the presence of such motives as to produce choice, by necessity, or as they say, *certainty*, which certainty, as I have said, when explained, is nothing else than sheer necessity. There is no magic in words. To call it certainty, and then so explain the certainty as to make it sheer and absolute necessity, is only to trifle on a momentous subject. The fact is, their moral ability is nothing else than choice produced by necessity—motive producing choice in the same way, or by a connection of the same kind, that unites a physical cause with its effect. Now, if people are disposed to call this certainty, and tell us to remember that they mean certainty and not necessity, are we to throw away our common sense and even our intellectual perception of the fact that this certainty is nothing more or less than sheer necessity?

Then, so-called moral inability is an absolute *natural inability*. Observe, with them moral inability is the absence of sufficient motives to produce choice by this kind of misnamed certainty of which I have just been speaking. It is an inability to choose for lack of sufficient motives to produce choice, or which is the same thing with them, the sense of the most agreeable. In other words, they are unable to choose for lack of sufficient motives, and this is called a moral inability because it is an inability to choose. Now, why call this a moral inability, when it is self-evident that it is nothing else than natural inability. It is the highest and most proper and perfect kind of inability, an inability to will, and of course, and of necessity, an inability to act. Is it not nonsensical, by introducing the word *moral*, to attempt to distinguish this from a natural inability?

Gracious Ability Has No Grace.

The concept of gracious ability that the philosophers of this school adhere to has no grace whatever in it for the following reasons:

1. It is a first truth of reason that moral obligation implies the possession of every kind of ability which is indispensable to render the required act possible. For example, if God requires me to fly, He must furnish me wings. And this furnishing me with wings to enable me to obey the commandment to fly, is not, in view of the circumstances, a gracious ability. He is in justice bound (if He requires me to fly) to give me wings. And it is absurd and nonsensical to call this a gracious ability. Should He require me to fly without giving me wings, the requirement would be unjust, and it would impose on me no obligation. This is a first truth of reason. But if it is true that He will be unjust to require me to fly without giving me wings, it follows, of course, that the giving of wings in reference to this commandment would not be grace, but justice. Nor is the case at all altered if I have plucked my own wings, and thereby rendered myself unable to fly. For this He may punish me, but He cannot hold me obliged to fly until He restores my ability. So, if He requires me to raise the dead, He must give me power to do so. And unless He confers the power, the command would not be obligatory. Now, in view of the command to raise the dead it is nonsensical to call the bestowment of power sufficient to obey the command a gracious ability, for it is not grace but mere justice. These are first truths of reason. They need no proof, and to call for proof of truths of this class is absurd and nonsensical.

2. If people lost their ability to obey God by sin, and God should still demand service of them, He must, in the first place, in justice restore their ability. He might punish them for destroying their ability, but could not require obedience of them until their ability is restored. It would seem that this class of philosophers admits that God must in *justice* restore ability before He can require obedience. For they maintain that if the Atonement had not been made and divine influence vouchsafed, people would not have been under obligation to obey God. And that those in hell, from whom this divine influence is withdrawn, are under no obligation to repent and love and obey God. Now how nonsensical it is to maintain that without this ability people would be under no obligation to obey God, and still call it a gracious ability. It is what justice in reality demands according to their own view. For God to claim obedience, and yet while *justice* demands it at His hands they call it a gracious ability, what is this confusion of terms but nonsense. The very terms gracious ability are an absurdity, for what is *grace*? It is the bestowment of that which *justice* cannot claim. But *justice* does demand that a moral being should possess the requisite ability, what-

ever that is, to do and be what he is commanded to do and be. And the bestowment of this cannot be *grace* but *justice*.

3. Where the Gospel is preached and the Holy Spirit's influences are enjoyed, God may claim and does claim and ought to claim, corresponding service. But where He claims a higher service, in consequence of increased light, He does not consider the increased light in reference to the enlarged requirement *grace*, but *justice*. By this I do not mean that the Atonement and the influences of the Holy Spirit are not grace, but that they really are so, and that they are grace because people have not lost their natural ability to do their duty by sin; that, therefore, the Atonement and divine influence were not necessary to make men *able* to do their duty, but to induce in them a willingness to do it.

4. There is no inability whatever, under the moral government of God, to obey Him perfectly. Where the mere light of nature is enjoyed people are able to walk according to it, which is all that God requires of them, and for not doing so He condemns them. This Paul argues at length in his epistle to the Romans.

All moral agents in all worlds are able to obey, and consequently are bound to obey God perfectly, and perfect obedience in a heathen would be a living up in all respects to the law of nature as revealed in the works and providence of God. Perfect obedience in a child would be a living up in all respects in heart and life to the best light enjoyed. The same is true of people under the law and under the Gospel, of the angels in heaven, and of all moral beings in all worlds.

Now, we must examine what is intended by the language of the text and similar passages of Scripture.

Words are signs of ideas, and are always to be understood, of course, according to the subject matter about which they are used. For example, if I say I cannot create a world, everyone would understand me to mean by *cannot*, a natural impossibility. If I say I cannot take twenty dollars for my watch, no man in his senses would understand me to use the term *cannot* in the same sense in which I did before. He would understand me only as affirming that I was *unwilling* to sell my watch for that price. He would not so much as dream that I had not natural ability or power to consent to sell my watch for twenty dollars or less. Now, it is very remarkable that on other subjects such language is readily understood by common sense, and no where but on religious subjects do people seem so widely to depart from common sense in the interpretation of language as to make *cannot*, when applied to acts of will, imply an inability of any kind.

With respect to the language of the text, the connection in which it stands shows the sense in which Joshua meant to be understood when he said to the people, "Ye cannot serve the Lord, for He is a holy

God." Anyone who will take the trouble to read, will see that nothing was further from his intention than to affirm that there was either a natural or a moral inability in them to serve the Lord, for in the same connection he calls on them to enter into a solemn covenant to serve the Lord to which they consented upon the spot.

The whole connection shows that they did not understand him as teaching the doctrine of an inability of any kind in them to render an acceptable service to Jehovah. Joshua merely intended, and they manifestly understood him to affirm, that they could not render an acceptable service to Jehovah unless they became holy. And their ability to become holy is as strongly as possible implied in the whole connection and transaction.

Let a similar passage in Genesis 19:22, explain this. "Haste thee, escape thither; for I cannot do any thing till thou be come thither. Therefore the name of the city was called Zoar." Here Jehovah speaks of himself in similar language. He says to Lot, "Haste thee, for I *can do nothing* until thou be come thither." Who can believe that He intended to affirm of himself an inability of any kind to destroy Sodom before Lot arrived at Zoar? He manifestly intended merely to say that His mind was made up not to destroy Sodom till Lot was safe, and that therefore He was unwilling to rain fire and brimstone upon the devoted city until Zoar had closed its gates upon Lot.

See also John 1:12—"But as many as received him, to them gave he power to become the sons of God, even to them that believed on his name." In the margin of your Bible, you may see that the word *power* is rendered right or privilege. This passage has, not infrequently, been quoted as implying an inability in the sinner to become a Christian. But it favors no such idea. It only teaches that those who received Christ received themselves the privileges of adopted sons.

See also John 6:44, 45—"No man can come to me, except the Father which hath sent me draw him: and I will raise him up at the last day. It is written in the prophets, And they shall be all taught of God. Every man therefore that hath heard, and hath learned of the Father, cometh unto me." The 44th verse is often quoted in proof of the doctrine of natural or moral inability. But what inability is here intended? When the two verses are read together, we learn that no man is able to come to Christ unless he is enlightened or taught the way of salvation by Christ. It is certainly a plain truth that a person needs to be informed of the way of salvation by Christ in order to come to Christ. This text does not begin to teach any inability whatever in those who have been taught and understand the way of salvation by Jesus.

Here let me remark that to so explain the passages as to make them teach either a moral or a natural inability is to deny the freedom of the will. But that the will is free we have the testimony of our own consciousness. To come to Christ, to do our duty—in other words to be holy—consists in acts of will. Now to affirm an inability to will in any direction, in view of motives, is to affirm that as true which our consciousness teaches us to be false.

I might quote other passages that have been relied on to support the doctrine of inability, but I have said enough to give the candid reader a clue to the right understanding of them all. And for the mere debater I am not now writing.

The Work of the Holy Spirit

Perhaps now we can understand why the agency of the Holy Spirit is employed in inducing obedience to the moral law.

The Bible represents Him as exerting His influence over mind by or through the presentation of truth to the mind. In other words, as exerting the influence of a divine moral persuasion. Consider these passages: "Seeing ye have purified your souls in obeying the truth through the Spirit unto unfeigned love of the brethren, see that ye love one another with a pure heart fervently: being born again, not of corruptible seed, but of incorruptible, by the word of God, which liveth and abideth for ever" (1 Peter 1:22–23). "Of his own will begat he us with the word of truth, that we should be a kind of first fruits of his creatures" (James 1:18). "Sanctify them through thy truth: thy word is truth" (John 17:17). In these and similar passages, we learn that the manner and kind of influence which He exerts is that of persuasion and not of compulsion.

The thing which He is employed to do is not to make people able, but to induce in them a willingness by a persuasive influence to submit themselves to God.

With many, to deny a *physical* divine influence in regeneration, to deny that the Spirit of God is employed to make people able, and that He only employs His agency in persuading them to be willing is to deny the divine agency altogether. What do they mean? I am afraid of these men. It seems as if they were determined to hide away themselves under the plea of inability, and to screen others under the same refuge of lies.

To represent God as requiring impossibilities on pain of eternal death is to hold up His character and government to irresistible abhorrence. People are so constituted that by an unalterable law of their reason they affirm intuitively, irresistibly and indignantly, that for any government, human or divine, to require natural or moral impossibilities is unjust and tyrannical. And until the very nature of people is altered, this must forever be the case. Not long ago a doctor of divinity in the Presbyterian Church publicly affirmed that moral obligation did not imply any kind of ability whatever to do our duty. Now a more shocking and revolting contradiction of reason, common sense, and the Bible could hardly be stated in words. Such statements are in exact accordance with the spirit and policy of the devil.

It has always been the policy of Satan to misrepresent the character and government of God. He prevails by falsehood. He sustains his dominion in this world by gross misrepresentations of the character of God. It has always been of the greatest importance to him and his cause to deceive the church and induce the leading minds to entertain and publish to the world views of the character and government of God which are at war with reason and the Bible. He very early succeeded in this under the Christian dispensation. And who that is acquainted with the opinions and dogmas of the Christian fathers does not know that they very early began to inculcate the most absurd and revolting dogmas concerning the character and government of God? One of the leading minds among them could say of a certain doctrine "It is absurd and therefore I believe it." In every age of the Christian church, Satan has succeeded in influencing a certain class of minds to adopt and shamelessly avow, and zealously to inculcate dogmas as the truth of God, against which the very nature of man cries out with vehement indignation. And this many of them do not pretend to deny, but on the contrary boldly affirm it, and insist that the very nature of man must therefore be changed before he can love God. Instead of representing man as needing to have the voluntary state of his mind changed in respect to God, they represent him as needing to have his very nature changed by a creative act of physical omnipotence. And what sentiment can please the devil better than this?

When good but unlearned people have listened to such distorted misrepresentations of God and His government, they have hushed down their rising indignation under the impressions that it was a mystery. They have piously chided themselves for having a thought of the injustice and unreasonableness of such dogmas enter their minds. And often they have diverted their attention and found it indispensable to abstract their minds from the consideration of these dogmas to prevent the rising remonstrances of their deepest nature against the injustice of requiring of people natural or moral impossibilities on pain of eternal death.

It is remarkable to what extent unconverted but thinking people have become skeptical in view of such representations of the character of God. And ministers that maintain such sentiments are very little aware of the extent to which they preach their unconverted hearers into infidelity. Millions of souls have been ruined by the false representations of the character and government of God which they have heard from the pulpits not only of notorious heretics but multitudes of self-styled orthodox preachers.

Since the doctrine of entire sanctification in this life has been so much and so pointedly insisted on, multitudes of ministers and others who have heretofore professed to believe and teach the doctrine of ability in every moral agent to do his whole duty, are retiring back to the ranks of those who deny the doctrine of ability. They see and acknowledge that the doctrine of entire obedience to the law of God, or in other words, of entire consecration and sanctification, is only the legitimate application of the doctrine of ability to all the conduct of Christians; that if people are able to obey God perfectly, there is no reason why they should not, nor any ground for the affirmation that they will not. But let not those brethren think to find a resting place or an apology for sin under the doctrine of inability, for it is abundantly easy to show that of all the absurd doctrines that ever were broached, not one is more contrary to the Bible and to common sense, and more easily refuted than the doctrine of inability.

From what has been said, you can see that the dependence of sinners and of Christians upon God is of such a nature as to afford no excuse whatever for their sins. If the doctrine of inability were true, and the Spirit of God were indispensable to make them able to do their duty, then their dependence would be an apology for their sins. Or what is still more proper to say, until the divine agency was granted they could not begin to sin, inasmuch as sin must imply the power to be holy. But if, as has been shown, the sinner is able to obey, and the whole difficulty lies in his unwillingness to do his duty, and if the Spirit is employed only as a persuasive agency to induce a willingness to comply with duty, it is abundantly plain that the sinner's dependence upon the Holy Spirit affords him not the least shadow of excuse for ever having sinned or for ever indulging in another sin.

Until people are willing to confess their sin, they are able but unwilling to obey God. Until they are ingenuous enough to own that their difficulty does not lie in an inability but in a pertinacious obstinacy, until they perceive and allow that the Spirit is not needed to make them able, but only to overcome their voluntary rebellion, they have no reason to expect a divine influence to lead them to Christ. But they have every reason to fear that God will give them up to the agency of Satan, and send them strong delusion, and confirm them in the belief of inability, until they become so utterly blinded as that they cannot "deliver their souls, or say, have I not a lie in my right hand."

And now sinner, will you be as ingenuous and as courageous as the Israelites were when Joshua uttered the words of the text? If you read the context you will see that they believed and avowed their belief that they could render to Jehovah an acceptable service. And when Joshua put the question plainly home to them, whether they would, that day, choose and enter upon the service of God, they rose up and signified their determination to serve Jehovah. And from the history of that generation, it is manifest that many of them, to say the least, were sincere and whole-hearted in the avowal of their purpose. Is it not time for you to decide? Will you become holy? Will you serve the Lord? Will you do it now? Answer in your inmost being upon the spot. If you say no, or if you refuse to answer at all, remember that God may take you at your word; but if you say yes, and mean it, if you let your heart go with your words, your name shall be written in the Lamb's Book of Life.

12

GOD UNDER OBLIGATION TO DO RIGHT*

"Shall not the Judge of all the earth do right?" (Genesis 18:25b).

In discussing this subject I will show what the term *right* signifies, what is implied in God's doing right and that God is morally obligated to do right. Furthermore, we shall see that all moral beings are obligated to will that God should do right, and what that implies. I will close by looking at the state of mind that is indispensable to salvation.

The term *right* expresses the *moral quality* of disinterested benevolence. Benevolence is good-willing or willing the highest good of being. Disinterested benevolence is willing the good of being as an end, or for its own sake, or, in other words, on account of its intrinsic value. A thing is good, that is, naturally good, because it is valuable in itself. Such, for instance, is happiness. Happiness is a good in itself, that is, it is valuable. Every moral being knows by his own certain knowledge that happiness is valuable, that it is good. To will, therefore, the highest happiness or the highest good of being for its own sake is benevolence. Benevolence, then, consists in willing according to the nature and relations of things. Reason universally affirms that to will thus, to will good for its own sake, to will it impartially or disinterestedly, or in other words, to will every good of every being according to its relative value, is *right*. Right is the term by which we express the moral quality of disinterested benevolence. The terms right, virtue, and holiness, express the same thing. They denote the moral quality of disinterested benevolence or of that love that constitutes obedience to the law of God. Understand, then, that disinterested benevolence is always right, and that nothing else is right, and that whatever is right or virtuous is only a modification of disinterested benevolence. Nothing

---

*The Oberlin Evangelist, September 14, 1842.

is virtue or right that is not in compliance with the law of disinterested benevolence.

When God Does Right

We must know what is implied in God's doing right. Doing right in God, His nature and relations being what they are, must imply the doing of several things by Him that would not be implied in the case of any other being. Let us notice these:

First, He is naturally able to do many things that no other being can do. For example, God alone possesses creative power.* Benevolence in Him, therefore, implies not merely willing the good of beings already existing, but that He give existence to as many beings as He wisely can. The law of benevolence would certainly require Him to exert His infinite attributes in the promotion of good. If He did not do so, His own conscience would condemn Him.

Second, His nature and relations are such that benevolence in Him requires the establishment and due administration of moral government. He has created a universe of moral beings. The highest good of the universe demands that a moral government should exist. God is able to establish and administer a moral government. Therefore, doing right in God implies the establishment and administration of a moral government over the universe.

God is under a moral obligation to do right. The Scriptures represent God as a moral being. If He is a moral being, He must be the subject of moral obligation. If He were not under a moral obligation to do right, benevolence in Him would be no virtue. Indeed there could be to Him no such thing as right and wrong, unless He were under a moral obligation to do right. Doing right in any being consists in complying with moral obligation. Right, virtue, holiness, in any being, always implies moral obligation. If God were not under a moral obligation, He could have no moral character. He could be neither praise nor blameworthy. Nothing would be virtuous nor praiseworthy in Him unless it sustained a relation to moral obligation.

Nothing could be wise or virtuous in God that is not demanded by the law of benevolence. If God should do anything that was not required by the law of benevolence, it would be neither wise nor virtuous. If the creation of the universe were not required by the law of benevolence, then the act of creation was not virtuous. But it is impossible that the universe should not have been created in compliance with the law of benevolence. The evidences of a benevolent intention on the part of the Creator are so manifold in all the works of God as to render

---

*Finney uses "creative power" in the sense of creating out of nothing.

it certain that it was created in obedience to the law of benevolence. In other words, the creation of the universe was an expression and a carrying out of the disposition of God to do good.

I do not mean that God was under an obligation to anyone above himself, for no such being exists. But His own self-existent nature is such that He is His own law-giver, and imposes obligation on himself. His own reason eternally and intuitively affirms that He ought to be benevolent, that He ought to wield His own infinite attributes in the creation of beings and the promotion of their good. He is therefore under a law to himself, His reason and conscience always imposing moral obligation upon himself. Compliance with this obligation in Him is virtue. A refusal would be vice.

In the text, Abraham assumes that God is under moral obligation to do right. God had informed Abraham that He was about to destroy Sodom. Abraham's reply was, "Perhaps fifty righteous persons shall be found therein. Wilt thou also destroy the righteous with the wicked? This be far from thee to destroy the righteous with the wicked. Shall not the Judge of all the earth do right?" (Gen. 18:23–33). Here Abraham plainly assumes that God was under a moral obligation to distinguish between the righteous and the wicked, and that He had no right to deal with them alike. Or in other words, Abraham assumes that it was the solemn duty of God to deal with the righteous and the wicked according to their respective characters—that to do so would be right, and that not to do so would be wrong in God.

God does not resent this assumption of Abraham, that He was under a moral obligation, but most fully acknowledges it. He did not say to Abraham, "How dare you assume and insinuate that I am the subject of moral obligation; that anything is obligatory on me; that I can be called to the discharge of duty?" He gave Abraham no such reproof as this, but freely and fully admitted the assumption of Abraham and proceeded to give him to understand that the Judge of all the earth would do right, and that He knew too well what was obligatory upon Him to consent to destroy the righteous with the wicked.

Some people seem to feel shocked at the supposition that God should be under moral obligation. But they may just as well be offended with the supposition that He has moral character. If He does not owe obedience to the law of benevolence, then benevolence in Him is not right. It is no virtue. If God is above law, He is above virtue. If He is above moral obligation, He is above having moral character, and above being praised or blameworthy for anything.

The conviction has often crowded upon my mind, that the religion of a great multitude of its professors is mere superstition. They are shocked with any rational view of God's character. They are offended with His being represented as the subject of moral obligation. They seem not to know at all why He is praiseworthy, and if their view of the subject were true, He would not be praiseworthy. Multitudes of professors seem to praise Him for doing that which they suppose Him under no moral obligation to do. But if He were under no moral obligation to do it, if the law of benevolence did not require it at His hands, it would not be either wise or virtuous for Him to do it, and therefore for doing it He would deserve no thanks.

Whenever I see people manifest a spirit of opposition to the idea that God is under law, the subject of moral obligation, and that virtue in Him is not as in all other beings, only a compliance with the great law of benevolence, I know that the religion of such persons must be superstition. It cannot be that they have the true knowledge of God, of His character, relations, and government, and that they either praise or respect Him for any good reason. God must consider the reasons they worship Him as injurious and insulting.

The Bible takes it for granted that right and wrong are as applicable to God as to any other being, and that virtue in Him as in every other being is a compliance with moral obligation.

Hence let me say again, *He is not, as we are, under obligation to one above himself, for no such one exists*. But He is under obligation to the law of benevolence as it is imposed on Him by His own reason.

God's Arbitrary Will Is Not the Law.

Some seem to suppose that the reason God cannot sin is that He is above law, that His arbitrary will is law, and that whatever He wills or can will must be right simply because His will is law. But such people do not consider that if this theory were true, He can no more be holy than He can sin, for if there were not some rule of conduct obligatory upon Him, He has no standard of action, nothing with which to compare His own conduct, and can in fact have no moral character. Now the reason God cannot sin is not because He is naturally unable to sin, nor because selfishness in Him would not be sin. He cannot sin because He is voluntarily holy and infinitely disposed not to sin.

All Moral Beings Are Bound to Will That God Should Do Right.

If God is under a moral obligation to do right, no one can have any right to object to His doing right, for this would be absurd. It would imply the existence of contradictory rights or obligations—that God was under a moral obligation to do that which other beings were under a moral obligation to prevent if they could. It must be that whatever the law of benevolence requires of God, whatever the highest good of being demands that He should do, all moral beings are bound to be willing that He should do.

Being willing that God should do right implies the love of right for its own sake. It implies a willingness that He should require of all His subjects just what He does require. He never legislates without good reason. He has no right to do so, and never does enact any laws that are not required by the highest good of being. He therefore does nothing, more or less, than to comply with His own duty in requiring of every moral being just what He does. To be willing, therefore, that God should do right, is to be willing that He should require just what He does in all instances, and for the very reasons for which He requires it.

We must have a willingness to do whatever He requires. He requires of everyone just what He ought to require, and if you are willing that He should do right, you are of course willing that He should require this of you. And if you are willing that He should require it, it must be that you are also willing to do it. Outward doing is necessitated by inward willing. Therefore a willingness that God should do right implies the actual doing of whatever He requires of you, so far as you know it.

You must be willing that all events should be disposed of according to His sovereign pleasure—that He should send the finally impenitent to hell, for this is right; that He should send your own children, if they be finally impenitent, to hell, or that He should send you to hell, if the law of benevolence requires it at His hands. If the rule of right, if the highest good of the universe demanded that you be sent to hell, it is God's duty to send you there, and you have no right to object, but are bound to consent with all your heart.

Willing what God wills implies in you a spirit of perfect benevolence. No one who is not disinterestedly and perfectly benevolent is willing that God should in all things do right. You must have in you a spirit of the same uprightness that there is in God. You must love right as He loves it. You should be actuated by the same motives that actuate Him, and in your measure you should have the same regard to right that He has. In other words, you should be willing that God should in all things do right, and in your measure have the same perfection of willingness that there is in God.

This state of mind is indispensable to salvation, because nothing short of this state of mind can be virtue at all. If in anything you are unwilling that God should do right, you are in rebellion against Him. If in anything you are unwilling that God should do right, it is impossible that for the time being you should have a supreme regard to what is right, or to the authority or will of God. There cannot possibly be any virtue or holiness in one who is unwilling that God should in all things do right. To be willing that God should in all things do right, is essential to happiness, and therefore indispensable to salvation. God will do right whether you are willing or not. If you consent to it and are joyful in it, you can be happy under His government. But if you are unwilling, He will do His duty without asking your permission, however much it may fret or distress you. His doing right will extend to all beings. And if in anything you are crossed or offended by His doing right, there is no remedy for it, for He will do it although it may be the means of destroying you forever. All moral beings will know that God does right, that He does universally and perfectly right, and no one can prevent it. It is self-evident that no one can be happy or saved who is not supremely pleased with His doing universally and perfectly right.

Strictly speaking there is no such thing as a work of supererogation in God or in any other being. By a "work of supererogation" I mean doing something that one was not of right under obligation to do, something not required by law. In morals, a work of supererogation would be something not required by the law of benevolence. Now, if there were any such thing as a work of supererogation in God or any other moral being, it could not be benevolence or virtue. It could not be praiseworthy. If it were not required by the law of benevolence, it could be neither wise nor good. But if required by the law of love, it is not properly speaking a work of supererogation.

The common notion of the imputed righteousness of Christ, by which many maintain that the saints are to be saved, is a papal superstition. It has no foundation whatever in truth. The fact is that Christ did no more than to comply with the great law of universal benevolence. Both as God and man, His obligation to be universally and perfectly benevolent was complete. He did no more than under the circumstances was His duty to do, no more than the exigencies of the government of God required, no more than to comply with the great law of universal love. Had He done anything more or less than this, it would neither have been worse nor good.

Do not understand me to say that sinners would have any cause of complaint if He had not died for them. They had forfeited all claims to favor. So far as they were concerned, He might have visited upon them the penalty of the law. But to His own nature He owed the obligation of perfect benevolence. To himself and to the virtuous universe He was under an obligation to make a sacrifice of himself, if by so doing He could promote a greater good than the evil He suffered.

If there could be such a thing as a work of supererogation; that is, doing that which the law of benevolence did not require, such a work would be sin and not holiness. The spirit of the law and of the Gospel is identical: both require universal and perfect benevolence. There is no proper distinction between law and equity. This distinction in morals has no foundation.

Strictly and properly speaking there is no distinction between what is lawful and what is expedient. And when Paul says, "All things are lawful unto me, but all things are not expedient," (1 Cor. 6:12; 10:23) we are to understand him only as speaking in a general way, and not as designing to affirm that in the most proper sense a thing might be lawful, and yet not expedient. Expediency is that which, under the circumstances, is demanded by the highest good. But this is identically the spirit of the law. A thing may be contrary to the *letter* of the law which is expedient. But the spirit of the law requires that every interest should be treated according to its relative value; that of two evils, one of which is unavoidable, the least shall be suffered; that of two goods, but one of which can be secured, the greatest shall be preferred. The letter of the law and real expediency may be at variance. But the spirit of the law and true expediency are always identical.

There is no law of right separate from the law of benevolence. Justice is only a modification of benevolence. And nothing is just or right that is not in accordance with the law of benevolence. *By justice and mercy nothing more is intended than benevolence acting in different relations—the end always being the same, the promotion of the highest good.*

God sends the wicked to hell for the same reason for which He takes the righteous to heaven; that is, in both cases He designs to promote the highest good. When sinners come into such relations that the highest good demands that He should send them to hell, He does so for that reason. And when the righteous come into such relations that the highest good demands that He should take them to heaven, He does so for that reason.

The Atonement and all that God does for the salvation of sinners is done by Him in compliance with the great law of benevolence. Had it not been a compliance with duty it would not have been virtue.

The Sovereignty of God

Notice from this subject what constitutes the sovereignty of God. Many seem to speak and think of the divine sovereignty as if it consisted of God's acting arbitrarily, without any regard to moral obligation; that in His sovereign acts He has no other reason than it seems good in His sight. They speak of His sovereignty as if He had no good reason for willing as He does, but that such is His pleasure, entirely irrespective of the reason why it is His pleasure. Now this is a most odious and injurious view of the character of God. God's sovereignty is and can be nothing else than benevolence acting independently. It consists in His doing His duty without asking the permission of any one. It consists in His doing right without authorization or hindrance from anyone.

Those who are not pleased with the sovereignty of God when they rightly understand it cannot be Christians. If they are not willing that God should consult His own wisdom and do what He regards to be His own duty, they are rebels and the enemies of God and of all good.

God will never punish the wicked to gratify any feelings of resentment in the proper use of the term. The very nature of God demands that the finally impenitent should be punished. Our reason affirms that the one who is wicked ought to be miserable, and that God could not consult the highest good, could not promote His own happiness, nor the happiness of holy beings, unless He acted in conformity with this affirmation of His own reason and of the reason of every moral being, and inflicted merited punishment upon the incorrigibly wicked. If God is a moral being, as we have shown, we know from our own consciousness as moral beings that from the laws of His very nature, His reason affirms the justice of inflicting punishment upon the wicked. We know that punishment and sin ought to go together, and that God cannot be satisfied with himself, and holy beings cannot be satisfied with Him, unless He inflicts punishment upon the finally impenitent. The highest good must demand that He punish the wicked. This is implied in what Abraham says: "Wilt thou also destroy the righteous with the wicked? This is far from thee. Shall not the Judge of all the earth do right?" Here it is plainly implied that to punish the wicked is right.

Do not think that God or any holy being has pleasure in the infliction of pain for its own sake. Misery never is and never can be regarded by a moral being as a good in itself. It can never be chosen for its own sake. It can never be chosen as an end by any moral being, but only as a means of promoting the blessedness of the universe. Such is the nature of moral beings that they affirm by a law of their nature, over which they have no control, that sin deserves punishment, and that if sinners persevere in sin they *must* be punished. And although by a law of their own nature, they look upon misery as an evil in itself, yet under a moral government they look upon the punishment of finally impenitent sinners as a less evil than impunity in sin.

God punishes sinners for public reasons. The nature of moral beings is such that public justice promotes the highest happiness of the universe. For this reason and for this reason alone God punishes the finally impenitent.

For the same reason God forgives and saves the repentant sinner; this recognizes the fitness of public justice. Everything considered, upon the whole it is best, reasonable and right in view of the Atonement of Christ and the repentance of the sinner that God should not inflict the penalty of the law, but that the sinner should be forgiven and saved. Therefore in the salvation of the repentant sinner, public justice is not set aside, but in saving him, God acts upon the principle of public justice; that is, His so doing under the circumstances is in the highest degree conducive of the public interests. Hence, the apostle John represents the salvation of the contrite as an act of justice. "If we confess our sins, He is faithful and just to forgive us our sins, and to cleanse us from all unrighteousness" (1 John 1:9). The law of right requires that God should punish the wicked as much and as long as the public good requires.

In a government that is to last throughout eternity, the punishment of sin must be endless for very important and manifest reasons. There will need to be under such a government, a steady, perpetual, and eternal monument upon which the nature, the demerit, the history and the results of sin shall be recorded. Truth is the great instrument of controlling the mind.

Let the history of the Temperance Reformation illustrate what I mean. Under a moral government, I suppose it was impossible for God to bring about the Temperance Reformation, until the nature and tendencies of the use of alcohol could in some way be known. But when its nature was developed, its tendencies perceived, and its history written in the blood of millions of souls, there was then sufficient materials on hand with which to assail it and push it back—shall I say to hell from whence it came? The monster intemperance came up upon the length and breadth of the land clad in a mantle of light. He found his way into every habitation and smiled, and dealt out excitement and deceived the nations. Alcohol was regarded as a friend. Its presence was deemed indispensable to health and happiness. It was prescribed by the physician almost as a medicine. It was taken even by the clergy as an auxiliary in the discharge of their holy functions. All classes supposed themselves to be blessed by it. And until it destroyed its millions, so deep were its deceptive influences people could not be awakened to regard it as an enemy. But now its mask is off. It is known. Its history is written in blood, and who does not know that for the use of future generations this history is an indispensable safeguard? Should the present or any future generation succeed in banishing alcohol from the world by exhibiting in every country its true history, who does not know that except these records be preserved, and the public mind kept sufficiently awake, that the same scenes will, in future, be acted over again, and that nothing can prevent so dire a catastrophe but the keeping in perpetual memory the nature, the history, and the results of using alcohol. As moral beings, it is impossible to preserve future generations of mankind from intemperance except by the universal presence of information upon this subject.

Now for the same reason that the history of alcohol will need to be kept in perpetual memory, for the same reason will the endless history of sin in its details and results need to be kept before the public mind. Something must be done that shall be a virtual penciling of the history of sin in characters of light upon every part of the whole universe. His dealings must be so public and so perpetual as never to be forgotten. It must be a record that cannot but be read by every moral being. It must teach a thrilling and perpetual lesson to all moral beings in all worlds as long as moral beings shall exist. And if at any time His public dealings with sinners should cease and fall into forgetfulness, the impression would of course be done away upon the universe. And who can say that all the horrors of another apostasy from God would not be the result?

Those who are not willing that God should send the wicked to hell cannot be saved. If the execution of the sentence upon the finally impenitent will make them miserable they must be miserable. No one is willing that God should do right who does not do right himself. This is self-evident. Unless doing right is supremely pleasing to you, you cannot be saved. Anxious sinners are often distressed for fear God will do right. If they remain in sin God will certainly send them to hell. This would be right. This it would be His duty to do. But this is the cause of the sinner's anxiety. He fears God will do what He ought.

Do you see what true submission is? It consists in a willingness to have God do, in all things, with us and ours, through all the universe and to all eternity, what is right—to dispose of all we have and are just as the highest good of the universe shall demand.

What a glorious consideration it is that the supreme, universal Judge of all the earth will do right. He cannot be mistaken. He cannot be bribed. He cannot be deterred. He cannot be prevented. He will never change. He will never cease to be. What a glorious consideration to be under the government of such a being!

If His providential designs are displeasing to you, you cannot be saved. He deals with you just as He does, because it is right, because, under the circumstances, the highest good of the universe demands it. Thus He will not ask your permission. If you are pleased with it, it is well. If you are displeased, there is no help for you. God is equally good in all He does, for the best of all reasons. He has the same ultimate reason for all He does, namely, the highest good of the universe demands it. In other words, it is right.

God deserves as much praise for sending the wicked to hell as for taking the righteous to heaven. He deserves just as much praise for what are called His judgments as for what are called His mercies, for sickness as for health, for death as for life, for hell as for heaven, for pestilence, earthquake, and tornado under the circumstances in which they occur, as for their direct opposites under other circumstances. One law governs Him in all these things. One principle of action, one motive or intention accounts for the whole. If He sends you to hell, all heaven will be under an obligation to praise Him for it. If He sends your companions or children to hell, you will be under obligation to praise Him for it. If he sends your children or even yourself to hell, you will be under eternal obligation to praise Him for it. It will always be true that He did it because it was right, because the public good demanded it, and it was therefore His duty to do it. He did it in compliance with the great law of perfect benevolence. And shall you not praise Him for being benevolent?

There is no good reason for being shocked at the idea of God's being the subject of moral obligation, and acting in accordance with the dictates of law and of conscience. Unless you are, according to your knowledge, as upright as God is, you are not willing He should do right, you are in rebellion against Him and cannot be in a state of justification with God.

Sinners are so selfish that they would be saved at all events. Whether it would be right or wrong on the part of God to save them they neither consider nor care. If God should save sinners, forgive their sins, and treat them as they desire Him to treat them, He would ruin the universe. The prayers of unrepentant sinners for forgiveness are among the blackest sins in the universe. Nothing is more common than for impenitent professors of religion, and impenitent non-professors to pray that their sins may be forgiven. But to forgive their sins while they are unrepentant would not be right but infinitely wrong on the part of God. Such prayers are a virtual asking of God to commit a great sin, to abandon the public good, to ruin the universe for their sake. Remember that if you pray for forgiveness, when you do not repent and forsake your sin, you are guilty of the grossest insult to God, and of the highest rebellion against Him and His government.

In view of the promises of God and the Atonement, your salvation is consistent with what is right, if you accept Christ. By this I do not mean that upon the principle of distributive justice you might not be justly punished. But I do mean that upon the principle of public justice, your salvation, upon these conditions, is consistent with and demanded by the highest good. Unless you comply with these conditions you must be damned, and all the holy ones of God will thank Him for sending you to hell. How sweet it is to think of God as the Judge of all the earth. And how deep and permanent is the consolation that in all things He will do right. Every holy being in all worlds, at all times, is ready to cry out, "Let the judge of all the earth do right. Amen and Amen."

13

ORDINATION OF MINISTERS*

*"Take heed unto thyself, and unto the doctrine; continue in them:
for in doing this thou shalt both save thyself, and them that hear thee"*
(1 Timothy 4:16).

In remarking upon these words I shall point out some of the respects in which a minister should take heed to himself, some of the respects in which he should take heed to the doctrine he preaches, show what is intended by continuing in these respects, and what it means that he shall save both himself and those who hear him.

Respects in Which a Minister Should Take Heed to Himself:

The minister should not take heed to his own self-interest as the great end of pursuit. If a minister gives himself up to look after his own interest instead of the interest of God, he will be worse than useless as a minister. He should not take such heed to his reputation as to have his eye continually upon that, constantly raising the inquiry how such and such a thing will affect his reputation. With such a state of mind, the minister would be a perfect slave to public sentiment rather than the freeman of Jesus Christ. There is scarcely a more hateful character under the sun than a minister who is constantly taking heed to his own reputation, preparing his sermons, preaching them, and regulating all his movements with an eye to securing a reputation among people. This is a most detestable state of mind and renders a man worse than useless.

Nor should a minister take heed to his own ease. If ministers are

---

*The Oberlin Evangelist, September 28, 1842. Preached at the ordination of fourteen young men on August 22, 1842 and published by request.

afraid of wearing themselves out, afraid to lay out their strength for God—if they are indolent, effeminate and self-indulgent, they are never likely to be of any use to others, nor any honor to God. Ministers should not take such heed to themselves as to indulge any form of selfishness. Selfishness is the direct opposite of holiness, and so cannot exist in the same heart with holiness. If, therefore, a minister should not be totally depraved, he should not indulge any form of selfishness.

Ministers should take heed to the motives by which they are actuated in entering upon the great work of the ministry. Be careful, brethren, that you make no mistake on this point. See that your eye is single to the glory of God—that disinterested benevolence is the actuating principle of your life. Unless your eye is single, and your intention supremely and disinterestedly benevolent, you are ungodly and have no business in the ministry.

Take heed that you are truly converted—not merely a convicted sinner, but regenerate, men whose hearts are right with God, and whose great motive in entering the ministry is to glorify God in the salvation of others. Remember, if you are not converted when you enter the ministry, you are almost certain to go to hell yourself, and, so far as you have influence, to take your hearers with you. Remember, it is altogether too common to assume that ministers are really converted men. I must say, and dare not say less, that every year's experience and observation forces upon me more and more the conviction that it is becoming alarmingly common in these days of pressing so many young men into the ministry, for multitudes to enter upon that sacred office who are not truly regenerate men. We have had, in this place, instances, not a few, of young men coming to this institution to prepare for the ministry, who have turned out to have no religion at all. They have been here convicted and for the first time converted—young men who had been supposed in churches from which they came, and by which they were recommended, not only to be truly converted men, but young men of more than common piety and promising candidates for the Christian ministry. And if not for those powerful revivals in this institution which broke up their delusions, numbers of them would no doubt have been this day in all their sins and engaged in the sacred office of the ministry. Take heed then to yourselves, brethren, that you *know what it is to be born of God,* and that you *know what it is to have an eye single to His glory in entering upon this sacred work.*

Take heed that you are called by God to this work. And let me beseech you not to treat the subject of a special call to the ministry lightly, and as an antiquated notion no longer to be heeded. You are not to take it for granted that Christ has called you to the work of the ministry because He has called you into His kingdom. But let your mind be well satisfied that it is the will of God for you to be separated to the work of the gospel ministry. You should be as well satisfied of this as you are that you are converted.

If you ask how you are to obtain this evidence, I answer, from the indwelling Spirit of God. If you ask again whether you are to give yourself up to be directed by impulses, I answer, No. You are not to be directed by impulses, but by the sober dictates of your judgment in respect to the path of duty. If God really calls you to the ministry, you will hear His voice; for if He does not call loud enough so that you can hear Him, you have no right to go. If He designs you for a minister of the Gospel, He will give you such views of himself, of the worth of souls, of the great importance of your engaging in this work; in short He will give such an inclination to your mind as to fasten the conviction upon you that it is His voice, and that He calls you to preach the Gospel. Men may call you to the ministry, but do not consent to go unless God calls you. Too many young men already have been called of men, and what are they doing in the church but increasing its sectarianism and grasping after power? We want God-made ministers. Take heed then to yourselves, I beseech you, brothers. See to it that God puts you into the ministry.

Take heed that you are especially anointed by God to this great work, and do not confound a *call* to the ministry with an *anointing* to the work. Christ's disciples were called to the work long before they were specially anointed and endued with power from on high for its effectual prosecution. Remember, conviction is one thing: regeneration is still another. A call to the ministry is distinct from both. And a special anointing to the work of which I am speaking is another, and a gift distinct and by itself. The peace of the Gospel, the rest of faith and communion with God are entirely distinct from that power from on high with which a minister needs to be clothed to be efficient in his work.* A man may be truly pious, ardently so, and know what it is to live and walk with God without that Spirit of power which a minister needs to make his words cut like a two-edged sword. Indeed the grand distinction between efficient and inefficient ministers consists more in this than in anything and everything else. A man may be learned and pious, and yet inefficient as a minister. He may be unlearned, in the common acceptance of the term, yet with a special anointing for the work, and be a most efficient minister. I beseech you, then, let this be well settled in your mind, that unless you take heed to be anointed with a special anointing of the Holy Spirit to this work, you will do but little good, and that if we hear from you at all, it will be that you are doing pretty well, but that there is nothing special under your ministry.

---

*To learn more about the power from on high, see *The Believer's Secret of Spiritual Power*, by Andrew Murray and Charles Finney.

Brothers, you ought to have such an anointing that whenever you open your mouth to preach, the people will feel that you are sent of God. You ought to know that there is such a thing as that. If you are anointed to the work, your hearers will feel that you speak with authority and with power. And by power I do not mean vociferation and noise, but that your words will be sharp, like a two-edged sword.

Take heed that you give yourself wholly to the work. Remember, if you are called to the ministry, this is a labor by itself. You are not to be diverted from this work without being plainly directed by God. And here let me warn you against being lightly drawn aside to engage in agencies for benevolent societies and objects. I say *lightly*, because I suppose it is sometimes true that Christian ministers may be devoted to the performance of some particular branch of Christian reform. But I have long been persuaded that it is a very serious thing for a minister to leave the direct work of preaching the whole Gospel for the purpose of engaging in an agency that will confine him almost exclusively to one department of religious truth. One of the evils of such a course is to beget in his mind a monstrous development of that particular truth. He soon loses the symmetry and proportion of a Christian man. He becomes too much a man of one idea, and he loses sight in a great measure of other branches of reform. He is in danger of becoming censorious toward all others in whose minds there is not the same monstrous development of that particular truth. This is a dangerous state of mind, exceedingly injurious to his own piety and usefulness, and dangerous to the church of God. Such men are found not infrequently to be loudly denunciatory in respect to all Christians and ministers who are not swallowed up, as they are, in that particular branch of reform. They go up and down through the churches lecturing, making their particular topic a test question, and measuring everything and everybody by the importance they attach to the particular branch of reform in which they are engaged. To them it appears that no one else is doing any good—that nothing else is at the present time of much importance, and that little or nothing can be done for the salvation of the world until that particular branch of reform is perfected. These brethren seem not at all aware of the state of mind in which they are. They seem not to consider that they have so long dwelt upon the bearings and influence of one branch of reform that it has in their mind grown all out of proportion as compared with other branches of Christian reform. I beseech you, brethren, take heed lest you come to be among the number of those of whom I am speaking.

Do not understand me as speaking against agencies or agents, for no doubt these agencies need to be engaged in. But I would earnestly warn you against being drawn away from the whole work of the ministry to engage in them without an obvious call from God. And if you should be called to engage in them, I beseech and warn you to be on your guard against the tendencies of which I have been speaking. Without being at all aware of it, many of the lecturers of different societies have diffused a very unhappy spirit through the churches, and wherever they go they seem to plant a root of bitterness, and to get up a kind of faction, and to embitter the minds of certain classes of professing Christians against the church in general, and the ministry, and in short against all who have not a single eye to that particular department of reform.

Take heed to yourself that you are studious. Do not suppose that you can run about without study or reflection during the week, that you can engage in light reading and frivolous conversation, and, for any length of time, interest your people on the Sabbath. You must be deeply studious. You must think much, think correctly, and see that you are master of every subject before you present it to your people. By this I do not intend that you should neglect pastoral visitation and other parochial duties, but I do mean that your people will never be truly benefited by your taking so much time for visitation or other duties as to neglect thorough study. A good minister must be a student.

Take heed that you do not encumber yourself with unnecessary cares. Take upon your hands no business or labor that shall interfere with your high calling. Many ministers, no doubt with the sincerest intention to do good, allow many responsibilities to be thrown upon them which greatly hinder them in the main work to which they are called. They will undertake to board and prepare young men for college, or engage in society matters. They will allow the lay brethren to throw upon them many things of a secular nature to which the laymen should themselves attend, which greatly hinders them in the work of the ministry. Indeed, some ministers seem to take upon them the work not only of the ministry, but also of the elders, in looking after the delinquents in the church; of the deacons in looking after the poor; of the sexton in seeing that the bell is rung and the house in order for worship. In short, some ministers seem to be minister and session and deacon and chorister and sexton and trustee, and almost everything else that has any care and responsibility attached to it. In this way they wear themselves out with doing a little of everything and yet nothing to any advantage.

Take heed that you do not encumber yourself with an unsuitable companion for a wife. See that you do not unite yourself with a worldly woman, one who is fond of dress, or property or worldly society. If you do, she will greatly injure your influence, if not entirely ruin it. Take heed that you do not get a covetous wife. If you do, she will never prevail for you in prayer. She will be constantly instituting comparisons between you and other ministers, will be envious and jealous lest other ministers should be more highly esteemed than you are, will be a trouble to you, and a disgrace to herself and to the church of God. If you have an occasion to employ an evangelist to labor with you, she will be in the way. She will be on tiptoe lest you should be thrown into the shade and the evangelist be exalted above you in the estimation of the people. If his labors should be blessed among your people, she will be thrown into an agony lest it should be thought that her husband is not the great instrument of performing the work.

Take heed that you do not get a self-indulgent wife, one who is afraid of self-denial, afraid of being poor, afraid to work herself or have you work hard for the good of souls. Some minister's wives are always afraid of trouble, of labor, of poverty, of care—so much afraid their husbands will overwork themselves as to be always in their way. Take heed to yourself that you do not become united to such a woman as this.

Take heed that you do not get an indiscreet wife. By indiscretion I mean imprudence. Many women and men seem to lack common sense as to what and when they should speak. Indiscretion in a minister's wife is often a source of much trouble in a congregation. Should the providence of God lead you to marry, choose a wife who is naturally discreet and heedful of the use of her tongue. Take heed that you do not get an incompetent wife—one whose education is in any respect so defective as to be an unsuitable companion for you. By education, I mean not only school learning, but let her be also what a wife and a housekeeper needs to be.

And above all take heed that you do not get a woman of superficial piety. The wife of a faithful minister will naturally have great trials. In a world like this, a faithful minister must meet with great opposition. In its present state, he may expect opposition from the visible church as well as from the world. His wife must share it with him. Take heed then, brethren, that you obtain a wife for whom grace has done so much that she can stand the shock of opposition without being intimidated on the one hand or made angry on the other.

Take heed that you have a thorough experience of the power of the Gospel in your own soul. Do not preach Christ by hearsay. Your preaching will reflect the character of your Christian experience. If you have only superficial experiences of the grace of the Gospel, you will naturally preach a very superficial Gospel. If you know but little of the power of Christ working in you, you will convey to your hearers but a faint impression of what the Gospel really is. I have long been convinced that the grand defect of the Christian ministry in the present day is the lack of a thorough Christian experience. Ministers judge the power of the Gospel by their own Christian experience. Their opinions and preaching manifest the most deplorable deficiency in this respect.

Much that has been written and said by them lately against the doctrine of entire sanctification in this life shows that they have very little experience of the power of Christ working in them to deliver them from sin. I say it with the utmost kindness, yet for the cause of truth and the benefit of the church it ought and must be said that the great difficulty in the way of ministers understanding and believing the doctrine of entire sanctification lies in a defective Christian experience. When they come to be filled with the Spirit, they will soon get over their philosophical difficulties and embrace and declare the truth upon this subject as it is. But with so superficial a Christian experience as many of them manifestly have, they will neither understand nor believe it, and should they embrace it as a matter of theory, it might only bring them into deeper condemnation without benefiting the church or themselves.

Ministers that preach Christ from hearsay, as a mere matter of learning without a thorough experience of the power of the cross to deliver from sin, often remind me of the seven sons of Sceva the priest, who undertook "in the name of Christ whom Paul preached," to exorcise evil spirits. "And the evil spirit cried out, 'Jesus I know and Paul I know, but who are ye?' And the man in whom the evil spirit was, leaped on them, and overcame them, and prevailed against them, so that they fled out of that house naked and wounded" (see Acts 19). So ministers who know little of Christ except by hearsay are easily overcome by Satan. Take heed to yourselves, brothers, that you have a thorough and personal acquaintance with Christ and the power of His Gospel.

Take heed that you realize your dependence upon Christ.

Remember that He has expressly told you that unless you abide in Him, you can do nothing, but that if you abide in Him you shall bring forth much fruit (see John 15). Do not depend upon your education, your eloquence or the strength of your intellect. Remember, the eloquence of an angel would not effect the conversion of a sinner nor the sanctification of a saint. And if you possessed the intellectual endowments of an angel, without Christ you could do nothing. Take heed that your dependence upon Christ is not a mere matter of theory, without being realized and felt by you. Let this be with you a settled matter of fact, that without the power of Christ dwelling in you, and working through you, you will never convert a sinner nor effect the sanctification of a saint. Let this be so thoroughly settled in your mind that you no more expect to live without Christ constantly dwelling in you, than you expect to live without your daily food—that you make no more calculation upon neglecting Christ or upon doing anything without Him, than you would calculate upon living without your daily food.

Take heed that you do not neglect much secret prayer. Unless you are in the habit of coming to your people from the mount of communion, you will do them little or no good. Pray much or you will cease to pray at all. Pray honestly. Pray earnestly. Pray perseveringly. Pray in faith. Pray effectually. Pray in the Spirit. Pray without ceasing, or you will cease to pray at all.

Take diligent heed that you grieve not the Holy Spirit of God. Remember, in every stage of your ministry you are in danger of doing this. If you grieve away the Holy Spirit, you are a withered branch, a cast away minister—laid aside as useless. You will only live to swell the number of unprofitable ministers who are seeking in vain for a field of labor, and inquiring in vain for a vacant church, and who are so obviously without the Spirit of God that if all the churches in the land were vacant they would still be out of employment. If this were the place, I might enumerate the many ways in which you, as ministers, are in danger of grieving the Holy Spirit of God and coming into such an attitude that God must disown you as a minister. I can only mention in general this: Take heed that you do not array yourself against any branch of Christian reform. If you do, the Spirit of God will leave you. If light is within your reach, it does not matter what rationale you use to do this. If you array yourself against the efforts of those who are endeavoring to reform the church and the world, or stand aloof and refuse to come to their help, you may expect the Spirit of Christ to leave you. So well is this settled in my own mind, from my observation of the facts, that when I see a minister get on to the wrong side and array himself against any branch of Christian reform, I naturally expect that his ministry will be barren and his soul will be in darkness whether he knows it or not until he repents and lays his hand to the work of universal reform.

Take heed that you rule your own spirit. "He that is slow to anger is better than the mighty; and he that ruleth his spirit than he that taketh a city" (Prov. 16:32). If a minister cannot govern his temper, he will likely do very little good in the world. It is the curse of many ministers that they give way to passion and often manifest ill temper. Take heed that in this respect you are not in fault.

Take heed that you govern your tongue. Few things in the world do so much mischief as an unbridled tongue in the mouth of a minister. Take heed that you preach out of the pulpit as well as in it—that your whole demeanor out of the pulpit shows that you mean what you say when you are in the pulpit. If this is not so, though you may be called a grand preacher, you will be a bad minister. It has been said of some ministers that when they were in the pulpit it seemed as if they never ought to go out, and when they were out it seemed as if they never ought to go into the pulpit.

Take heed that you are an example in all things to the flock. Do not content yourself with preaching well, but do well whatever you do.

Always be punctual to the hour and moment of your appointments. Never be late to a meeting. Never be behind with any of your engagements. If you have a house, a garden, a barn, a fence, or whatever you have, see that it is in order just as it ought to be.

Take heed that you do not seek ecclesiastical power. Be not among those who are endeavoring to concentrate ecclesiastical power, and who through the influence of presbyteries, synods, associations, consociations, conferences, and councils, are endeavoring to "lord it over God's heritage." Such ministers are a curse to the church. Do you know one of them who possesses the Holy Spirit? Not one of this class seems to be promoting the peace and purity of the church or the salvation of the unrepentant. Now mark me, brothers, avoid this or you will grieve away the Holy Spirit. It is no doubt one of the reasons why ministers of the present day are so barren. There are so many efforts among them to grasp at ecclesiastical power. I beseech you, brethren, by the mercies of God, that you keep clear of this shameful business.

Take heed that you avoid schisms. You know, brethren, that the church is bleeding at every pore under the influence of sectarianism, and what is most shocking and revolting is that ministers are shamelessly supporting sectarianism and even glory in promoting it. Presbyterians exhorting their people to be consistent Presbyterians, and Baptist ministers exhorting their brethren to be consistent Baptists, and Methodist ministers exhorting theirs to be consistent Methodists. Congregationalists, Episcopalians, and Roman Catholics engaged in the same work, while comparatively little is said to induce them to be consistent Christians.

Take heed that you are not vain. Vanity is the besetting sin of many. Scarcely anything is more disgusting or wicked than vanity in a minister. And it is remarkable to witness the extent to which even ministers sometimes indulge vanity. Their affected pronunciation, their mincing, their gestures, their attitudes and the whole costume of their services and pulpit address, as well as their manners and habits out of the pulpit, testify to their insufferable vanity. Their egotism and constant efforts in seeking adulation and flattery, in angling for compliments upon their services and talents—all conspire to render them odious and ridiculous in the estimation of thinking men and of God.

Take heed that you are not flattered. It is the sin and curse of many churches and congregations that they spoil their ministers by flattering them. They compliment them about their splendid sermons, their profound learning, their great eloquence, and even sometimes go so far as to compliment them on account of the elegance of their personal appearance. Ministers are often very little aware of how much they are influenced by such things. I have sometimes thought it was the policy of the devil, and have not been without my fears, that it was the policy of certain leading members of churches and congregations, to tie the hands of ministers by flattering them. Everyone knows how difficult it is to willingly disoblige or thoroughly reprove or rebuke one who has been so much our friend as to often express his approbation of what we have said or done. We come insensibly to feel that the approbation of such a one is of great importance to us, and to have an eye in what we say and do to the manner in which it will affect him. Now, brothers, if you permit yourselves to be flattered by your hearers, you will find yourselves unwilling to deal faithfully with them. They will soon come to be your dictators, and to lay down rules by which you shall preach, instead of your laying down rules by which they shall live. They will become your masters instead of your spiritual pupils. Do not forget that you are much more in danger of being overcome by flattery than you are of being put down by direct opposition. Flattering ministers is especially the sin of city churches.

Take heed that you do not become enslaved by the influence of your ministerial brethren. For years and with great pain I have beheld the growing influence of ministers over each other, and have often thought that I knew of no set of men so servile in this respect as ministers. They form themselves into ecclesiastical bodies, and then either flatter or brow-beat each other until one or two leading minds in an ecclesiastical body will lord it over all the rest, and thus there is a pope in nearly every ecclesiastical body in the land—one, who by flattery or abuse or great talents will come to have an almost unlimited influence over his ministerial brethren. Where there happen to be two or more such minds in an ecclesiastical body, it will almost infallibly work division, and the body will either be torn asunder or live in a state of almost perpetual jangling.

Ministers will often flatter each other in such a manner as to become exceedingly afraid of displeasing each other. It is becoming common for the ministers in a city, town, or region of the country to so unite themselves together that one dares not adopt any measure, preach any doctrine or pursue any course, without the consent of his brethren. And sometimes they really seem to be slaves to each other, and not to have the moral courage to act independently upon any question of moment. Let me beseech you by the mercies of God that you avoid all such things as these.

Take heed that you do not become censorious. When viewed as a state of mind, censoriousness is a disposition to censure and impute blame to persons. It often manifests itself in an unwillingness to receive any such explanation of an action or course of conduct that will show that there was no wicked intention in it. I have observed that many who complain much of the censoriousness of others are themselves exceedingly censorious. They will take up an evil report of a brother and publish it, and afterwards refuse to receive and publish an explanation, obviously intending to fasten blame upon one whose conduct they have misrepresented. A censorious spirit also often manifests itself in a disposition to unnecessarily publish a brother's faults. A censorious spirit often manifests itself in a harsh and intolerant manner of speaking of others. I beseech you to take heed in this respect lest you grieve the Spirit of God and render yourself useless as a minister.

Take heed that you preserve a conscience void of offense toward God and man. If you violate your conscience in anything, you will in that proportion lose your confidence in God and in yourself. You will cover your own face with confusion and tie your own hands so as to prevent you from fearlessly attacking sin in high and low places.

Take heed that you cultivate a tender conscience. Your preaching will be of a very superficial character so far as reaching the hearts of men is concerned, unless you cultivate a tender conscience. If your own conscience is asleep, you will be very ignorant of your own spiritual state and of the spiritual state of those around you. You will be blind to the existence of many forms of sin, both in yourself and in those to whom you preach. But if you cultivate and secure a tender conscience, it will render you sharp-sighted in respect to sin both in yourself and others, and tend to give that searching character to your preaching which is imperiously demanded by the state of the church and of the world.

Take heed that you do not fear men, "which kill the body, but are not able to kill the soul: but rather fear him which is able to destroy both soul and body in hell" (Matt. 10:28). Many ministers are afraid of men, and do not embrace or preach the whole truth without seeming to be at all aware of their being in this state of mind. They seem to think themselves fearless in the discharge of their duty, when, at the same time, it would throw them into a desperate agony to know that in rebuking sin they had offended certain people in their congregation. Rather than offend someone, they immediately qualify, explain away and apologize for what they said until they have neutralized the truth.

Take heed that you are not rash. Some ministers are exceedingly rash and hasty in forming and expressing their views and opinions on almost every subject. They are impetuous and unguarded in their measures. They are stiff and stubborn in the positions they take. They can never be long employed as ministers in any one place. They will almost always leave their people in a divided state. This may be true of a minister who thoroughly does his duty and nothing more; but it may be and often is because of downright rashness and indiscretion in the minister. Not long ago, a young minister observed to an elderly one that "he was determined to drive the devil out of the church in which he was preaching." The aged man replied, "See that you do not attempt to cast out the devil through Beelzebub the prince of devils, and act yourself like the devil in banishing him from your place." Ministers should always take heed that in opposing Satan, they do not come to possess his spirit.

Take heed that you hold not the truth in unrighteousness. Remember that you do this whenever you preach what you do not practice. Remember that the "wrath of God is revealed from heaven against all ungodliness and unrighteousness of men, who hold the truth in unrighteousness" (Rom. 1:18). They hold the truth in unrighteousness, they know what it is, they hold it and admit it, yet do not obey it. And no one is more guilty of doing this, and more sure to have the wrath of God revealed against him from heaven, than the minister who preaches the Gospel and does not obey it.*

Take heed that you hold your entire being in a state of entire and universal consecration to God. Remember that you are called to the work of the ministry. You are about to be set apart by the laying on of hands, and request us to ordain you to this work in the name of Jesus Christ. And now take heed to yourself that when we consecrate you to this work, you consent with all your heart and consecrate your whole being to the work. And take heed that you do not at any time desecrate from this service a precious moment of your existence. Remember that you are God's ministers, set apart by prayer and the laying on of hands. And what is more than all, by the Holy Spirit, to the work of the "ministry of reconciliation" (2 Cor. 5:18).

Now, I want to show you in what respects you are to take heed to the doctrine.

Be sure you have a thoroughly developed idea of what constitutes true Christianity. Nothing is more common than for ministers and people to make a mistake here. It is truly astonishing to see how almost universal the opinion seems to be that Christianity consists in emotion or mere feeling instead of consisting in unselfish good-willing. Where ministers preach, pray and talk as if they supposed Christianity to consist in mere feeling, they preach anything but the Gospel, and give anything but a correct representation of what constitutes true Christianity. The thing I wish to impress upon you here, my brothers, is that you have in your own mind a correct and thoroughly developed idea of what true Christianity is, as distinguished from everything else; that is, true Christianity consists in the supreme ultimate intention of the mind and not at all in feelings or outward actions except as these result necessarily from right intention or good-willing.

Take heed that you thoroughly develop this idea in your hearers.

---

*For two lengthy and vital sermons on Romans 1:18, see *Principles of Victory* and *Principles of Liberty*.

Observe closely their daily walk to see whether they are benevolent. Mark their prayers and conversation, that you may understand whether they distinguish the difference between a religion of feeling and outward action and a religion of supremely disinterested benevolent intention. See whether their religion is a religion of soul principle, or consists only in the occasional effervescence of excited feeling. I am more and more astonished every year to find how few professing Christians understand what true Christianity is.

See that you do not lose the idea of true Christianity, nor allow those to whom you preach to lose it. Remember that selfishness is so rife in this world, and there are so many forms of selfishness that look very much like benevolence, that people are in the utmost danger of letting slip the true idea of Christianity.

Take heed that you understand the whole Gospel. Do not confound it with the law, nor suppose that it does not embrace the law. I beseech you to understand thoroughly the distinction between the covenant of works and the covenant of grace, and keep these distinct in your own minds. Understand what is intended by a religion of works and what is intended by grace. Never confound these in your preaching or conversation. Never leave this distinction out of view; for if you do, you will promote legality on the one hand or Antinomianism on the other.

Take heed that you preach the whole doctrine of the Gospel. Many ministers seem able to preach sinners into conviction of sin, but can go no further. They can make sinners see their sins, but cannot tell them how to get rid of them. Others still can tell sinners how they may be forgiven, but cannot tell Christians how they may be sanctified. And here let me say, brothers, that with very few exceptions, the standard of religious experience in your congregations will not be above your own standard. Here and there the Spirit of God may lead a praying soul into regions so far above you that this will be a source of annoyance to you. You will look upon them to be verging strongly to ultraism, and to be a little inclined to derangement. But as a general thing, the members of your churches will not rise above your standard. If you are yourself a spiritual child or skeleton, so they will be. You must be qualified to preach to them the higher doctrines of grace, and to preach them from your own experience, or you can do them comparatively little good.

Take heed that you live out the doctrine of Christ. Remember that the doctrine of the Gospel is not taught merely in the pulpit. It is often most emphatically and impressively taught out of the pulpit by the temper, spirit and life of a disciple.

Take heed to avoid looseness in your statements. Many seem to consider very little the importance of a sound and strictly correct phraseology in stating the truths of the Gospel. Loose, unguarded statements and expressions in prayer, preaching, and conversation will soon be instrumental in begetting in the minds of your hearers a loose indefinite and unintelligent manner of thinking and consequently a lax manner of living. You cannot be too much on your guard in this respect. On all doctrinal questions be sure to be strictly accurate in the use of such language so you will convey exactly the right idea of the doctrine, and then examine your hearers in every way within your power to see whether they get the true meaning of your language. Analyze their prayers and phraseology, if you perceive it to be loose and indefinite, correct them. Remember that your great business is to develop correct ideas of Christianity in the minds of your hearers. This also is the work of the Holy Spirit, and you can be no further a co-worker with Him than you use "soul speech," and are correct in your statements of the doctrine of the Gospel.

It is amazing that many theologians who call themselves new school consent to use and allow their people to use old school phraseology. They often preach, talk and pray as if they supposed human nature to be in itself sinful, and regeneration to be a physical change and wrought by a physical influence. They hold the doctrine of ability, and yet preach, talk and pray as if they believed in inability. Indeed, many of them seem to study to use old school phraseology, lest they should shock the prejudices of the people, when in truth they do not mean by this phraseology what they are understood to mean and what the language naturally imports. It is amazing that many ministers are even contending for the use of old school phraseology while they reject old school opinions. They seem to expect to correct the opinions of men while they studiously use a phraseology that has become stereotyped in the minds of the people. They will find it forever impracticable to correct the opinions of the people unless they correct their phraseology. They must use different words or they will not convey different ideas.

See that you understand the true spirit and meaning of the law of God. The real intent and meaning of the law is that every interest is to be regarded and treated by every moral being according to its relative value, so far as that value can be understood by the mind. Now, brethren, remember that this is the rule and the only rule of action for moral beings. It is the sum of the law of God. It is of universal application. The rule is plain, and your business is to make an application of it, and to show how it is to be applied to every concern of life. Remember, brethren, there is a vast lack of practical preaching. You may preach faith and repentance, and repentance and faith, sanctification, consecration, or whatever you choose to call it, but unless you descend in detail into the practical application of the law of love to all the concerns of life, you will leave your people after all to blunder on under the influence of many gross and injurious mistakes.

Take heed that you do not leave out of view either the rule or law of love in all its detailed applications to the concerns of life on the one hand, nor on the other, the efficient influence by which obedience to this rule is to be secured. If you present Christ, and leave the law out of view, you will promote Antinomianism. If you present the law and leave Christ out of view, you will promote legality. These two great truths must always be presented in such a manner as to keep thorough possession of the mind. The law is the rule of life, but it is weak and inefficient in itself in promoting obedience. The mind is able to apprehend and perceive the meaning, propriety, and importance of the law; but its motives are inadequate to secure in man, since the fall, the love which is required. The love of Christ, His Atonement, the divine influence of the Spirit secured to man through the Atonement, are the great and efficient truths that are able to secure obedience. Christ as the wisdom, righteousness, sanctification, and redemption of the soul must constantly be held up as the indispensable means of securing conformity to the law of love.*

See that you preach a full Gospel. Do not satisfy yourself with the mere conversion of sinners. Aim at the entire and universal sanctification of saints. Preach a Gospel suited to this end. Show what is "the length, and breadth, and height, and depth of the love of God," and that He "is able and willing to do exceedingly abundantly above all that we can ask or think." Preach not merely justification, but sanctification in all its length and breadth.

You ought to understand, brethren, that the doctrine of justification by faith, as it is now generally held by the orthodox churches, is a modern invention and was unknown to the ancient church. It is this, that men are justified by faith in Christ while they are not sanctified. In other words, that faith is so substituted for holiness that they are accounted as righteous while in fact they are not so, but are living in the daily and hourly practice of sin.

The doctrine of the primitive church was that people are made righteous by faith. In other words, that they are sanctified or made holy by faith, and that they were justified only so far as they were made just by the grace of God through faith. Now this must be the truth. And take heed to the doctrine, brothers, that you do not convey the idea that people are justified while living in sin.

Briefly, we must see what is meant in our text by "continue in them." The apostle says, "Take heed to thyself and to the doctrine; continue

---

*Finney demonstrates this in a practical way in the devotional book on the names of Christ, titled, *Principles of Union With Christ*.

in them: for in so doing, thou shalt both save thyself and them that hear thee."

By "continuing in them" is meant continuing to take heed to yourself and your doctrine. Do not take it for granted that if for some time, or for any length of time, God shall be with and bless you, that He will therefore always do so, whether you continue to take heed to yourself and to the doctrine or not. Remember that if at any time, or under any pretense, you neglect to take heed to yourself and to the doctrine, to continue in them, He will cast you off: "Be not high-minded, but fear" (Rom. 11:20).

Finally, look at what is intended by the phrase, "In so doing, thou shalt both save thyself, and them that hear thee."

This may be understood either as a declaration or a promise. It may be regarded either as a declaration, that those who take heed to themselves and their doctrine shall save both themselves and their hearers, or as a promise that upon this condition such shall be the result.

The language is general and not universal. We are not to understand the apostle as affirming strictly a universal truth, that all who hear such a minister shall be saved. Judas listened to Christ, who certainly took heed to himself and to His doctrine, and yet he was not saved. The Bible teaches a general truth that upon this condition ministers shall not only be saved themselves, but shall be instrumental in saving their hearers. There may be exceptions among their hearers, as there was one exception among the immediate disciples of Christ. But these shall only be exceptions to a general rule.

This passage of Scripture is the faithful minister's stronghold, his consolation amid his trials, his strength and his support. Let him persevere in the fulfillment of the condition and the result is as certain as the truth of God. Here let me say, some ministers greatly mistake on account of our limited views of things. Sometimes, in inculcating the truths of the Gospel, it seems to us for a time, that the people are waxing worse and worse. We become greatly discouraged and are ready to abandon the field as if the people were given up of God, when a more extended and correct view of the subject would show that at the moment when things looked most dark and discouraging the way is rapidly preparing for a general and glorious change among the people. Be not stumbled by appearances. Keep hold of this and similar promises. If the people wax rebellious and resist the truth, hold on in mighty prayer and effort, and press them still the more and you will see the salvation of God. I have often seen great changes take place in a most wonderful manner in the midst of the most discouraging appearances, and doubt not that ministers often quit the field in despair just at the time when mighty faith and prayer would have secured the blessing.

Remember that you are to exercise faith in this and kindred promises: To expect the salvation of your hearers as much as your own salvation; to plead the promise of God in respect to them as well as in respect to yourself.

Always remember the condition upon which this and other promises are given. You are to believe the promise as a universal condition, and fulfill whatever other conditions may be expressed or implied. In this case you are not only to believe the promise, but remember that you are to take heed to yourself and to your doctrine.

If you neglect either condition, you will fail. If you take heed to yourself, and do not take heed to your doctrine; or if you take heed to the doctrine, and do not take heed to yourself, or should you do both these and still disbelieve the promise, in either case, you will fail and the blame will be your own.

It is in the best interest of any people that a minister should comply with these conditions. How unjust the minister is to the people, as well as rebellious against God and injurious to his own soul, if he neglects to take heed to himself and to the doctrine.

What an infinite blessing a true and faithful minister is to a people. From what has been said, plainly, as a general truth, the minister has it within his power not only to secure his own salvation but also the salvation of those that hear him. What a blessing, then, to any people to have a faithful minister.

We see what to think of those ministers who are not instrumental in saving their people. I heard of one minister whose preaching was so manifestly and uniformly unsuccessful in winning souls to Christ that it is said he came to the conclusion that he was commissioned to prepare souls for hell and not for heaven. To meet his case, this text should read, "Take heed to thyself, and to the doctrine; continue in them: for in so doing, thou shalt damn both thyself and those that hear thee."

I have not intended to make the impression that the most faithful ministers can save their hearers without their consent, or that God will or can convert them if they refuse to be converted. But God knows what can be accomplished by the use of moral means. And when He has promised to secure an end upon a certain condition, we may rest assured that upon the fulfillment of that condition, He knows himself to be able to accomplish it. Therefore, let it be your abiding consolation that if you take heed to yourself and to your doctrine, and continue in them, you shall save both yourselves and those who hear you.

14

WISDOM JUSTIFIED OF HER CHILDREN*

"But wisdom is justified of all her children" (Luke 7:35).

The dress and manner of life of John the Baptist were typical of the state of repentance and humiliation to which he called the Jews, and to which every soul is called before he receives Christ, gospel liberty and joy in the Holy Spirit. The prophets of Israel very commonly adopted modes of life that were typical of the particular truths they were commissioned to announce.

Jesus Christ does not appear to have differed in his dress and dietetic habits from the masses. Remember, however, that among the eastern nations, modes of dress were not perpetually fluctuating as they are in the West. Obviously, Christ observed the innocent civilities of life. He attended marriages and politely accepted the hospitality of all classes for the purpose of doing them good. He observed the rites of the ceremonial law, since they were typical and that dispensation had not ended. However, He paid no other regard to the superstitious traditions of the elders than to rebuke them and to reject their authority.

John the Baptist's austere habits and manner of life, his severe rebukes and denunciations, were a stumbling block to the self-righteous Jews. Since they were righteous in their own eyes, and did not in their own estimation need repentance and humiliation, they neither understood his preaching nor the typical design of his dress, diet and manner of living. From all these, they concluded that he was a railer and possessed an evil spirit.

Christ's preaching and manner of life were no less a stumbling block to them. Knowing nothing of gospel liberty, and not understanding that all things belonged to God's children and were to be wisely

---

*The Oberlin Evangelist, October 12, 1842.

and temperately used by them with thanksgiving, they accused Christ of being a glutton and a winebibber. John's preaching and manner of life were designedly legal, in the sense that they were designed to make the Jews feel that they were in a state of condemnation instead of being in a state of justification by faith in Jesus Christ. Christ's manner of life was a perfect specimen of gospel liberty in opposition to the legal and conscience bound state in which the Scribes and Pharisees lived.

In the context of our text, Christ illustrates the manner in which the Jews had first treated John and afterward Jesus himself: "And the Lord said, Whereunto then shall I liken the men of this generation? And to what are they like? They are like unto children sitting in the market-place, and calling one to another, and saying, We have piped unto you, and ye have not danced; we have mourned to you, and ye have not wept. For John the Baptist came neither eating bread nor drinking wine; and ye say, He hath a devil. The Son of man is come eating and drinking; and ye say, Behold a gluttonous man, and a winebibber, a friend of publicans and sinners! But wisdom is justified of all her children" (Luke 7:31–35).

Jesus says that John called you to mourning, but you would not mourn. You resisted his rebukes and appeals, and said he had a devil. Then He says, I called you to liberty and rejoicing, and you rejected this as antinomian and latitudinarian by accusing me of gluttony and intemperance. So, you are displeased and stumbled by whatever is done for you.

While the great mass of the Jews were stumbled, and would have been stumbled whatever might have been done for them, it was nevertheless true that the actually wise were edified and saved.

In this sermon I will show what wisdom is and those who are wise; then that those things which are wise and true will be justified and approved by the wise; and finally, that selfish souls will stumble at what is wise and true.

What Wisdom Is and Those Who Are Wise

Wisdom consists in devoting ourselves to the promotion of the best ends by the best means. This is exactly synonymous with true Christianity. Virtue, holiness or true Christianity consists, as I have often shown in my lectures, in disinterested or unselfish benevolence. Benevolence consists in good-willing, choosing or intending; or, in other words, in devoting one's self to the promotion of the highest good of being for its own sake. True Christianity is the devotion of one's being to the glory of God and the highest good of His kingdom. This is wisdom. Therefore, all true Christians are wise. In the Biblical sense of the term, "fools" devote themselves to some unreasonable end and course of life.

Those things which are wise and true will be justified and approved by the wise. All the truly wise or truly pious have one and the same end in view. This fact distinguishes them as pious persons. They will substantially agree as to the means of promoting this end, because they all have spiritual discernment. "But he that is spiritual judgeth all things, yet he himself is judged of no man" (1 Cor. 2:15).

Similarly, they are free from the bias of selfishness. They have no self-righteous and legal prejudices to blind them. They have no idols to consult or lusts to gratify. Insofar as their eye is single, they will naturally and readily apprehend the truth as it is. From the very constitution of their mind, they are less likely to misunderstand the truth by how much less they are influenced by any selfish considerations. They are more likely to understand it rightly by how much more single their eye is to the glory of God. Jesus Christ says, "My sheep hear my voice, and I know them and they follow me. But a stranger will they not follow, but will flee from him, for they know not the voice of strangers" (see John 10:4–5). Here Christ plainly teaches that those who are truly His sheep will not follow strangers; that is, they will not be led away into a fundamental error. The apostle, in one of his letters, plainly teaches the impossibility of deceiving the elect.

The fact is, to those who are truly wise, the works, providence and Word of God are one harmonious revelation of His natural and moral attributes. Having the same end in view that God has, they naturally and easily understand Him. Being benevolent themselves, having their hearts set on doing the utmost good in their power, with their attention being directed to that end, they are naturally struck at every turn with the manifestation of benevolent design that everywhere appears in the works, ways and Word of God. Turn their eyes where they will, their attention is immediately arrested with the fact that God evidently has the same end in view which they have. He has gone before them in laying the trains by which their benevolent plans may be carried out. God is in innumerable ways cooperating with them in the promotion of the great end they have in view. They, therefore, very naturally come to an easy interpretation of the works, providence and Word of God. These speak a familiar language to them. It is the language of benevolence. And shall not the benevolent understand it? Does not love understand the language of love? I tell you that wisdom is justified of all her children.

To the truly wise, the law and Gospel are one consistent scheme of revelation and salvation, and not contradictory and conflicting schemes. A truly pious person will behold at a glance the wisdom and benevolence of God in the typical manner of teaching the Gospel under the Old Testament dispensation. He sees at once that through those types and shadows a future Christ and justification by faith in Him were taught. Truly pious persons see no difference in the way of salvation under the two dispensations: They only differ in this, in the Old Testament Christ was presented through types and prophecies as a future sacrifice, while in the New Testament He is presented in the simple form of history, as having lived and died and risen from the dead, thus setting aside the necessity of the typical manner of teaching the Gospel. To them God is the same in both dispensations, and the spirit of all that He has ever done or said is one and the same.

Selfish minds will stumble at what is wise and true. Their state of mind, or the end for which they live, has a powerful tendency to beget misunderstanding. Being selfish, they naturally overlook the benevolence of God as it is everywhere manifested in the works of creation. They have their eye upon the promotion of their own private interests and see no benevolence in anything that does not favor the particular end they have in view.

They are often fretted with the providence of God. Like the owl in the fable that wondered why the sun was created with so much light that he could not see to catch a mouse, the selfish sinner looks upon everything as very untractable and ill-natured that does not fall in with his peculiar ends and aims. In this state of mind, he naturally misunderstands almost everything that God does and says. If God commands him to glorify Him, he is apt to understand God as being selfish and ambitious, just as the sinner knows himself to be. He does not understand that God is purely and disinterestedly benevolent in such a requirement. He naturally understands all God's commands, promises and threatenings as founded in selfishness. He knows his own to be, and therefore he naturally thinks of God as being altogether such a one as himself. Furthermore, when God promises reward to virtue and threatens evil to vice, he understands these as appeals to his selfishness.

The sinner misunderstands the providence of God at every step. If it should happen to fall in with his favorite pursuits and schemes, he looks upon God as being very partial to him. Perhaps he thanks God, as we often hear selfish professing Christians do, for being so much better to him than He is to others—for being so very partial to him in a great many respects. But, on the other hand, if God's providence does not happen to favor his particular pursuits and schemes, he is apt to look upon God as prejudiced against them, and as indulging some pique—as acting toward them upon the principle of retaliation and revenge. Being conscious to some extent of the principles by which they know themselves to be actuated, they very naturally attribute the same motives to God. Thus, they perpetually deceive themselves in regard to the divine character.

God's works, providence and Word are universally good. They tend to one ultimate end: The highest good of being. God aims to promote every interest according to its relative value. He proceeds upon a vast scale of benevolence which induces Him to cause His sun to rise and His rain to descend upon the evil and the good. The very fact that God is pursuing one end and the sinner another leads the sinner, almost continually, to misinterpret God's ways, works and Word. The wisdom and virtue of God so conflict with the sinner's selfishness, they keep him in almost a continual fret.

The sinner's selfishness naturally tends to make him misunderstand the moral law, to overlook its spirituality, and to consider obedience to consist either in outward acts or inward feelings. And seldom do sinners understand obedience to the moral law to consist simply in universal disinterested (unselfish) benevolence.

Their selfishness led the Jews to misunderstand and misinterpret the ceremonial law—to look upon it as a religion of works. Instead of understanding it to be a system of typical instruction, by and through which the most spiritual truths were taught, their selfishness led them to regard the splendid temple and the vast round of rites and ceremonies and costly sacrifices, as a splendid, costly, gorgeous set of rites, such as the great Mogul might institute, or some human deity might cause to be observed in relation to himself.

Those in a selfish state of mind do not understand the spirit of the Old Testament. God appears to them, under that dispensation, to have been malignant, revengeful, selfish and bloody. Under the Gospel, He appears to them as at the opposite extreme of selfishness, and as exhibiting such an overweening fondness for people as to be far from exercising even needed severity in justice. They seem unable to understand how the same God and the same state of mind manifests itself under both dispensations. They do not realize that the same benevolence which required the exterminating wars in the days of Moses, Joshua and Samuel, poured out the Savior's life's blood upon the cross and manifested such vast forbearance in the days and in the person of Christ. Their selfishness is such that they do not understand how benevolence manifests itself in all the variety of ways in which God has dealt with people at different times. They do not understand that it is the same benevolence manifesting itself in regard to the public good which sends sinners to hell and takes the righteous to heaven. The spirit of benevolence in Samuel led him to hew Agag in pieces before the Lord, in other circumstances the same Spirit led Jesus Christ to stand in the midst of the fiery furnace of persecution even unto death, unangered and sweetly quiet as a lamb.

Legalists

One class of selfish minds are legalists. Having been convicted of sin, their selfishness takes on that peculiar type. They are, perhaps, remarkably strict in the outward observance of the Sabbath and the ordinances of God's house. They seem to be always dissatisfied with themselves and with everybody else—they are vexed and harassed with the consideration that they do not meet the demands of their own conscience. They are always confessing their heart sins, but they never forsake them. Having no faith in Christ, they know nothing of gospel liberty. Not knowing what it is to eat and drink for the glory of God, their table becomes a snare, a trap and a stumbling block to them. They are uncomfortable with themselves, and render those around them so. Cheerfulness looks shocking to them and appears altogether like unbecoming levity. Encouraging any of the arts appears to them like conformity to the world, and even the temperate enjoyment of such things as are required to health, comfort and usefulness appears to them inconsistent with benevolence. They do not seem to know that all these things are parts of benevolence, but look upon them as a spirit of self-gratification, just as a man who knows nothing in his own experience of eating from any other motives than self-gratification, would not, of course, understand how others could do the same things only as they were influenced by the same motives.

Antinomians

Another class of selfish persons are antinomian perfectionists. They have so much faith, as they vainly dream, that they can violate law without sin.

A third class, and a much larger class, are antinomian anti-perfectionists. They expect to be saved by imputed righteousness. They do not intend or expect to be holy or sanctified. They disclaim all pretensions to anything more of personal holiness than barely enough to support a faint hope that they have been regenerated. If they have been regenerated, they believe they are in a state of perpetual justification on account of their once having exercised faith in Christ. They do not pretend to obey the law of God themselves, but as they understand it, Christ obeyed it for them and His personal obedience is imputed to them. They acknowledge the law to be obligatory upon them, but suppose themselves to be justified by the Gospel while they live in disobedience to the law. Instead of regarding the Gospel as the means of inducing entire obedience to the law, they regard it as opposed to the law in such a sense as really to justify one who continues to disobey the law.

The same doctrines are understood differently by different people according to their different states of mind. Some do not understand that the doctrine of self-denial means the deposing of self and the enthroning of God in the heart, the devotion of the whole being to Him, and doing everything, even eating and drinking, for His glory. To them, the doctrine of self-denial is a system of penance, of outward retrenchments, of bodily mortifications, a denial and trampling down of the very nature of man. Fastings, celibacy and multitudes of monkish tricks seem to be indispensable to their ideas of self-denial. They do not understand that in all these things, to whatsoever extremes they may be carried, there is not necessarily one particle of Christian self-denial. These are oftentimes nothing else than the manifestations of a legal spirit. Sometimes we see they are connected with an acid and vexed state of mind, a spirit of complaining and censoriousness—a disposition to complain about everyone who does not fall in with their particular views and come up to their particular standard.

Others understand the doctrine of Christian self-denial to mean nothing more than abstinence from outward extravagance. And to abstain from extravagance with them is to keep a little back from going beyond everyone else in self-indulgence.

Those who are wise understand the doctrine of self-denial to be what it is: A total renunciation of selfishness in all its forms—a doing, using and being everything for the glory of God. They understand the doctrine of self-denial to require them to hold everything, even life itself, at the absolute disposal of God in so high a sense as not to count their own lives dear to them if the cause of Christ demands that they should be given up. While they thus hold their lives and their all at the disposal of God, they do not wantonly and recklessly cast their lives away as a thing of nought, but carefully preserve and enjoy their lives while in the providence of God they are permitted to do so. And so too in regard to everything else which they have and are. While everything is held at God's disposal, they do not recklessly cast away and squander or give away to be squandered by the improvident around them the useful things which God has put in their possession, but they temperately and thankfully use such of them as can contribute to their health, comfort or usefulness until the providence of God shall call for the relinquishment of some or all of them for His glory. They count these things not dear to them, but yield instant possession not only without gainsaying but with joyfulness.

To one class of selfish minds, the doctrine of Christian liberty is synonymous with the doctrine of indulgences. With them, liberty is license. The denial even of their lusts is legality and bigotry. They have so much faith, and such Christian liberty, that they can violate the laws of their being, use with impunity the most unhealthful kind of diet, and in the most extravagant and unhealthy quantities use narcotic drinks, and even take opium and alcohol as though these were some of the good things that God has made for their enjoyment. I know a woman who is a most pertinacious smoker of tobacco. When expostulated with for using it, she calls it her Isaac, says she once laid it upon the altar, and the Lord gave her the privilege of using it. And she imagines that her faith is such that she can use it without sin. Paying any attention to dietetic reform, or almost any branch of reform, is to this class of persons considered to be legality. Because they are allowed things healthful, comfortable, convenient, they rush into the extremes of self-indulgence. To this class, Christian liberty is regarded as a license to extravagance and intemperance in almost all things.

There is another class to whom the doctrine of true Christian liberty looks suspicious and at least to border upon self-indulgence. Their legal spirit is grieved with it. But the wise understand and are edified by it. To them the doctrine of Christian liberty is only that of living, eating, drinking, dressing, being, using, and enjoying all really good and useful things for good and useful purposes and for the glory of God. To them there is no tendency to extravagance or intemperance or licentiousness in this doctrine at all.

To some, the doctrine of Christian forbearance, as taught by Christ and illustrated by His life, is synonymous with the doctrine of ultra nonresistance—that no government, family, state, or clergyman has a right to use force for the public good. To them, force, even in the suppression of mobs, insurrections, or to prevent the most horrible crimes, is inconsistent with Christian forbearance.

To others, Christian forbearance means nothing more than that you are to appeal to the civil law instead of the bayonet or the fist to secure your selfish ends. To the wise, the doctrine of Christian forbearance is nothing more than the true application of the law of universal benevolence to human conduct. There is a considerably large class of people whose attitude is such that they put such a construction upon particular precepts of Christ as to make them flatly contrary to the spirit of the law as expounded by Him.

Christ has summed up the requirements of the moral law, and included all moral obligation in the two great precepts: "Thou shalt love the Lord thy God with all thy heart, and thy neighbor as thyself." Now, all agree, so far as I know, that the true spirit and meaning of the law of God as thus explained by Christ is that every interest shall be regarded and treated according to its relative value. Consequently, a lesser interest should always be sacrificed to a greater: Of two evils, the least is to be preferred, and whenever a lesser interest comes in conflict with a greater, the lesser is to be given up and the greater secured. This is the principle upon which all just governments are administered. And no power in the universe can render it unlawful to inflict penalties by physical force where the highest good demands it. But this class of persons would understand the precept, "resist not evil," to require that governments are not to suppress mobs or rebellion by physical force, that evil should not be resisted under any circumstances, even in cases where we have all the evidence we can have that resistance is indispensable to the public good. Thus, they array Christ against himself. They represent Him as giving such an exposition of the moral law as to require every interest to be regarded and treated according to its relative value, and at the same time say that whatever the public good may demand, and whatever interest may demand it, evil is not to be resisted.

The doctrine of government and of self-defense under circumstances where the law of benevolence demands it is to some a license to revenge. To others, it is an antiquated relic of barbarous times— something that would do under a former dispensation when God was not as benevolent as He is at present, or when the severe Father and not the benevolent Son of God laid down rules of conduct. But with them, the present dispensation is one of an entirely different spirit, as if another God ruled the universe, and as if the present dispensation was designed to rebuke the former. But to the wise, the doctrine of government, the infliction of penalties for the public good, of self-preservation and defense, where the law of benevolence plainly demands it, is only the true application of the law of love.

The Truly Wise

The truly wise may be known by the manner in which they are affected by the truth. Preach to them whatever doctrine you will, if it be true they will understand it, be edified by it, and be sure to make a wise improvement of it. Self-denial, or Christian liberty, Christian forbearance, or whatever doctrine you choose will find its counterbalance in their minds—it will not carry them to extremes, but will be the instrument of their sanctification. Those who are not truly wise or religious will be injuriously affected by almost every truth you preach. Either they will not be moved by it in any direction, or they will go to such extremes as to develop a monstrosity of character. "Wisdom is justified of all her children." I understand this to be a universal truth. And that this is the real characteristic, not only of some of those, but of all of those who are truly wise.

The selfish will of course misunderstand the wise. When they pursue outwardly the same course of conduct, they will be supposed to do so for the same motives. If they eat, drink, marry, or are given in marriage, build houses, cultivate land, pursue business of any kind; if they labor or rest, journey or stay at home, walk or ride, sleep or wake, or whatever they do, although this is also done by those who are selfish, it will be understood by them to be done from the same motives by which the wise are actuated. But in this they are entirely mistaken. They give themselves credit for just as much piety as any have or can have who do outwardly the same things. Their mistake lies in this: They suppose others to be actuated by the same motives as themselves.

None but spiritual minds understand what Christian liberty is. The apostle Paul understood what it was to be free from the restraints and constraints of the ceremonial law. And yet there was no tendency in his mind to a lax morality. A true Christian alone understands what it is to eat and drink, to dress, to walk and ride, to wake and sleep, and live, and be, and do, all for the glory of God. He alone knows how to use the things of this world without abusing them, and understands the secret of owning all things and yet selfishly indulging in the use of none of them.

Those who have been truly convicted of sin and have seen the spirituality of the law of God, and are truly converted, if they fall back, they will generally fall into a state of legality and find themselves in grievous and iron bondage. Others, who have only been excited and not truly slain by the law and converted, will, when they fall from this excitement, almost always fall into latitudinarian Antinomianism. This last is the largest class of professors of religion.

No doctrine of the Gospel can be fully preached by an enlightened and benevolent mind without frequent and painful apprehensions of the results on certain classes. He must watch with unspeakable solicitude the developments that are made in different minds as an almost certain indication of whether they are converted or not.

Whenever the mind has fallen into a misapprehension of any doctrine, and has consequently received a wrong bias, any attempt to correct that bias by the exhibition of the truth will shock, prejudice and give pain. For example: Let one who has embraced the ultra doctrine of the non-resistants listen to a correct exhibition of the rights, necessity and duties of government, the true principle of self-defense and self-preservation, and he will feel almost as much shocked as if he should witness the fighting of a duel. So let one who has embraced the idea of the doctrine of self-denial, which has been entertained in different ages of the church by many persons, as requiring little less than a system of mendicancy—let such a one listen to a discourse on the doctrine of Christian liberty, and he will feel almost as much shocked as if you were granting indulgences to extravagance. Notice that some have imbibed wrong notions on the subject of Christian retrenchment, that Christians are required to give up everything but the mere necessaries of life (with whom it is a violation of Christian principle to use elliptic springs upon a wagon, or a top, or boot; with whom to build a cornice on a house or to have a button on your coat where you do not need to use it is extravagant; who will not allow anything to the eye or the ear—such as improvements in the arts, the cultivation of music, painting, poetry, improvements in the style of building, in orders of architecture, in short almost all improvement in the physical condition of mankind); they regard things beyond necessity with jealousy if not with pain. Such a person would listen with unutterable pain to a discourse in which a true application of the law of God should be made to all such things, principally because of the perverted state of his mind and by a false view of the subject.

The wise feel relieved and refreshed with truth when mist has been thrown around any subject by those who are in error. They may have been thrown into doubt and embarrassment for a time, but when the light comes they will receive it and be edified and sanctified by it.

Every prominent doctrine of the Gospel seems to be set for the rise and falling again of many. The spirit of reform is abroad in the land. The wise are temperately but firmly pushing these reforms. The rash misunderstand them and go to extremes. The conservatives misunderstand them also and go in an opposite direction. It is curious to see how things move forward under the government of God. The doctrines of the abolitionists to some minds lead directly to and result in the most ultra views of non-resistance. The doctrine of entire sanctification in this life in some minds leads to antinomian perfectionism. But the wise understand. "Wisdom is justified in all her children." And multitudes see no tendency in abolition principles to ultra non-resistance, nor in the doctrine of sanctification or the doctrine of antinomian perfectionism. They hold on the even tenor of their way in pushing these wholesome reforms upon the attention and to the hearts of men. May the Lord speed them. Amen.*

---

*For Finney's continuation of sermons from 1843, see *Principles of Holiness*.

APPENDIX

This appendix lists all of the sermons and lectures which Bethany House Publishers has printed to date, both in alphabetical order and in the order of original publication. If the sermon came from a book published in a distinct year, or if I only had the year of original publication and not the month and the day, I have put January 1 for the day and the month. The appendix does not include Finney's sermons and lectures that I have put into a monthly devotional format. For example, the devotions in *Principles of Union With Christ* have not been included, but the one sermon in the appendix of that book has been included. We are tremendously indebted to Timothy Smith, who published the first collection of Charles Finney's sermons, *The Promise of the Spirit*, with Bethany House Publishers. Interest in Finney's sermons has increased ever since. I have included this appendix for those who would like to study how Finney modified his views or his expression of them over the course of many years. As far as I can tell, Finney never changed the substance of any of his central teachings, but he would modify his expressions as he gained new light. Throughout his life, Finney remained teachable, and he learned much during the thirty or more years these sermons and lectures represent. My prayer would be that we can take the best of what he taught and put it into practice in the way we live and witness.

INDEX OF ABBREVIATIONS:

TITLE	ABBREVIATION
Lectures on Revival	Lec.Rev.
Principles of Consecration	P/Con.
Principles of Devotion	P/Dev.
Principles of Faith	P/Faith
Principles of Holiness	P/Holi.
Principles of Liberty	P/Lib.
Principles of Love	P/Love
Principles of Obedience	P/Obed.
Principles of Revival	P/Rev.
Principles of Salvation	P/Salv.
Principles of Sanctification	P/Sanc.
Principles of Union With Christ	P/Union
Principles of Victory	P/Vic.
Promise of the Spirit	Pr.Spirit
Systematic Theology	Sys.Theo.

FINNEY'S SERMONS IN ALPHEBETICAL ORDER

SERMON	TEXT	DATE	BOOK	PAGE
Ability and Inability	Jud 24:19	08/31/42	P/Con.	187
Acceptable Prayer	Mat 6:10	05/12/50	P/Dev.	109
Affections and Emotions of God	Hos 11:8	10/09/39	Pr.Spirit	216
All Events Ruinous to the Sinner	Rom 8:28	01/20/47	P/Lib.	119
All Things for Good to Those That Love God	Rom 8:28	01/06/47	P/Vic.	128
An Approving Heart—Confidence in Prayer	1Jo 3:21	03/03/47	P/Dev.	271
Atonement		01/01/51	Sys.Theo.	194
Attributes of Love, 1		01/01/51	Sys.Theo.	71
Attributes of Love, 2		01/01/51	Sys.Theo.	81
Attributes of Love, 3		01/01/51	Sys.Theo.	93
Attributes of Love, 4		01/01/51	Sys.Theo.	102
Attributes of Selfishness, 1		01/01/51	Sys.Theo.	119
Attributes of Selfishness, 2		01/01/51	Sys.Theo.	132
Backslider in Heart, The	Pro 14:14	01/01/35	Lec.Rev.	267
Be Filled With the Spirit	Eph 5:18	01/01/35	Lec.Rev.	72
Being in Debt	Rom 13:8	07/31/39	P/Lib.	157
Being in Debt	Rom 13:8	07/31/39	Pr.Spirit	175
Benevolence of God, The	1Jo 4:16	12/06/43	P/Holi.	231
Blessedness of Benevolence	Act 20:35	06/03/40	P/Obed.	51
Bound to Know Your True Character	2Co 13:5	01/01/37	P/Salv.	30
Carefulness a Sin	Phi 4:6	05/08/39	Pr.Spirit	125
Christ Our Advocate	1Jo 2:1	01/01/54	P/Faith	159
Christ the Husband of the Church	Rom 7:4	01/01/37	P/Vic.	99
Christ the Mediator	1Ti 2:5	05/19/50	P/Faith	171
Christian Affinity	Amo 3:3	01/01/36	P/Rev.	189
Christian Perfection, 1	Mat 5:48	01/01/37	P/Holi.	17
Christian Perfection, 2	Mat 5:48	01/01/37	P/Holi.	38
Christian Warfare	Gal 5:16	03/01/43	P/Holi.	105
Christians, the Light of the World	Mat 5:14	08/12/40	P/Obed.	93
Communion With God, 1	2Co 13:14	08/26/40	P/Obed.	105
Communion With God, 2	2Co 13:14	09/02/40	P/Obed.	117
Conditions of Being Kept	1Pe 4:19	05/26/41	P/Con.	107
Conditions of Being Saved	Act 16:30	01/01/48	P/Salv.	121
Conditions of Prevailing Prayer, The	Mat 7:7	05/21/50	P/Dev.	135
Confession of Faults	Jam 5:16	11/04/40	P/Obed.	155
Conformity to the World	Rom 12:2	01/01/37	P/Vic.	156
Conscience and the Bible In Harmony	2Co 4:2	01/01/55	P/Faith	43
Conversion of Children	Joh 4:35	12/16/50	P/Salv.	278

242

244

FINNEY'S SERMONS BY DATE
OF ORIGINAL PUBLICATION

DATE	BOOK	PAGE	SERMON	TEXT
01/01/35	Lec.Rev.	116	A Wise Minister Will Be Successful	Pro 11:30
01/01/35	Lec.Rev.	72	Be Filled With the Spirit	Eph 5:18
01/01/35	Lec.Rev.	225	Directions to Sinners	Act 16:30
01/01/35	Lec.Rev.	207	False Comforts of Sinners	Job 21:34
01/01/35	Lec.Rev.	277	Growth in Grace	2Pe 3:15
01/01/35	Lec.Rev.	176	Hindrances to Revival	Neh 6:3
01/01/35	Lec.Rev.	145	How to Help Your Pastor	Exo 17:11
01/01/35	Lec.Rev.	128	How to Preach the Gospel	Pro 11:30
01/01/35	Lec.Rev.	29	How to Promote a Revival	Hos 10:12
01/01/35	Lec.Rev.	237	Instructions to Converts	Joh 21:15
01/01/35	Lec.Rev.	94	Means to Use With Sinners	Isa 43:10
01/01/35	Lec.Rev.	84	Prayer Meetings	Mat 18:19
01/01/35	Lec.Rev.	38	Prevailing Prayer	Jam 5:16
01/01/35	Lec.Rev.	62	Spirit of Prayer	Rom 8:26
01/01/35	Lec.Rev.	161	Strategies to Promote Revival	Act 16:20
01/01/35	Lec.Rev.	253	Teaching Young Converts	Joh 21:15
01/01/35	Lec.Rev.	267	The Backslider in Heart	Pro 14:14
01/01/35	Lec.Rev.	193	The Necessity and Effect of Union	Mat 18:19
01/01/35	Lec.Rev.	50	The Prayer of Faith	Mar 11:24
01/01/35	Lec.Rev.	11	What Is Revival?	Hab 3:2
01/01/35	Lec.Rev.	20	When to Expect Revival	Psa 85:6
01/01/35	Lec.Rev.	105	Winning Souls Takes Wisdom	Pro 11:30
01/01/36	P/Rev.	189	Christian Affinity	Amo 3:3
01/01/36	P/Rev.	173	God Cannot Please Sinners	Luk 7:31
01/01/36	P/Rev.	59	How to Change Your Heart	Eze 18:31
01/01/36	P/Salv.	96	Love of the World	Joh 2:15
01/01/36	P/Rev.	13	Sinners Are Bound to Change Their Hearts	Eze 18:31
01/01/36	P/Rev.	203	Stewardship	Luk 16:2
01/01/36	P/Rev.	115	Total Depravity	Rom 8:7
01/01/36	P/Vic.	109	Total Depravity	Rom 8:7
01/01/36	P/Rev.	89	Traditions of the Elders	Mat 15:6
01/01/36	P/Rev.	157	Why Sinners Hate God	Joh 15:25
01/01/37	P/Salv.	30	Bound to Know Your True Character	2Co 13:5
01/01/37	P/Vic.	99	Christ the Husband of the Church	Rom 7:4
01/01/37	P/Holi.	17	Christian Perfection, 1	Mat 5:48
01/01/37	P/Holi.	38	Christian Perfection, 2	Mat 5:48
01/01/37	P/Vic.	156	Conformity to the World	Rom 12:2

248